Nova Scotia

SHAPED BY THE SEA

A Living History

LESLEY CHOYCE

VIKING

VIKING
Published by the Penguin Group
Penguin Books Canada Ltd, 10 Alcorn Avenue, Toronto, Ontario, Canada
M4V 3B2
Penguin Books Ltd, 27 Wrights Lane, London W8 5TZ, England
Viking Penguin, a division of Penguin Books USA Inc., 375 Hudson Street,
New York, New York 10014, U.S.A.
Penguin Books Australia Ltd, Ringwood, Victoria, Australia
Penguin Books (NZ) Ltd, 182–190 Wairau Road, Auckland 10, New
Zealand

Penguin Books Ltd, Registered Offices: Harmondsworth, Middlesex,
England

First published 1996
10 9 8 7 6 5 4 3 2 1

Printed and bound in Canada on acid free paper ∞

Canadian Cataloguing in Publication Data

Choyce, Lesley, 1951–
Nova Scotia: shaped by the sea

Includes index.
ISBN 0-670-86507-9

1. Nova Scotia – History. I. Title.

FC2311.C56 1996   971.6   C95-933112-3
F1038.C56 1996

Illustration credits appear on page 305.

"Don't brood on what's past,
but never forget it either."

Thomas Raddall

Acknowledgements

Special thanks to the following who
helped make this project happen:
Dana James, Emily White, Jennifer Wessel, Peggy Amirault,
Erin Dunn, Dean Jobb, Malcolm Ross, Claudia Pinsent,
Gary Shutlak, Dan Paul, Barrie Clarke, Karen Smith,
Charles Armour, Cynthia Good, Terry Choyce
and the people of Nova Scotia.

Contents

Nova Scotia

SHAPED BY THE SEA

Chapter One

The Sea That Surrounds Us

Driftwood and dune grass on the Eastern Shore of Nova Scotia.

In the winter, the "beach" at Lawrencetown Beach disappears. Formidable storms assault this northern coast, pounding the land with waves that gouge and suck at the sand until it is pulled out to the deep. In the summer, it's a different story. The sea kindly returns the sand to the shoreline and on a crisp, clear August morning at seven o'clock you can find me alone on this beach, walking the edge of the North Atlantic, a sea that is as placid as a mountain lake, with water as transparent as a pane of glass. To anybody watching, it might appear that I'm searching for something, but the truth is I've already found what I was looking for. It's been more than twenty-five years since I made my personal discovery of Nova Scotia, and having moved here and staked my claim on a five-acre homestead at Lawrencetown Beach, I can say in all honesty that I have also found myself.

When I immigrated to Nova Scotia, it was clear in my mind that a geographical move would enhance my life. My goal was to become a Nova Scotian and it was secondary that I need also become a Canadian. I didn't mind all that much really, given the fact that my allegiance to this coastal province was so strong that I was ready to swear allegiance to any flag or Queen necessary. Hugh MacLennan once mentioned to me that as recently as the 1950s, passengers disembarking from ships in Halifax Harbour were asked by the customs men if they were foreign, Canadian or Nova Scotian. Hugh had always answered the latter and I can understand why. Every state or province undoubtedly nurtures loyalty to its soil, but a land nearly surrounded by water and steeped in a history of the sea suggests kinship between the salt in the blood and the salt in the air.

Because I live a rural life, I like to think that I am more closely linked with the past than those who live in cities. I'm not a historian but I live inside the history that is this place. My two-hundred-year-old farmhouse is a window into the past. One day when I was cutting through a wall to put in a new door, I uncovered an alarming fact. I discovered that my house was built those two centuries ago with wood that had already been used before. Whoever had fashioned this home, above this once lonely stretch of salt marsh, sand dune and sea, had been a scavenger like me. Some closer investigation reveals that it was not a mere barn that had been torn down to provide the sills and beams, but the lumber recycled here was the wood of a sailing ship, ravaged by a storm and left stranded on the beach. My house was once a ship. And with the original captain long dead, I'm the only one here to sail her on into the twenty-first century, complete with the aid of satellite dish, on-line information networks, fax, modems and call-waiting.

Historians often speak with some despair of this province as a place that has been out of step with major industrialized development and the inherent blessings that come along with that. There is for me, however, great comfort in this thought that the world has passed us by. Now I can live here with fewer frills, fewer distractions, a limited amount of noise and observe the madness from a distance.

But this is also a province of people who still long for the good old days, the Golden Age of Sail, that sort of thing. Not far from where seventy-foot schooners once carved their way along this coast on serious business, I now scoot along with the wind in a mere plaything of a sailing ship, less than five metres long with a hull of fibreglass and a Dacron sail. I'm a novice in the hands of the wind and grow to respect its many moods as I tack east and west, learning that the quickest route from point A to point B is not necessarily a straight line.

In my immediate neighbourhood, whole headlands have been and gone in a matter of decades. Human history has made only a little dent in this community on the Eastern Shore a mere thirty-two kilometres from the city of Halifax. But the sea has carved and scraped the coast with such serious intent that cartographers might just as well start all over with their work of aerial mapping every five years. The sea has created the history of this place more than colonial politics, more than Confederation and even more than all the demands of the twentieth century. To live by this powerful North Atlantic is to be intimate with the dreams and fears of seafaring men who sailed this coast and also to laugh with the gulls or shudder with the pounding waves at the many facets of the ocean.

Wind and water and wave. Three of the great personal and literary influences in my life. I share a passion for the sea with the fishermen and sailors of the previous centuries, but I doubt that I have suffered the hardships that they have. I started surfing when I was thirteen, further south on a warmer shore. Now I surf a cold but immaculate wave, summer or winter, a stone's throw from my doorstep. The waves form as the wind pushes against the water some one hundred and sixty kilometres off shore. The storm subsides, but the waves drive on through deep waters until they reach a stony reef along the rib of land that is Lawrencetown Beach. If I've walked the morning shoreline and observed that the waves are plentiful, then I give up my meditative trek along the sand and put on my wetsuit, grab my board and paddle out to meet them. As they rear and sometimes rage in their final challenge of the coastline, I paddle hard and tag along to feed off their strength and energy. If you don't mind cold water, Nova Scotia is a surfing paradise. The waves make their long pilgrimage here and rise up from the depths as they hit the shallows along the shore. In their end is my beginning, because I begin as many days as possible out on the beach or out on the waves and I feed off their positive energy until I am fully recharged for another day of work.

Lawrencetown itself, for all of its obscurity, is a place of historic beginnings, and my link to the past here is my relationship to the elements that shape this place. As for all of Nova Scotia, the sea has demanded pre-eminence in the history books, even in the story of this town.

The first peoples of this province, the Mi'kmaq, came to my beach in the summers for fish and mussel, and the salt-water lake beyond my garden was known as *Negsogwakade* or the "place of the eel traps." This was a fertile, generous destination to spend the warm summer months feeding on eels, gaspereaux, smelt, salmon, clams, quahogs and waterfowl. But each year, the Mi'kmaq sensibly retreated away from the coast, further into the spruce forests to avoid the hostility of winter storms.

Early attempts by Europeans to settle Lawrencetown ended in failure. The first white people to try and make a go of it were the French. They were not as intrusive as the English who were to follow and did not mind that this area had no great harbour for big ships. English surveyor-general Charles Morris, in his official report of 1752, missed the advantages of this area altogether, reporting that "the harbour to the [French] settlement is but indifferent, it being a salt water river or creek, with a shoal at its entrance." The Acadian settlers, however, had already been finding sustenance from the fish and shellfish and most likely built an aboiteau, a style of dyke, so as to control the tidal flow on the marsh and allowing for plentiful salt hay.

In search of the remains of anything Acadian, my daughters and I have often set sail in my second-hand Laser across the wide, shallow base of Lawrencetown Lake, which drains into the sea. The forest has long since swallowed up anything remotely resembling a community. There are no signs of the Acadians.

To simply name a place is to instil a level of significance to that geography, to foster a history or a mythology (sometimes it's hard to separate the two). I'm thinking of this town named for Lawrence. I can't say that I'm happy about who we are named after. Charles Lawrence was an English military leader who governed Nova Scotia in the 1750s. Considered by many of his peers to be a military genius and great commander, history at various times paints a picture of a man of heroic proportions. Rethinking the past, we see a different man altogether. For it was Lawrence who ordered the deportation of all Acadians in Nova Scotia and the burning of their farms.

Worse yet, Mi'kmaq historian Dan Paul points out that there is a reasonable case to be made in comparing Governor Lawrence to Adolf Hitler for his effective program of mass genocide. In Lawrence's proclamation of May 14, 1756, he issued "a reward of thirty pounds for every male Indian Prisoner above the age of sixteen years, brought in alive; or for a scalp of such male Indian twenty-five pounds and twenty-five pounds for every Indian woman or child brought in alive." Dan Paul points out that women and children were probably not spared the scalping as it was often not possible to determine the sex or the age of the valued scalp.

And so I feel some sympathy for those currently in the province lobbying to rename the towns that have immortalized some of our most barbaric founders. Some of my surfer friends refer to this place simply as "Larrytown," a lighter moniker to place on the geography than that of the man who caused so much human grief to the French and Mi'kmaq.

It was in 1754 that Governor Lawrence and his council decided to create a settlement in Lawrencetown. He granted twenty thousand acres of Mi'kmaq and French land and was even willing to underwrite the cost of settlement, providing not only land but soldiers, cattle, sheep and pigs. A road was cut from Dartmouth and a stockade of sorts built. Concerned about the moral character of the first citizens of Lawrencetown, Lawrence declared that those chosen must be "sober and industrious people, rather than crowd their settlement first with worthless wretches…" An argument had also been put forward that the creation of the settlement of Lawrencetown would give the Native people a foe in their own backyard and perhaps dissuade them from travelling further down the road to harass the thriving communities of Dartmouth and Halifax.

The fort went up near the river here, the French apparently having moved on or been driven off. The Mi'kmaq were not so easily put aside. Bloody fights broke out between the Englishmen building the palisades and the Mi'kmaq men who could not abide this invasion of their homeland. Four settlers and three soldiers were killed. The settlement persisted, however, until one year into the Seven Years' War. On Thursday, August 25, 1757, a new order went out to withdraw settlers and troops and burn Lawrencetown to the ground. It was simply a burden on the limited finances of the colony, too costly and difficult to defend. Not everyone left. But by 1767, there were only fifteen people living in and around Lawrencetown: four English, one Scot, three Americans and five Germans. Animals were a bit more abundant with eight oxen, thirty cows, eighteen cattle for meat, fifteen pigs and some chickens.

In later years, despite the influx of Loyalists to Nova Scotia, Lawrencetown did not flourish. Thomas Chandler Haliburton, in 1808, indicated that there were only fifty people in the entire area.

Here, near the tail-end of the twentieth century, Lawrencetown has a population of less than three thousand souls. Despite the fact that we live not far from the suburbs, growth here has never been dramatic. In the summer, fog sits heavy on the land for weeks or even months, discouraging those who would rather be in the sunlight, a mere nine kilometres inland. In some ways, the sea has conjured this cloaking device to protect us from rapid growth. The water is cold as well. Even on an inviting summer day, the sea might still stab at your feet with what feels like hot knives, the water is so bloody cold. But this has not discouraged the many fellow wave riders who come here from Australia, England, South Africa, California and Hawaii who recognize the unique and ecstatic business of surfing cold pure North Atlantic waves at the foot of a ragged headland.

Lawrencetown Beach has been recognized before as a place of beginnings. Earlier this century, the National Film Board was out here shooting the opening scenes of a film called *The Railroader*, where Buster Keaton emerges from the sea riding a bicycle up onto the shore. Not far away he catches the train and he's off for a trek across Canada.

The train no longer travels by the beach. About six years ago I watched a work crew tear up the tracks. The ties were sold for landscaping, the iron sent for scrap. The steel rail that tethered this place to the rest of Canada is gone. A forgotten steel spike or two and a trail of cinder and rock are all that remain. The old railroad bed is now a good place to ride mountain bikes with my kids as it snakes its way past the beach and along the shores of a brief Acadia and across to the site of Lawrence's military attempt to control this place.

But from what I can tell, all efforts to fully civilize and tame this shore have failed. Each winter the sea undoes the boardwalk and at least one storm will send wave plumes crashing down on the road by the headland. Protective boulders weighing tons, hauled here from inland to save the highway from extinction, groan and shift and sometimes give up and roll off into the deep. Even as the sea carves and reshapes this coast, it has reshaped my own life as well. As a result I feel twinned with the history of this province, this Nova Scotia that has been both victim and benefactor of the North Atlantic that surrounds us.

The sea, along with the weather that belongs to the sea, has been the great dictator of history in Nova Scotia. The foggy, cold weather where I live continues to slow the pace of development and progress. While Canadians across the continent consider moving to warmer places like that of coastal British Columbia, relatively few think of moving to the Eastern Shore of Nova Scotia because of the relentless effects of the sea. Were it not for the stiff southerly flow of the cold Labrador Current pushing the Gulf Stream away, we'd have a climate more like continental Europe. And the history here would be a whole other matter.

But things are getting warmer. For good or bad, the globe is changing and I can see these changes in my own lifetime. Every so often a monster of a tropical storm even lashes this coast and reminds Nova Scotians how little power we have over elemental forces, cold or warm. The classic case is the Saxby Gale of October 4, 1869, which hit the Fundy area the hardest and ripped up miles of forests near that coast.

This book is very much about the sea and about the people of Nova Scotia. It is episodic by design and parcelled up into small units for easy digestibility. In the research and writing of this project, the weight of history has sat heavily upon me as I found myself discovering more about what went wrong than what went right. There is joy here but there is also a long legacy of hardship and despair. Maybe the same can be said of the history of any part of the world.

The story of Nova Scotia inevitably encompasses the political and military conflicts involving the British, the French and the Americans. It also embraces the Mi'kmaq, the Acadians, the Blacks and the many immigrants who have found their way here. While war appears to be such a potent ingredient of this province's history, I have found myself less interested in military or political strategies and more intrigued by motives, personalities and the lives of civilians directly affected by war and politics. Rascals, rebels, reasoned men, feisty women, financial schemers and relentless dreamers have all shaped the human history of Nova Scotia. Despite my great love for this place, I was not about to cover up the legacy of tragedy and the flaws in our decision-making that have led to the ravaging of the sea and forest, the tragedies of Africville and Boat Harbour, as well as the sad fate of so many coal-mine casualties.

I have tried to create a book that would be of value to both readers who live here and those who have never set foot on Nova Scotian soil. For the record, I own up to certain biases that have shaped the story. Anything and everything regarding the sea was of paramount interest. Those individuals whose lives were enmeshed with the North Atlantic are given plenty of ink.

While the book is primarily organized in a chronological manner, I have felt the need to fashion specialized chapters about single subjects in order to provide a clear perspective on such topics as the early Acadians, coal mining or the death of the fishery.

The history of Nova Scotia is deep and broad and could be told in many volumes instead of one. Hard decisions were made as to what to leave in and what to leave out. I don't believe there is such a thing as "objective history." I have attempted to tell the story as truthfully as I could, but I agree with Samuel Johnson's observation that "Every man has a right to utter what he thinks is truth, and every other man has the right to knock him down for it." I am also grateful to my publisher who has given me licence to offer up not only what appears to be fact, but also some opinions where I see the need—to cheer the heroes on and curse the scoundrels when I see fit. My hope always has been to inform, entertain and exercise the writer's prerogative to question when necessary.

Chapter Two

The Story Begins in Africa

The earliest stories of Nova Scotia are written in the rocks.

The Drowned Coast

As I walk along the shoreline near my home, I am walking on a part of the continent that will be gone all too soon. It will be covered with water; the sea will have both risen and washed away the sand and rocks beneath my feet. I live on what geologists call a "drowned coast." It's drowning slowly—or rapidly if you want to figure it in geological time. Someday the people of Lawrencetown and Halifax and other coastal communities will have to retreat. It's that simple. I think it's a fair reminder to those of us who live here what a tenuous hold we have on this place. The sea is still ultimately dictating the future and I'm happy for that.

Someday "Farewell to Nova Scotia" will have a different meaning altogether. But then, much of the coastal world will have changed too. The seas are rising, the polar caps are melting. Or it could go the other way. Another ice age might actually help the continent to advance back into the ocean.

Continents in Collision

It's always good to begin a history at the beginning, so just to set the record straight, I'll mention that the earth is about four and a half billion years old. The first four billion years are not really recorded in Nova Scotia rocks, so I can't enlighten you much about these early days. Continents tend to build up from the centre and we're way out here on the edge, so our rocks are fairly young—prepubescent even. The oldest rocks stashed in the earth here are 570 million years old.

Now for the interesting part. Barrie Clarke, professor of geology at Dalhousie University, points out to me that the real history of Nova Scotia begins in Morocco. *What?* you say. *Morocco?* Yes, as in Africa, or to be more precise, its predecessor, the extinct supercontinent of Gondwana.

From his office at Dal, Barrie points outside to some loose rock walls that divide the campus. "See those stones out there. Those are sedimentary rocks and the sediments didn't come from the rest of *this* continent. They came from Morocco."

I tell him that it looks like the same loose slate that my house is built on. "Sure," he says. "You're living on a chip of Africa." And suddenly I feel a whole new heritage coming on that I'd never known. "The rock is made from material shed off the Saharan Shield and collecting on the margin of Gondwana—deposited sediment from 500 million years ago."

Gondwana was in the southern hemisphere and it was equatorial. But that was where my property was way back then. It started out as warm, dry desert land.

Not all of Nova Scotia was African. There's an identifiable place on the Trans-Canada where you leave the geology of old North America and enter into the leftovers of Gondwana. "There should be a sign on the highway near Londonderry," Clarke suggests. "Put up an information centre and hire a couple of students to say, 'You are now entering Africa.'" Barrie's been to Morocco. "Geologically speaking," he says, "it feels just like home."

I dug a well in my backyard once and hacked away at a lot of this African slate. It chipped and shattered and some of it was peppered with iron pyrite. I thought I'd found gold but it was the fool's variety. I never understood why the slate didn't lie flat; the sheets of it are nearly upright. It all had to with continental collisions. Yes, collisions. Bang—real slowly. Two continents literally crashing into each other. "Stuff gets really crumpled in a collision," Barrie says. "It gets pushed around from its original place. Some of it standing on end. Slate used to be mud, fine silts from the Sahara that got compressed then jacked upright."

The fault line in Nova Scotia, our own San Andreas, runs from Chedabucto Bay to the Bay of Fundy. There's a gorge along part of it. Everything on my side of that line is from Africa. Gondwana was jammed up against the old continent here, then pulled apart. Stuff got dragged along in its wake; and this chunk was left behind to give me Moroccan slate to carve a well into. I'll be darned. The big collision of the supercontinents happened about 400 million years ago. Three hundred million years ago, Nova Scotia was still on the equator and the pulling apart happened about 200 million years ago.

All that dragging apart and leaving behind has something to do with the ragged coastal shape of Nova Scotia, but the backbone of this place is solid granite—granite that had been in Africa/Gondwana for one and a half billion years before being left behind here as the supercontinent cruised slowly away. Barrie pulls out a geological map of the province and points to something—a "tension fracture" that almost broke and took the land back to Africa. It was a close call. We could have lost almost all of Nova Scotia.

I'm suddenly afraid that I don't have the whole picture. Do I really have the story from the very beginning? So he explains that in the beginning, the earth was hot, molten until the outer surface "froze," solidified and became a crust—like scum rising to the top of something boiling and then hardening there. Lavas keep breaking through, then solidifying. The earth, he points out, is always recycling, refining. "We're a dynamic planet—destroying, re-creating."

Destroying, re-creating. It's hard for me to see the big geological picture, but I guess it's like what I see each year along the shoreline. In the summer the sand is deposited at the beach where I surf. In the winter it's washed away. Then it comes back. But the beach keeps changing as well. Destroying, re-creating. That's what the natural forces have been doing to coastal Nova Scotia for a long time and will continue to do. Maybe man has done the same thing here. As the current fish crisis illustrates, however, we've put too much effort into the first half of the cycle and it's time to shift to the *re*-creation mode.

Land of the Mini-dinosaurs

The oldest dinosaur fossils in Canada have been found along the Fundy Shore, near Parrsboro, Nova Scotia. They date back 240 million years. The tides continually erode the shorelines of this part of the province and have allowed for wonderful discoveries of fragments from this distant, but certainly not lifeless, past. Two American researchers, Paul Olsen and Neil Shubin, made one of the largest finds ever for this time period in 1986 when they unearthed more than a hundred pieces of fossil bone. Along with Olsen and Shubin, scientists who have studied the fossils from this area are convinced that something catastrophic occurred way back then, causing a mass extinction of the dinosaurs.

Most Nova Scotia dinosaurs were not massive. They grew to be in the range of one to seventeen feet in length. The Otozoam, which slinked around the mud flats, was something like a contemporary crocodile. A lot of the creatures who ran around on the land were the size of turkeys or ostriches. At least one mini-dinosaur had a footprint of one centimetre, no larger than that of a robin.

Keep in mind that back then, well before the ice ages—Nova Scotia was located near the equator and covered in rain forests. Known as the Coal Age, this period of time 300–500 million years ago allowed for the build-up of organic materials that would eventually be crushed and formed into coal.

A million years ago, the ice that crept down from the poles to cover all of Nova Scotia was a kilometre and a half thick. The glaciers advanced and retreated five or six times and between these colder spells, animal and plant life would re-emerge. Right now, we may well be living in one of those benevolent periods of time between glaciers, some experts suggest.

Chapter Three

Cold Wars and Warm-blooded Mammals

Great sheets of ice scoured the land and left stark, beautiful monuments of stone as glaciers retreated.

Heavy Ice Gives Way to Glacial Rebound

Not long after all the depositing of materials from the collision and separation, Nova Scotia began to erode. Glaciers, in their advances and retreats, destroyed a lot of geological evidence. Ice ages came and went. Global temperatures went down, then up. Seas rose and fell, all affecting the shape of this coast. The most recent retreat of major ice was a mere 10,000 years ago.

If you fly over Nova Scotia, you can readily see what the scouring and grinding of glaciers has done to us. Sediment has been pushed off the land, leaving bare rock in many places. The lakes tend to run north and south. Glacial action has left drumlins, moraines and piles of till and kettle holes. Four-kilometre-thick ice sitting on the land squeezed it and made it bulge outward into the sea. You could have walked all the way to Sable Island on the ice that sat on dry land in those days.

Periods of glacial rebound followed those frosty times when the unweighted continents could push up as the land recovered. But the water along the coastline would also rise as the ice melted, drowning the coast again. Even now, we are seeing the results of glacial melting as the sea intrudes further into the land. As salt-water levels get higher, lakes will end up being inlets as the salt water connects to the fresh.

The lake in front of my house, Lawrencetown Lake, seems to be going in the opposite direction. It's filling up with sediment and has been for a long time. This body of water is shielded from the sea by a wide low marsh and a set of sand dunes ravaged by sand and gravel excavators of the 1950s. The sea will eventually have its way here, sediment notwithstanding. It will break through. The beach will retreat and then disappear altogether and if my two-hundred-year-old house continues to stand, the waves will lap at my driveway and a new breed of surfers will be riding waves where I once gardened Swiss chard and peas.

Here, drumlins, those whale-shaped hills of glacial debris, elongated and cigar-like, are abbreviated now along the Eastern Shore. Half of each of these soft-shouldered hills at Lawrencetown, Seaforth and East Chezzetcook are chewed off. The land has been gobbled, digested and is silting off toward the deeper sea bottom. Citadel Hill in Halifax is primarily a drumlin and it too may one day feel salt water slapping at its base. Barrie Clarke says jovially, "I already have the concession for gondolas in Halifax; as the city goes down, it will become the Venice of North America. You'll be able to cruise down Hollis Street in a boat." When all the ice melts, the sea level can go up as much as one hundred and fifty metres. "Farewell to Nova Scotia," the chorus sings, saying goodbye to a sizeable chunk of the most populated city of this fair province.

A Paradise for Fish

The riches of the sea were once our greatest resource. Through four ice ages, mud and sand were scraped from the land here and dumped off the coast, creating a fertile series of "banks." The soils that could have supported good farming were stolen from us and given to the fishes. As the ice melted, the sea rose over the banks of soil left out there, creating a great place for minute life to develop, leading to higher forms who fed on the lower ones until a massive population of fish cruised around the Grand Banks and George's Bank. It was here that the collision of the Labrador Current and the Gulf Stream took place, a fortuitous combination that enhanced the production of teeming sea life. The great Arctic current of the Labrador, 400 metres deep and 350 kilometres wide, is packed with rich minerals and tiny northern sea creatures. The Gulf Stream, which is positioned 400 to 800 kilometres off the coast of Halifax, mixes with the cold water here. The mineral-rich northern waters and the warmer southern waters provide perfect conditions for the breeding of plankton which are fed on by small fish such as capelin and small cod. They, in turn, feed the bigger fish that are harvested by man. Then man overfishes without regard to the future and suddenly something goes wrong. The cycle ends. Given time, the planet may repair itself. No one knows how much time this can take.

In the heyday of the Grand Banks, cod was harvested by the ton. A codfish can grow to 96 kilograms if left to survive into old age. A female codfish is (or was) enormously fecund, carrying as many as nine million eggs at once. They are omnivorous and have been known to eat seabirds, bars of soap, metal, whole scallops, lobsters or nearly anything. But drag the ocean floor for decades destroying the habitat and even they cannot continue to survive. Spawning must take place between one and a half and seven degrees centigrade. As global temperatures change, that too may make successful breeding impossible for the cod. And once the cod disappear, other species will not be far behind. The recent disaster in the fishery of the Atlantic suggests that we may not see the recovery in our lifetime. Perhaps it will take longer than our children's lifetime. As the history of Nova Scotia unfolds, the logic of this result seems all too, well, logical. The British and the French first came here to carry off whatever they could that was of value. They came to exploit and that destiny has been fulfilled for these several centuries in the fishery and to a lesser degree in the forests. Once the exploitation is over, it will be time, we hope, for repair and recovery. We may just now be entering that phase.

Mastodon, Moose and Men

Before the ages of ice, Nova Scotia had a rich diversity of animal and plant life. No major mountain ranges impeded the traffic of wandering creatures or emigrating plant life in any direction. Each inter-glacial period, however, saw less variety and intensity of life. There were times of tundra and vast fields of northern grasses with shrubs and sedge growing from the moraines and the glacial till. In the valleys grew sugar maple and hemlock, balsam fir, white spruce and white pine. The landscape of much of Nova Scotia six thousand years ago may have looked a lot like the barrens of Peggy's Cove today. Sable Island, however, probably has the same vegetation today as existed there 11,000 years ago. It wasn't until as recently as 5,000 to 3,500 years ago that the mixed forests of the province developed.

Well after the dinosaurs romped around, the mighty and hairy mastodon could be found here. In the early 1990s, workers at the National Gypsum Quarry near Stewiacke (previous claim to fame: "Halfway from the North Pole to the Equator!") uncovered not one but two mastodon that were about 70,000 years old. Mastodon, like the modern moose, preferred to hang out in lakes and swamps. Near Middle River, Cape Breton, an even "younger" mastodon from 30,000 years ago was unearthed. Cuts and scrapings on the bones imply that the beast was hunted down by men, suggesting that Nova Scotia was inhabited by tribes of hunters even then. Mastodons became extinct here about 10,000 years ago.

The ice may have been disastrous to plants and animals, but it allowed for an ice bridge to form across the Bering Strait, far away from Nova Scotia on the western fringe of Alaska. Migrating across this bridge came bison, moose, caribou and musk oxen, creatures most suited to cold climates who tended to continue moving east instead of south to warmer climes. Eventually they found their way to this far coast.

Other animals found here after the ice ages included white-tailed deer, black bear, beavers and ermine, to name a few. All still exist here today.

Humans had also crossed the Bering ice bridge, travelling throughout North America, retreating southward as the glaciers advanced, but moving back north when the land opened up. These peoples crossed over from Asia 13,000 years ago and their children began to move south along a kind of corridor that led them onto the Great Plains. Within two thousand years they had settled all over North America, including as far away as Nova Scotia. They travelled by land and when possible by water. The fragmented remains of a very early settlement is located near Debert. There these early Nova Scotians sustained themselves on caribou herds. Debert, the site of one of the earliest human settlements here, seemed destined to be the location of a final enclave of humanity had we not all survived the Cold War. In the 1960s, the Nova Scotia government built a massive underground bunker there to shelter the premier and a select band of men and women to keep civilization going should there be an all-out nuclear war. Had the bunker ever been put to use, the surviving politicians and bureaucrats would have emerged into a decimated Debert landscape, harsher than anything known by the Paleo-Indians who first came here.

Those earliest of settlers would have lived in animal-skin tents upon a tundra in a climate still chilled by receding glaciers. They hunted the mastodon and caribou with sharp stone-tipped spears. Other stone tools were used for preparing hides and chipping away at bone and wood.

Traces of human presence are absent between 10,000 and 5,000 years ago, probably due to rising sea levels and an unkind environment. For the following thousand or so years, human settlement again appeared along the coasts where people fished from the sea and the rivers and hunted beaver, moose and deer. We don't know a lot about these times, but spears and grooved axes, scrapers and knives have been found. In the period between 2,500 and 3,500 years ago, tools must have been very important not only for a livelihood but as part of one's identity. When you died, you were buried with your tools and painted in red ochre as part of your preparation to enter the spirit world.

Chapter Four

The Land of the Mi'kmaq

Mi'kmaq encampment on Dartmouth shore of Halifax Harbour; illustrated by Lt. Robert Petley, 1837.

Ten Thousand Years of Civilization

In his book *We Were Not the Savages*, Mi'kmaq historian Dan Paul writes eloquently about the history of his people, for the first time documenting the story of the Europeans' arrival and settlement of Nova Scotia from the Native North American point of view. So much of what is recorded by the European invaders is so slanted by Eurocentric, and ultimately racist, attitudes that it may be unreasonable to accept any of the early written accounts about the Mi'kmaq as fact. Like me, Dan has an inherent mistrust of history as it is reported to us. White heroes of yore now appear more like villains of monumental proportions. If Dan and other living Mi'kmaq leaders suggest that towns named for the likes of Amherst, Cornwallis and Lawrence be changed, it is not a simple complaint against nomenclature. It is a protest against the power of a dominating culture to distort what really happened. In a modern tribunal, all of the above would be rightfully convicted of not only murder but genocide.

The story of the Nova Scotian Mi'kmaq people and the arrival of white settlers is a tragic tale of the degradation of a near-utopian society. As Dan Paul points out, the European arrival was nothing short of a "total disaster" for his people.

It was 10,000 years ago the first Mi'kmaq settled in Nova Scotia. Having descended from other tribes which crossed the Bering Strait and spread out across North America, they had probably retreated south once or several times as the climate dictated. Now they were here to stay and prosper until their land was invaded by Europeans in the seventeenth century. Each Native culture evolved as it separated from the rest into a unique pattern of lifestyle, language and government. While Mi'kmaq and Maliseet bore strong similarities, for example, the Mi'kmaq and the Mohawk would be radically different.

Mi'kmaq culture was of a highly organized and civilized nature. It is reputed to have been an open and accepting society with no degree of racial élitism. Early French officers would worry about this openness, because it led to "reverse assimilation" as French soldiers became part of Mi'kmaq communities and families. Much earlier, it is suggested that even the notorious Vikings had been welcomed into Mi'kmaq culture, accounting for the presence of some very white Native people on hand to greet the English and French when they arrived.

Mi'kmaq villages were democratic, with an established legal system for resolving grievances. There were seven defined Mi'kmaq districts in the region and most people lived in communities of 50 to 500. By the seventeenth century, the Mi'kmaq population in Atlantic Canada stood at about 100,000. By 1843, this number had diminished to a mere 1,300 survivors of the disease, malnutrition and mistreatment that befell the people whose homeland was overtaken by men from across the sea.

According to Dan Paul, the Mi'kmaq were far too accommodating to the intrusive Europeans. The English really had little to fear from the Mi'kmaq until they began to outrage the local population with vicious acts against these people they viewed as "savages." The resulting Mi'kmaq backlash would be an effort of simple self-defence, a matter of survival against the militant British.

Mi'kmaq society was not warlike by nature. Men were competitive but it was a kind of contest to be the best provider for the community, not a competition for the greatest personal profit. The English leaders could not comprehend this principle. While the British notion of leadership hinged on enforced respect and punishment, Mi'kmaq leadership was based on hunting skills and character strengths.

Religion revolved around a personal and spiritual relationship to the earth and the inherent spirit in all things of the earth—from the rocks to trees and bears. The Mi'kmaq have always believed in an afterlife and the morality of the community was based upon religious beliefs embracing the inter-relationship of all things of the human world, the natural world and the spiritual world. Monogamy was dominant in the culture, although polygamy was permitted. Chrestian LeClercq, one of the first Europeans to document the Mi'kmaq way of life, notes that they were a very emotional people. Principles of honour played an important role in their lives, as did romantic love and a sense of duty to family and community. The attitude toward sex was very open and while premarital sex was not encouraged, no stigma was attached to someone born out of wedlock.

When Port Royal's first French settlers made unwelcome advances against Mi'kmaq women, however, word was quickly returned to the French leaders that such actions were offensive. Any white man who attempted to repeat the offence might be severely punished by the Mi'kmaq chief.

Of their dietary habits, explorer Nicholas Denys wrote:

> They lived without care, and never ate either salt or spice. They drank only good soup, very fat. It was this that made them live long and multiply much. They often ate fish, especially seals to obtain the oil, as much for greasing themselves as for drinking; and they ate the Whale which frequently came ashore on the coast, especially the blubber on which they made good cheer. Their greatest liking is for grease; they ate as one does bread and drink it in liquid.

While that may not sound to modern ears like a totally healthy diet, it was undoubtedly one that provided all the Mi'kmaq needed to lead a healthy life until access to such rich resources was cut off by the English.

Traditionally, if a Mi'kmaq villager was not able to find his own supply of these items or fish, berries, moose meat and other staples, then a kind of social safety net provided help. The sharing of food was a vital and sacred principle of life.

Among the early Native Nova Scotians were master canoe-makers who produced both river and ocean-going craft. Europeans were awe-struck by the maritime abilities of canoeists who thought nothing of paddling from Cape Breton to Newfoundland. In the 1700s it was even recorded that one Cape Breton chief gathered some Mi'kmaq leaders to paddle to St. Pierre to pay their respects to the governor there. The ocean, like the earth itself, was more ally than enemy. Mi'kmaq watermen had a great knowledge of coast-lines, tides, weather and navigation, all handed down in an oral tradition, which made ocean travel possible. Father Lallement, in a letter of 1659, speaks of the "savage mariners [who] navigate so far in little shallops, crossing vast seas without compass, and often without sight of the sun," implying that they could navigate on cloudy and foggy days as well as in good weather.

Summer was the time to live by the sea as the Mi'kmaq did here near my home at Lawrencetown. In winter, people would migrate to a more hos-pitable inland site, maybe fifteen or thirty kilometres from the sea. As Dan Paul suggests, "They invented the summer cottage business."

A Savage Assault

Life would change for the Mi'kmaq forever once the Europeans began arriv-ing. The French would get along with the Mi'kmaq much better than the English. As early as 1605, when Port Royal was abandoned by the French settlers, the site was left in the hands of Chief Membertou for safe-keeping. Once the French learned to be more civil around Mi'kmaq women, inter-marriage was accepted without much concern. Many young Mi'kmaq men would even travel to France for an education. Some stayed on there and were assimilated into Parisian life.

The English, however, arrived here with a preconceived fear of the Native people. They were leery of the Mi'kmaq's early friendship with the French. The English military leaders also mistrusted the democratic nature of the Mi'kmaq culture which stood in sharp contrast to their own style of keeping civil order among the soldiers and settlers. The Mi'kmaq leaders ruled only at the "pleasure of the people" and could thus be removed if they were not doing their jobs adequately.

Dan Paul argues that the alleged Mi'kmaq raids on white settlements in the 1700s and 1800s were "mostly propaganda." Some can be attributed to Mohawks, who were enemies of the Mi'kmaq and brought in by the English to help wipe out the local population. The English, obsessed with being masters over the Mi'kmaq, forced them to sign documents ensuring their own extinction. The English used bounty hunters to kill the Mi'kmaq in the 1600s and 1700s. Gorham's Rangers were brought in from New England in the 1740s to kill as many Mi'kmaq as they could find.

There would be a long string of treaties designed to rob the Mi'kmaq of their homes and to subjugate them. The treaty of 1725 was signed by most of the tribes along the northern seaboard as a working document to bring about peace. Unfortunately, most of the Native leaders didn't understand that it was to be peace by subjugation. The very nature of written treaties was an alien concept to the North Americans and the document itself had been translated from English into French but not into the many Native languages. The Mi'kmaq leaders thought they were signing an agreement of co-operation and peace, not a deal surrendering the rights to their lands. Whatever was agreed to, little tangible peace came from it. By 1744 all-out war was declared on the Mi'kmaq by Nova Scotia and New England. Governor William Shirley of Massachusetts offered money for the scalps of Native people. Again and again the English leaders would find excuses, often based on false information, to offer money for Mi'kmaq scalps, encouraging the wholesale slaughter of men, women and children for reward from the Crown.

In 1760, the Mi'kmaq were again forced to sign a treaty that would lead them into further poverty and a loss of their land rights. In 1763, General Jeffrey Amherst proposed to deal with the "Indian problem" by "inoculating" them by means of blankets. And so blankets infected with the small-pox from dead or dying soldiers were distributed to Mi'kmaq families. Amherst and his associates knew how deadly European diseases could be for the Mi'kmaq and he had determined the perfect treachery to kill off hundreds of the feared "savages" without incurring any danger to his men. Unaware of the deadly nature of the blankets, the local Mi'kmaq accepted this surprising token of English generosity with gratitude.

One of Nova Scotia's greatest political figures, Joseph Howe, would be struck by the immense horror of what had happened to these once-proud people. But his efforts could not offset the disaster that had already occurred. Upon Confederation in 1867, the Native people became the responsibility of the federal government, which adopted a paternalistic role. While not as deadly as infected blankets, the more modern tactics of integrating Mi'kmaq people into white society would continue to foster physical and spiritual hardships.

Chapter Five

Early Explorers: Myths, Legends and Maybe a Few Facts

Saint Brendan and followers encountering a giant fish on their Atlantic crossing; woodcut by Anton Sorg, 1476.

St. Brendan's Isle

By contemporary standards, we have come to accept the whole idea of the "discovery" of North America by Europeans as preposterous. The Mi'kmaq had obviously "found" a home in Nova Scotia long before anyone else came along. Over generations their ancestors had travelled here from Asia. Various European explorers as well made their way here long before those who would attempt permanent settlements. These brave voyagers of the distant past remain obscure but not forgotten. Given the tenuous proof concerning the journeys of John Cabot, who seems to garner a lot of credit for "finding" this place, it would not be fair to write off the claims of the Irish, the Welsh and the Orkneymen who may have come across the Atlantic before Cabot's official journey.

The Irish, for example, were adventurous seafarers and by the eighth century had sailed far to the north and west in the Atlantic. When the Norse arrived in Iceland in 870, they found an Irish monk already living there. Other Irish had settled there as well. One traditional tale relates that the Irish fled the hostile, heathen Norsemen and sailed on somewhere else for a little peace and quiet. They may have gone to Greenland to settle peaceably among the Native people there or even as far as the shores of the Gulf of St. Lawrence.

The only further "evidence" of these Irish settlers in the New World is the Irish legend of the Icelandic merchant, Gudleifr Gunnlaugsson. He left Dublin in a ship and was caught up in storms that drove him far away to a land in the west where he was captured by an unknown people of tinted skin. These people debated (in Gaelic!) whether or not they should kill what they saw to be a troublesome Norseman. An elderly white man came to Gunnlaugsson's rescue and set him free, then bid him farewell with presents and accurate directions for finding his way back to Iceland.

A number of legends speak about Irishmen venturing west by accident or with good intentions. A story dated around A.D. 700 tells of the voyage of Bran who has a vision of a beautiful woman and sets off in three curraghs (skin boats), arriving at a place he calls "The Land of Women." The queen there keeps Bran for a year until he can escape and return to Ireland. As he returns, he discovers that centuries have passed instead of years. A crewman who steps back on Irish soil dissolves into the sand, so Bran returns to the sea and is never seen again.

One of the more outlandish reports is that of the voyage (or voyages) of Prince Madoc, a twelfth-century Welsh prince who travelled to the Americas and sailed all along the coast from Nova Scotia to Mexico. The place impressed him so positively that he returned again with folks from Wales to establish a colony. He has been identified with Quetzalcoatl as a legendary white man who taught Native Americans to speak Welsh. Other reports surfaced among later American colonists that there were Indians who spoke Welsh but these curious people were never found.

Another voyage involves a chief's son named Mael Duin who sails in a curragh big enough for sixty men in search of a bandit who murdered his father. They come across many exotic islands and creatures including giant ants, exotic birds, monsters and mystifying creatures. At the furthest reach of the journey, there are no beautiful enslaving women this time, but simply a hermit who has the satchel of the great St. Brendan who has been there before.

And this leads us to the story most reported by the Irish, that of St. Brendan the Navigator, born around 489. Medieval maps show something called "St. Brendan's Isle" in various locations far across the Atlantic from Europe. All we can say with reasonable certainty is that Irish sailors, and probably monks as well, had already been living in Iceland when the Norse arrived. It would be a hopeful guess to say that Brendan actually made it to Nova Scotia on his voyages, but the possibility is not to be ruled out. Brendan's tale was written up three or four hundred years after the events were supposed to have occurred. The earliest story has him setting out on a quest for a quiet and peaceful place, failing once and trying it again, this time with success. A message from God later tells him to give up the peace and quiet of the New World and return to a less cloistered life in Ireland.

The twelfth-century version of Brendan's story sends him off with thirty men to an earthly paradise retreat. An angel has told him which direction to sail. Brendan encounters monsters, whales, mermaids and even devils as he sails from island to island only to return home after five years, never having found the promised land. What he really wanted to find was a place of no violence or death. Fearing that he might have failed because he was travelling in a boat made from the slaughtered skins of animals, he built a wooden one and set off with sixty men. This time he confronted more monsters, sea cats and pygmy demons, but he eventually arrived at yet another island, this one inhabited by a lone Irishman, a survivor of some shipwreck, who told him the way to the dream island. The narrative ends where Brendan arrives at the much sought-after coast to find a man wearing brilliant white feathers.

In the long narrative that is the story of Nova Scotia, this tale is probably of little concrete merit, except to show a healthy contrast to the motivation of so many of the explorers who were to follow. Here is an ancient Irishman plowing the seas in search of a little peace and harmony. Had such a tradition prevailed, Nova Scotia might have been populated by a wave of ancient European peaceniks craving a contemplative life. Instead, what followed was a long parade of aggressive men of commerce, lusting for riches and hoping to harvest and harass more than to homestead.

The Fierce Adventurers

While Newfoundland can probably lay a sincere claim to the arrival of the early Norse explorers, it is reasonably safe to say that these fierce, proud but violent people also came ashore on Nova Scotia where they established temporary settlements. The Icelandic sagas provide accounts of voyages to a place known as "Vinland the Good" and it has been widely debated as to exactly where Vinland was—perhaps as far south as Massachusetts or as far north as the coast of Labrador. The name "Vinland" may not have suggested grapes at all, but in translation, simply grass—a land of grass. The grassy expanse of L'Anse aux Meadows in northern Newfoundland fits that description and it is here that archaeologists have found the remains of homesteads created by Norse men *and* women.

The sagas include reports of encounters with Native North Americans called "Skraelings," who may have been Inuit, Beothuck, Mi'kmaq or some other Native group. While these people were considered by the Norse to be hostile and dangerous, a quick scan of many of these sagas and legends reveals that the Norsemen themselves were anything but easy to get along with. They were quick to anger, aggressive and likely to make enemies of whoever crossed their path and it's safe to assume that the Skraelings recognized the imminent danger of these newcomers and tried to defend their homes.

The Icelandic sagas were written in the fourteenth and fifteenth centuries and were based on oral tradition. Thus they are full of half-truths, exaggeration and even contradiction. Nonetheless, we know that Vikings certainly came this way, they settled, they fought, and they died or retreated. Unlike those other Europeans who were to follow, however, they understood the harshness of the cold North Atlantic winters and probably had made better psychological and physical preparation. They were a northern people, turbulent but resilient.

Although evidence of visits by Leif Eriksson and Thorfinn Karlsefni to Newfoundland is quite compelling, the case for Viking visits to Nova Scotia remains tentative at best. However, not far from Yarmouth a stone was discovered which is believed to have an inscription written in ancient Icelandic. Known as the Yarmouth Stone, this piece of rock has been deciphered by the researcher Henry Phillips to say "Harkussen Men Varu" or "Harko's son addressed the men." Harko was one of the men reported to have travelled with Thorfinn Karlsefni. In 1939 Olaf Strandwold, another researcher hot on the trail of the meaning of this rock, deciphered the message as "Leivur Eriku Resr" or "Leif to Erik raises," implying that the rock was a monument recording praise from Leif Eriksson to his father. One of Strandwold's critics, however, suggests that he was a man who was "able to find runes in any crevice or groove and decipher them," while others who have seen the stone suggest that the markings are more likely Mi'kmaq in origin.

The Wealth of Whales

Basque fishermen from the Bay of Biscay prided themselves as being great whalers and there is a record of whaling going on there as early as 1199, although it most likely goes even further back. In the thirteenth and fourteenth centuries, whaling was a Basque monopoly and their catch was plentiful along their own shores until the sixteenth century, when they had depleted their own stock and were forced to travel further for the kill. They went to Spain, Scotland, Iceland and Newfoundland. The European harvest of the sea has rarely been a cautious or concerned endeavour. The message was clear, even as early as this, that the sea did not provide a limitless resource, though this myth has persisted to our own time and may continue to do so until all species of commercial value are eradicated.

Whatever their environmental shortcomings, Basque fishermen were brave, industrious and willing to put up with the great discomforts of a cold North Atlantic crossing for a catch of seafood from the riches of the Grand Banks and beyond. Basque fishermen may have found their way to Newfoundland as early as the 1300s, but the first real documentation shows them here in the 1520s. Port-Aux-Basques in the southwest corner of the island bears their name. Basque whaling ships in the fourteenth century would have rivalled the size of even Columbus's largest vessels.

Basque fishermen fished for whales and cod, both off the shores of Nova Scotia and in the Gulf of St. Lawrence. Life aboard a whaling ship would not have been a pretty picture. There were no sleeping quarters, the provisions would often be rotting, a smell of decaying whale fat would permeate the hold, and beyond that was the danger of icebergs, storms and pervasive cold.

Life ashore in the temporary colonies on Île de Bacaillau (Island of Cod), as they referred to Newfoundland, must have provided some respite to restore their health as the Basques dried and salted their catch for return to their homeland.

The Basques seemed fairly unconcerned with holding down any piece of geography. They wanted the fish and Newfoundland provided a convenient place to go ashore and preserve the catch. The surrender of Newfoundland to the English in 1713 by the Treaty of Utrecht drove the Basques not only from Newfoundland but from the high seas as well. The more militant English, with their weapons and their naval vessels, had by then discovered the great profit to be made in whaling and wanted to have full reign to plunder without competition.

Henry Sinclair and the Holy Grail

St. Brendan, if he came this way at all, was not alone in his quest for new land for religious reasons. In recent years considerable ink has been spilled over the evidence concerning the travels and religious quest of Prince Henry Sinclair of the Orkney Islands. While reports of other adventures rest more in legend than fact, there is a credible story here with shreds of concrete evidence that cannot be dismissed.

Sinclair was the son of King John I and Philippa, daughter of John of Gaunt. In his 1974 book about Sinclair, Frederick J. Pohl writes with conviction of the authenticity of Sinclair's travels to Nova Scotia. The story goes as follows.

In 1398 Henry hears a tale about a fisherman who had disappeared into the western sea for about twenty-five years and then returned to tell of a strange but magnificent land where there was plenty of fish but cannibals as well. Not fearing the cannibals, but lured by the adventure, Henry and a sizeable crew set sail and arrive at Newfoundland (called Esotilanda), where an Icelander tells him of another island called Icaria that is ruled by an Irish king. Henry travels there and goes ashore but is attacked by Aboriginals and forced to leave. Sailing further along, they spot smoke coming from a hillside, causing Sinclair to send a hundred of his sailor/soldiers to see what was going on. The men return after eight days to report that the smoke came from a burning pitch-like substance that flowed up from a spring. They also report having found many inhabitants who were small in stature, timid, and living in caves.

Sinclair and some of his men decide to stay on here and send the others back. He may have intended to eventually build another sailing ship from the local trees for his own return voyage, although this plan seems a curious, brazen move that may have left him cut off from his home for good.

There's another facet of this story more intriguing than the journey itself. Michael Bradley, in *Holy Grail Across the Atlantic*, argues that Sinclair's journey was not purely for discovery. Henry Sinclair was a supporter of the Templar movement of Europe and provided refuge for those persecuted on the continent. Some believe that the Templars had inherited the Holy Grail—the actual cup used by Christ and passed around at the Last Supper. Bradley and other writers have put forward the notion that Sinclair came to Nova Scotia with his Templar refugees to hide the Holy Grail from enemies and also to establish some sort of new colony as a refuge for his persecuted friends. Bradley points out that early maps of Nova Scotia show some sort of castle near the centre of Nova Scotia that was similar to castles in Sinclair's homeland.

Adding to this amazing but far-fetched story is new research by a surveyor named William Mann, which includes exact details about where the Holy

Grail is buried in Nova Scotia and other clues to Sinclair's visits here that involve surveying techniques, stone carvings, Masonic codes and the mystery of buried treasure on Oak Island. Establishing the truth about what actually happened may be impossible after these many years, but the controversy surrounding this mystery will undoubtedly have a long life. If Pohl, Bradley and Mann are correct, then Sinclair hoped Nova Scotia to be a kind of New Jerusalem, a land of religious refuge and spiritual growth.

Chapter Six

Sailors Westward:
In Search of New Worlds

La Nuova Francia, *a 1556 map by Giacomo Gastaldi; an exotic portrayal of the New World.*

John Cabot: "Immense Quantities of Fish"

None of John Cabot's own writing has survived, so it is hard to tell his tale with supreme accuracy. In Cabot's day and in the years after, events were recorded in "chronicles," massive journals that bridged big chunks of history. Often one chronicler borrowed from another and stories had a habit of altering according to the mindset of the scribbler. Fact and fiction were meshed together but, of course, this can be said of reporting in our own time as well. So what we have is a story made up of fragments, opinions and guesswork about who John Cabot was and what he did.

My attempt here is to pull together some consensus of the man. The government of Nova Scotia has erected a monument along the Cabot Trail, where John supposedly set foot, but my guess is that this was a hopeful notion, geared toward tourism, not history.

John Cabot was most likely born in Genoa but had become a naturalized Venetian. He was of "plebian origin" and while we like the comfortable sound of the anglicized name, he has been recorded with many variants on his name including Cabot, Caboot, Cabota, Kabotto, Shabot, Tabot and Gabote among them. He had a wife who was Venetian and three sons— Luigi, Sebastian and Sancio. He was skilled as a seaman, navigator and merchant and believed the earth was a sphere, not flat. Cabot arrived in England somewhere between 1484 and 1490 and settled in the port city of Bristol. It is quite possible that his first voyage toward the New World was cut short in 1496 due to bad weather.

Certainly Cabot must have been a persuasive man. When he did set off on his successful mission, he had letters patent from the king permitting him and his sons to become governors of whatever new territories they found, reserving a mere one-fifth of all profits for the Crown. All British subjects would be forbidden to visit the new territory without Cabot's consent. The mission statement from the king has a haunting "Star Trek" ring to it, asserting that he was to, "Seek out, discover and find" whatever there was out there. But as the statement continues, it is imbued with the paranoia and cultural egotism of the day. Cabot was instructed to discover "whatsoever islands, countries, regions, or provinces of heathens or infidels, in whatever part of the world they be, which before this time were unknown to all Christians."

Although an adventurer, and a damn good navigator, Cabot may have been a businessman first. He had hoped he was headed toward Asia and could ultimately divert the spice trade from the Mediterranean. Jewels and spices were to be had somewhere across those cold northern waters, he figured wrongly. So, one wonders exactly what hunch this shrewd businessman was working on as he set off for yet another new route to the East. It could be that his life in England, and in Bristol in particular, had introduced him to the Icelandic sagas and reports of the discoveries of lands to the west. The English had had contact with Icelanders since the fourteenth century and had with them a healthy trade in fish, cloth, oil, salt and volcanic "brymstone." Bristol merchants would have heard the Norse tales, including the stories of Norse pioneers attacked by the "Skraeling savages" of Vinland. Cabot may have hoped that beyond the coastal "savages" were rich inland cities and even a sea route to China.

Cabot received no funds from the king, so he hoped to make a fairly cheap first expedition, a reconnaissance voyage, in 1497. The *Matthew* was a medium-sized vessel referred to as a "navicula," or more commonly known as a barque, with a crew of a mere eighteen, including his thirteen-year-old son, Sebastian. At least Sebastian wrote in later years that he was aboard, although this cannot be confirmed. There was also a Genoese barber-surgeon, a man from Burgundy and an assortment of English sailors.

On June 24 of 1497, Cabot landed somewhere and he found snares for trapping animals and a fishing-net needle, evidence enough that there was human life along this coast. Yet there must have been substantial fear that these inhabitants would be hostile. Cabot saw fish in great numbers as he sailed along the coast for about three weeks.

Cabot's friend Raimondo de Soncino later wrote to the Duke of Milan informing him that the new-found wealth of fish meant that England need not remain dependent on Icelandic fish. Clearly, fish was a hot topic in those days. There was money to be made—lots if it—in catching and shipping new sources. Not only had Cabot sighted an abundance of "stockfish," as cod was often called, but June 24 was probably a time when capelin would have been abundant along the shores.

Sadly, historians say there is no hard evidence to prove exactly what land Cabot found on this voyage or where he landed. His contract with the king did not grant him permission to sail southward from England, so Cabot may have misrepresented his trip in his own reports. One good estimate suggests that the trip across took fifty-five days at an average of a mere 2.5 kilometres an hour. According to the map drawn by Sebastian in 1542, his father landed them somewhere near the north end of Cape Breton, thus legitimizing the Cabot Trail. Sebastian labelled the land "Prima Terra Vista." He also mentions an island named "St. John" which could have been one of the Magdalens.

Much of what we know of this voyage is based on what Sebastian had to say about the trip. Unfortunately, the younger Cabot had at least a small reputation as a liar. At one time, he had said he was born in Venice but he also reported that he was born in Bristol. Reports suggest he also took credit for discovering the new land himself and yet on another occasion reported that he'd never visited this foreign place at all. Hence the following passage from the legend of Sebastian's map may be more fancy that fact. It seems unlikely to me that he would have seen all of the following at one single location, but it is vividly written and it is the sort of thing that would stir other adventurers with both fear and curiosity about the land beyond the Atlantic. In describing Prima Terra Vista, he writes:

> The natives of it go about dressed in skins of animals; in their wars they use bows and arrows, lances and darts, and clubs of wood, and slings. This land is very sterile. There are in it many white bears, and very large stags like horses, and many other animals. And like in manner there are immense quantities of fish—soles, salmon, very large cods, and many other kinds of fish. They call the great multi-tude of them baccalaos; and there are also in this country dark-coloured falcons like crows, eagles, partridges, sand pipers, and many other birds of different kinds.

With such abundance of everything, I can't help but wonder exactly what he meant by "sterile." But if he saw nothing else, I'm sure that Sebastian saw fish, fish and more fish.

Before the voyage was over, John Cabot, flexing his ownership of the new land, gave an island to his Burgundian cohort and another to the Genoese barber-surgeon. Back home in England, Cabot was made an admiral and given a pension of twenty pounds per year.

Much of what has been reported about Cabot comes from *The Chronicle of Robert Fabyan* as rendered by Richard Hakluyt in his *Divers Voyages*, printed in 1582. Fabyan's document no longer exists, so what we have is really an interpretation of an interpretation. In it Hakluyt seems to have confused John Cabot with his son, which again might make us wonder about credibility. Hakluyt is also the one who stated that Cabot brought three Native people back to England. Of the prisoners (or guests?) he writes, "These were clothed in beastes skinnes, and ate raw flesh, and spake such speech that no man coulde understand them, and in their demeanour like to bruite beastes, whom the king kept a time after."

And so began the propagation of the lie that Native people of the Americas were savages. Hakluyt seemed genuinely surprised that they were not speaking English on the other side of the ocean. Reports of the mysteri-ous three Indians occur again in John Stow's *Chronicle* of 1580, only this time it was Sebastian who brought them, not his father. And so it goes.

Some scholars question whether Sebastian inscribed the information on his map or whether it was added later as an embellishment. Whatever the case, it's clear that the earliest English images of the New World were shaped more by fancy than by fact, illusions and delusions being far more tantalizing to the imagination than a long, slow and eminently dull trip across a cold, grey ocean.

In 1498, John Cabot shipped out of Bristol again to return to his new land. No mention is made of his sons, but Thomas Bradley and Lancelot Thirkill, fellow merchants with a passion for exploiting the riches of the unknown, accompanied him. Storms drove at least one of the five ships back to port in Ireland. The latter-day chronicles suggest that Cabot saw icebergs in the north and revelled in constant sunlight in July and somewhere between Newfoundland and Nova Scotia encountered vast quantities of fish. History does not reveal any hard evidence that Cabot made it back to England, although there is a record of his "pension" being paid up until September of 1499.

Some speculators suggest that Cabot returned, but having failed to find his way to China and Japan, he was somewhat in disgrace. Alas, fish were not the same exotic commodity as gold and spice.

A map circulating in Spain in 1500 showed a fairly detailed coast from Cape Breton to Long Island. Cabot may have actually covered much of this territory on his second, longer voyage. Whatever the case, Cabot's voyages did not set off a wave of enthusiasm for this uncharted land. The royal family may not have been enthusiastic about the myriad of cod that could feed the population of England many times over, but rumour of these great fishing grounds circulated from one coastal port to another in England and beyond in Europe. Perhaps that is Cabot's legacy—one that would ultimately lead to the final decimation of the Grand Banks cod in the 1980s and even a kind of fish war between the European Community and Canada involving gunboat diplomacy in 1995.

Jacques Cartier Forges Further West

Like other European explorers, Jacques Cartier was searching for a route to Asia that would lead him to gold, spices and fabulous wealth. On his first voyage, he sailed to the coast of Labrador, and traded with the Mi'kmaq people at the Bay of Chaleur. The next year he set off again from France with three ships and 112 men. With the help of friendly Iroquois guides, he ventured further up the St. Lawrence and was told stories of fabulous riches to be had in the land beyond. On his return voyage to France in 1536, he made a curious diversion as he was sailing homeward out of the Gulf of St. Lawrence. East of the Magdalens, he noticed the striking mountainous coastline of Cape Breton. He sailed south, then north, in a sort of hairpin turn, giving him a closer look at the coast from Inverness to Cape North. But that was probably as close as he came to Nova Scotia. Nonetheless, Cartier's expeditions would eventually set in motion political and expeditionary activities leading France into the ensuing power struggle for Nova Scotia that would continue for well over two centuries.

Cartier set off again in 1541 and stayed on in the New World through a debilitating winter. He was convinced, however, that he had discovered gold and diamonds and returned to France with what turned out to be false evidence. After this fiasco, Cartier retired to a quiet life in Saint Malo, and France more or less lost interest in the New World for another fifty years.

Chapter Seven

Port Royal and the Order of Good Cheer

Logemens des artifans.	F Paliffade de pieux.	rebaftir, & y logea le fieu
Plate forme où eftoit le ca- non.	G Le four. H La cuifine.	Boulay quand le fieur d Pont s'en reuint en Franc
Le magafin.	O Petite maifonnette où l'on	P (1) La porte de l'abitation.
Logement du fieur de Pont- graué & Champlain.	retiroit les vtanfiles de nos barques; que depuis le	Q (2) Le cemetiere. R (3) La riuiere.
La forge.	fieur de Poitrincourt fit	

Samuel de Champlain's drawing of fort at Port Royal, 1613.

Hazards of the Acadian Winters

In 1524, Giovanni da Verrazzano used the term "Arcadie" on a map he created of the northeast coast of North America. The name referred to a legendary land of tranquillity and beauty. Map makers over the years had moved this label to several locations as maps improved, until it eventually stuck to the territory that includes present-day Nova Scotia, New Brunswick and parts of Quebec. The original moniker may have been mixed with the Mi'kmaq term for a safe harbour, "cadie," resulting in the French adopting "Acadie" to put on the maps.

By the early seventeenth century both England and France believed the new lands could be exploited for profit. Colonies could provide a new form of wealth, and expansion of territorial rule might prove of military importance in the future. There was a degree of stability in France under Henry IV and rivalry with Spain was taken care of with the Edict of Nantes in 1598. True to the spirit of business exploitation, a Protestant merchant named Pierre du Gua de Monts was put in charge of French colonization. Henry magnanimously granted de Monts authority over all the territory between the fortieth and forty-sixth parallels and threw in a ten-year monopoly to trade with the Native people there. In terms of geography, Henry really had little idea of what he was granting.

One might wonder how both England and France could proceed to give away (or license proprietorship over) something they had not fully charted, indeed something they had no right to own. It would be an alien and absurd notion to the Mi'kmaq or to any fair-minded citizen of this century, yet property ownership in Nova Scotia to this day can be traced back to all the various "grants" of land that would be made to the English as they superseded the French with their appropriation of land. Since a Mi'kmaq lived *on* the land and *with* the land, he saw no need for ownership. The European mind would see things differently.

De Monts could have chosen to establish a colony in any number of places between the fortieth and forty-sixth parallels, but he chose Acadia because of its proximity to the sea, benevolent Native people, good agricultural lands, the prevalence of fur-bearing animals and hopes that the nearby waterway of the St. Lawrence might yet be found to be the route to Asia. This colony would also be positioned relatively close to the Grand Banks fishing grounds.

In 1604 de Monts began his two-month voyage along with the wealthy nobleman Jean de Poutrincourt and Samuel de Champlain, who would act as geographer. Because of his later efforts on behalf of the king, Champlain would be referred to as the "Father of New France," allowing him to receive much of the glory and some of the blame for the colonizing of Acadia.

Champlain was born in 1567 at Brouage, the son of a sea captain. As a soldier and a sailor, he crossed the Atlantic in 1598 to the West Indies and Mexico, then wrote and illustrated a book about the trip that much entertained the king. Champlain would make ten voyages in all to what he called "the Great River of Canada." His first voyage to Acadia, however, under the direction of de Monts, would not be an easy crossing. There were horrendous storms, a close call involving icebergs and a near grounding on Sable Island before reaching Cap de la Have on the South Shore of Nova Scotia. As they travelled south and west along the coast, they came across a Captain Rossignol trading with the Mi'kmaq. Today Port Rossignol bears his name, although we know little about how this brazen trader came to be there. Further along they decided to go ashore at Port Mouton, named thus because a sheep fell overboard there and drowned.

Rounding the southernmost tip of Nova Scotia, Champlain and de Monts entered what they called Baie Française (the Bay of Fundy) and soon were delighted to find the smaller protected bay that Champlain would describe as "One of the finest harbours that I have seen on all these coasts." Here would be the site of the future Port Royal.

They sailed further to the Chignecto Peninsula, then back down the Bay of Fundy and wintered over on Sainte Croix Island in the Ste. Croix River,

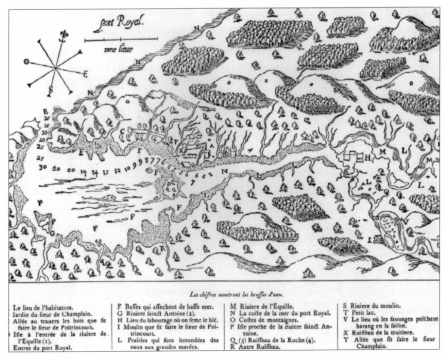

Samuel de Champlain's map of areas surrounding Port Royal, 1613.

a decidedly bad choice. They would have to travel continually to the mainland for firewood, fresh water and food supplies. Their homes were poorly built with many cracks that allowed the winter winds to invade. Despite some knowledge of a Native herbal tea that warded off disease, thirty-five of the seventy-nine men died of scurvy. Owning up to the fact that Sainte Croix Island was a poor place to live, Champlain ventured further along the coast of Maine but found it less than inviting. He and de Monts agreed that the outpost be moved back to that previous harbour across the Bay of Fundy that Champlain had found so desirable.

On both sides of the bay, the French encountered Native people: the Penobscot, the Maliseet and, near Port Royal, the Mi'kmaq with whom they would strike up a most beneficial alliance. Apparently the Mi'kmaq welcomed the French to Port Royal with open arms. Their leader was a man named Membertou, described by one of the settlers as being "of prodigious size, and taller and stronger-limbed than most, bearded like a Frenchman while not one of the others had hair on his chin." Membertou said he was over a hundred years old and that he had previously encountered Jacques Cartier.

De Monts returned to France to report to the king and to bring back supplies. The colony of forty survivors was left in the charge of Lieutenant François Pontgrave who saw his men through a somewhat milder winter that killed only a dozen of them. Still not convinced that they had chosen the most comfortable location, Pontgrave set off in the spring of 1606, again in search of a more suitable, warmer place further to the south for a permanent colony. But there were more problems. First there was a "navigational accident." Then Pontgrave suffered a heart attack, and finally his ship "ran aground and broke to pieces." Discouraged all round, they decided to abandon Port Royal. Two Frenchmen agreed to stay behind and look after things. The rest of the men would try to return to France on fishing boats working near Cape Sable. There the Port Royal refugees heard of the news of fresh supplies and more men on their way to Port Royal. The ships arrived under the command of Poutrincourt, who had replaced de Monts. With him were Marc Lescarbot, a poet and lawyer, as well as Claude and Charles de La Tour.

"The Spice of Fortune's favour"

Under Poutrincourt, further explorations took place as the French continued to look for a more comfortable colony site. New England proved inhospitable to them with unfriendly Natives, strong winds and unsafe harbours. Downhearted, Poutrincourt arrived back in Port Royal in November of 1606, feeling like a failure. Fortunately for all concerned, Lescarbot was feeling more like a poet rather than a lawyer. He decided to lift Poutrincourt's spirits by writing and staging a play, a masque called *le Theatre de Neptune,* the first bit of theatre for the New World. Lescarbot admitted it was simply "French rhymes penned in haste," but it helped to raise the spirits of all concerned. Lescarbot appeared as Neptune in a boat, accompanied by four French "Indians."

It was a kind of tribute to Poutrincourt and everyone who had survived the dangers of sea travel and adventure, sounding at times like a prototype for tourist brochures promoting sea travel. Lescarbot seems also to have established the first public-relations office in the New World as he wrote:

> If man would taste the spice of fortune's savour
> He must needs seek the aid of Neptune's favour
> For stay at homes who doze on kitchen settles
> Earn no glory than their pots and kettles.

It would be a long winter but already it was clear that things would be different. If bad feelings and even talk of insurrection could be quelled with a little theatre, it was decided that even more concerted efforts toward entertainment might help them through an otherwise cheerless winter. And so Port Royal would become a party town. The Order of Good Cheer (L'Ordre de Bon Temps) was founded to help keep everybody happy and even healthy. Fifteen men would sit at Poutrincourt's high table on a regular basis and each would have a crack at preparing a meal designed to outdo the last.

No European women lived in Port Royal at that time, so it was a true "buddy" club. But neither were there priests on hand to temper the good times with solemnity. Certainly religion was not forgotten as Poutrincourt and Lescarbot continued to plan ahead for the colony's survival so far from France. Had European politics not returned to haunt the shores of Nova Scotia, it is conceivable that the Order of Good Cheer could have provided a mildly hedonistic and happy model for the foundations of a new society, one that could have readily been sustained by the food resources available.

They ate well and they ate plentifully of what was available: wildfowl, sturgeon, moose, beaver, otter, wildcat and raccoon. There were also peas, rice, beans, prunes, raisins, dried cod to be added to the menu, and wine was not in short supply. Lescarbot noted that he was particularly fond of bear flesh, which he found "very good and tender," as well as "delicate beaver's tail" and "tender moose meat." For dessert there was "certain small fruits like small apples coloured red, of which we made jelly."

Chief Membertou was treated as an equal and partook of the feast with the French. Twenty or thirty Mi'kmaq men, women, girls and boys were often on hand to watch the entertainment. Lescarbot says they "beheld us doing our offices," as the French feasted and partied. The audience was given free bread but nothing more, although Lescarbot had high regard for their civility, remarking that they were more mannerly and polite than the French.

The Poet and the Chief

Unlike the English who would follow, the French did not push the issue of ownership of land with the Mi'kmaq even though de Monts had paperwork from a distant king laying claim to it. Each day the "Habitation" had visits from the Mi'kmaq and our trusty reporter of the day, Lescarbot, says that Chief Membertou had described his counterpart Poutrincourt as a "great friend, brother, companion and equal." These are happy words but haunting ones since very little would be made of *equality* in the politics of the century to follow.

During that first winter, at least six Frenchmen lived with the Mi'kmaq people nearby, the first of the French *coureurs de bois* who would take up Native ways in years to follow as they travelled to the interior of the continent. Lescarbot painted the Mi'kmaq as "truly noble" and praised them for their lack of "vain-glory, ambition, envy, and avarice."

Despite such admiration, the French often referred to them as savages, since they were not Christians. Lescarbot studied their songs and prayers and fancied their spirits to be aligned with the devil and powers of darkness. They were to his mind, alas, "destitute of all knowledge of God." Poutrincourt would attempt some degree of Christian conversion, but didn't have the luxury of trained clergy to help out in the task. Among his own ranks, the great impresario Lescarbot would lead a Sunday sermon to help keep Christianity alive.

The French and the Mi'kmaq shared meals that first winter and the relationship was certainly a fruitful one for both sides. While the Mi'kmaq could not possibly have foreseen the invasion of French and English that would follow, they noted with displeasure the arrival of a new creature into their midst. Rats came ashore from sailing vessels, perhaps the first ever to find their way to North America, and they adapted well to the new territory. There is no record that Lescarbot or Poutrincourt ever made apologies for such an unwanted gift.

In May of the following spring a ship arrived from France to inform the tiny colony that de Monts' contract to control this land had been revoked due to political pressure at home. De Monts had never really been able to establish the monopoly on furs that he had planned. Rumours suggested that his company's treasurer, De Bellois, along with Pontgrave and de Monts himself, had defrauded the company of money. The entire fur business was also in question. It had created some tensions with Native people elsewhere for the obvious reason that foreigners were killing off the source of their livelihood. Some Frenchman had also dug up the dead in Native burial grounds to rob them of the furs they had been buried with. These complaints, along with other more political reasons, led the king to revoke the privileges he had granted de Monts.

On July 17, 1607, Poutrincourt, Lescarbot and the entire party left the fort at Port Royal, heading for Canso. Membertou and his people were left ten barrels of flour and possession of the Habitation if they cared to use it. History does not reveal whether any Mi'kmaq jumped at the chance to move into a slightly used French fort. Most likely they would have found those dark, stark dwellings inhospitable compared to their own homes.

Champlain, who had survived his life at Port Royal not much worse for wear, had the opportunity to put his map-making skills to work again as they sailed around the southern tip of Nova Scotia and on toward Canso. In particular, he noted "a very sound bay seven or eight leagues long, where there are no islands in the channel save at the end." He referred to this body of water as "*une baie fort saine*," or "a good safe bay," and it would one day be known as Halifax Harbour.

Chapter Eight

A Charter for New Scotland

Sir William Alexander.

Absentee Owners and Hesitant Settlers

England had laid claim to virtually all of North America as a result of the explorations of John Cabot, but there seemed to be little ambition or political will to do anything about it until 1583 when Sir Humphrey Gilbert sailed from Plymouth and eventually arrived at the present location of St. John's, Newfoundland. Here he "took possession" on behalf of Queen Elizabeth I. He decided to explore further, but something went wrong and he went down with his ship, *The Squirrel*. Gilbert's brother-in-law, Walter Raleigh, took renewal of the Queen's patent to continue exploration. Raleigh went further south, eventually making the fateful decision to create a settlement on Roanoke Island in what is now North Carolina. Raleigh returned to England with Francis Drake, leaving his settlement behind. It was three years before he could return with supplies, only to find that the entire community had mysteriously vanished.

In 1606, big business came into the picture. The London and Plymouth Trading companies were granted the right to control a big chunk of the Atlantic coast from Port Royal and all of Acadia down to Cape Fear. Jamestown, in Virginia, was settled in 1607.

The newly formed Virginia Company created a settlement in Newfoundland as early as 1610 and Virginian John Smith (of Pocahontas fame) made a fairly extensive exploration of the Northern Atlantic coast, including Acadia, in 1616. He reported good land and favourable weather, but could not muster up an attractive enough picture to encourage settlement at that time.

Despite the fact that the English were not all that excited about inhabiting Acadia, there was money and hostility enough for the Virginia Company to launch a raid far northward from their southern colony to destroy the tiny French encampment of St. Sauveur in Maine. Under Samuel Argall, the English ships then sailed on to the empty fort at Port Royal and rather than occupying it, they ruthlessly demolished it.

Monsieur Poutrincourt had hoped to return to Port Royal and re-establish trade there. He heard the bad news in France and returned to see the ruins, which discouraged him sufficiently to give up on the idea of revitalizing Port Royal. However, he did leave Biencourt behind to maintain a fur trade. The French occupation of Acadia would remain just a string of small fur-trading outposts for years to come.

Renewed interest in this land, however, came from a Scotsman this time. William Alexander was a titled Scot, a friend of James I and a tutor of his son. He was also a prolific poet, although he was never a very popular one. As secretary of state for Scotland, he was a powerful and influential man who had visions of establishing his own colony, independent of that in

Virginia or Newfoundland. He persuaded his friend King James, also a Scot, that there should be a "New Scotland," just as there was already a New England, New France, etc.

The king liked the idea and granted a charter in 1621 to Sir William. In Latin, the land would be called Nova Scotia. It included mainland Nova Scotia, what would later become New Brunswick and parts of Quebec. Both the king and Alexander simply ignored the fact that this was the same land that the French had already claimed and called Acadia. It also meant taking land away from the grant given to the Council of New England. Obviously, Alexander was highly thought of at court, because he moved things even further along and successfully lobbied for a second grant of land—Cape Breton Island—for his friend Sir Robert Gorden.

Alexander himself was too comfortable in his own country to consider shipping off across the Atlantic to see his new property. In fact, it was a tough sell even to find volunteers to go across the sea for whatever opportunities might await them. Everyone knew of the inherent danger of territorial fighting that might break out at any time with the French. Nonetheless, a hesitant first expedition of farm hands, a minister and a blacksmith left Scotland in June of 1622. They ran into a raging storm just as they sighted Cape Breton in the early fall. This persuaded them to go ashore at St. John's, where many of them died during the bitter winter that they were not prepared for.

Another ship was sent across in 1623 and took on the ten survivors in Newfoundland. They sailed to Nova Scotia, all the while wrestling with difficult winds and impertinent fog. They explored much of the coast and then returned to England with a cargo of Newfoundland fish. Oddly enough, these hearty souls must have decided to put a positive spin onto the tale of their misery and woe, for they told Alexander enthusiastic stories of fertile land, rivers, abundant wood, furs and, of course, lots of fish.

Undoubtedly, Sir William was being told what he wanted to hear and the news was enough to continue his efforts to settle Nova Scotia. The only problem was that the first two voyages had used up what available money he had. It would not be the last time in history that Nova Scotia would encounter financial hardship. Alexander decided to put his poetic skills to work to muster interest from the Scottish landholders for his endeavours. He penned a neat little bit of propaganda that he called "An Encouragement to Colonization," and spread the good tidings of this already precarious business venture.

Conspiring with King James, Sir William came up with a sure-fire gimmick to raise the needed cash. For three thousand "merks" a gentleman could become a "Knight Baronet of Nova Scotia," complete with a whopping 30,000 acres of land. The gentlemen would, however, be obliged to send settlers west to occupy the foreign estate. Land to Sir William was cheap and disposable, even though it's hard to figure exactly how he had any moral ownership to any of it—he'd never even been there.

A Conflict of Claims

In 1625 James died and his son, Charles I, took the throne and continued to support the idea of baronets. By May of that year, there were eight baronets in all; the order kept going until 1638 and it earned a lot of money for Sir William. One sticky part of the deal was that you could not fully become a baronet until you actually stood on Nova Scotia soil. The would-be buyers complained that Nova Scotia was simply too far away, that the journey would be uncomfortable and dangerous and they shouldn't have to put up with such inconveniences. Before he died, King James and Sir William fine-tuned the agreement by declaring part of the castle yard in Edinburgh as Nova Scotian soil, which it remains to this day. So all you had to do was pay the cash, get touched on the shoulder with the sword of the king in down-town Edinburgh and receive your credentials as a knight. Even at that, it was a tough sell.

Nonetheless, enough money was raised to send ships and men for another attempt at settlement. Two groups were sent off. William Alexander the Younger (Sir William's son) was in command of one and Lord Ochiltree was in charge of another. Along with the less-than-enthusiastic colonists, Ochiltree's group arrived at Baleine, near Louisbourg on Cape Breton Island. They started to clear some land and build a fort for protection from the French. Lord Ochiltree, however, anxious to see some profit from his charter as baronet of this new territory, set about collecting a tax of one-tenth of all the fish caught by foreign vessels off these shores. This turned out to be a decidedly bad move on his part.

The French, of course, had also laid claim to Cape Breton. One day, a French captain by the name of Daniel became separated from his fleet and was sailing off the coast of Cape Breton. From the fishermen he met, he heard of the tariff imposed by Ochiltree and was incensed by the audacity of this less-than-diplomatic Scottish lord. His ship assaulted the fort at Baleine, destroying it and taking all of the settlers as prisoners. They were carried to St. Ann's, and treated to hard labour but finally put on ships and sent back to Scotland. Lord Ochiltree and a few others were put in prison in France and then released two years later.

William the Younger had gone on to settle at the vacated site of Port Royal where his group actually did quite well for a couple of years.

Chapter Nine

Carving Up Acadia

The coat-of-arms of Charles de St.-Etienne, Sieur de La Tour; from a letter dated 25 July 1627.

One Hundred Associates

Despite the pull-out from Port Royal, the French had not entirely given up interest in Acadia. If there was profit yet to be made there, then someone was sure to take up the cause for control and colonization. After the death of Biencourt, the lands under his control were passed on to his friend Charles de La Tour. Charles and his father, Claude, had spent some time at Port Royal and Charles was in charge of the fort at Cape Sable, as well as other Acadian lands. Charles ended up in control of almost all of Acadia by 1631.

It was an age of paranoia as well as mercantile expansion. Had the English not been worrying about the French and vice versa, it's probable that the colonization of Nova Scotia would have slowed to a snail's pace. Weather, starvation and fears of a potentially hostile Native population discouraged many from setting out across the sea. In the 1620s the population of New France was minuscule and spread thin. French businessmen relied mainly on Mi'kmaq labour to trap furs and, in effect, there was little need for a significant French population to keep up the trade on that front. It was apparent, however, that the French were falling behind in the business of exploiting the potential for wealth across the Atlantic. The English and the Dutch both had "companies" to expand colonization and trade in the New World.

In 1627, Cardinal Richelieu, perhaps more intrigued by commerce than God at this point in his life, created something called the Company of One Hundred Associates to get serious about economic growth in French territories. The lucky one hundred would have a virtual monopoly over land and trade in New France.

Competition in the New World may have fuelled apprehension and hostility between the European powers, but there was some attempt to establish peace and define boundaries to ease tensions—at least on paper. On April 29, 1629, a peace treaty was signed between France and England. All former colonies, including Port Royal, were supposed to revert to France. William Alexander was flabbergasted. Of course, what was written in ink was not necessarily binding. England had agreed to return Quebec, but partly because of Sir William's New World interest, the English weren't really all that keen about giving up Acadia. There were also some ill feelings here over a marriage that somehow complicated the territorial ownership issue. The King of France had not yet *paid* England for Charles's marriage to his daughter, Henrietta. A deal was a deal and, marital bliss notwithstanding, an English king felt a certain right to see the cash as well as the bride. On top of such grief, Charles was embroiled with various battles in his own Parliament and would rather not concern himself with peripheral interests in the New World if at all possible. Another treaty in 1632 saw England agreeing again to pull out of Acadia altogether.

Treaties, I suppose, establish some sort of historical fact—a document at least that can be read, fondled and referred to. Yet they don't always reveal intention, nor do they necessarily reflect action. News travelled slowly, as well, across the seventeenth-century Atlantic and what a king says or does one day may have no effect at all for many months.

The King of France chose Commander Isaac de Razilly to take charge of recolonizing Acadia after the 1632 treaty, replacing Charles de La Tour who had been the king's lieutenant-governor there. Razilly was a military man; La Tour was a businessman. It was obvious that Acadia was vulnerable to New England, with its ever-growing English population, and the king wanted a soldier there to hang onto the returned territories. So Razilly set sail for Port Royal in a well-armed warship, ready to blast the current Scottish settlers out of there if they were not ready to abide by the new treaty.

The ship first stopped at La Have to establish some new settlers in that rather comfortable spot and then went on to Port Royal, then under the command of the English captain Andrew Forrester, whose men had only recently sacked and burned La Tour's fort on the Saint John River across the Bay of Fundy. Forrester did give up Port Royal and his people were put on a French ship that returned them to Europe, although reports indicate that some of the Scots settlers were so happy in Acadia that they stayed on and blended in with the French.

Acadia Divided

As of 1635, French Acadia was divided roughly into two halves. Razilly had control over Sable Island, La Have, Port Royal and the St. Croix River area. La Tour controlled Cape Sable and Fort La Tour on the Saint John River. Both held titles as lieutenant-governors and were supposed to report to the One Hundred Associates. There was no great conflict here because Razilly's business interests were in lumber, fishing and farming, while La Tour was concentrating on the fur trade.

When Razilly died, his authority went to his cousin, Charles d'Aulnay, who decided to move the La Have settlers to Port Royal and to bring new blood from France. He built a new improved fort on the other side of the Annapolis Basin on what is now the site of Annapolis Royal. With the English and Scots temporarily out of the picture, rivalry flared between Charles de La Tour and d'Aulnay. La Tour, after all, had been given a grant from the king and so had d'Aulnay. There was supposed to be a clear division of lands, but each was jealous of the other. D'Aulnay had also become more interested in the fur trade. It seems that he wanted it all. In 1638, the king elevated d'Aulnay to La Tour's rank and declared that the potentially lucrative fur trade should be divided equally. The king failed to have a good grasp of the geography of Acadia and ended up creating an overlap of ownership between the two men, escalating the problem.

Across the Bay of Fundy from Port Royal, La Tour had built a trading post and fort. On a visit to Port Royal in 1639, there was a quarrel over the rights to trading furs. It led to one of La Tour's men being killed. Back at his own fort, La Tour then imprisoned some of d'Aulnay's men. La Tour also personally went to Port Royal and attacked d'Aulnay. D'Aulnay wanted to get rid of La Tour and sailed to France to air his grievances, stating that La Tour had become an enemy of France. D'Aulnay was persuasive and he had been instructed by the king to seize La Tour and then take over all of Acadia. La Tour refused to submit and left with his family for Fort La Tour. Out of spite, d'Aulnay attacked the Cape Sable settlement that had been under La Tour's control and burned La Tour's family home to the ground.

La Tour had been having friendly trade relations with New England and this obviously complicated things. He too sought help from his friends in France who were among the One Hundred Associates. His wife, Françoise Marie Jacquelin, personally went to France and brought back ammunition and supplies. La Tour had also sought help from New England. The Puritans there did not want to become embroiled in the struggle, but they were nonetheless willing to look for some profit from it, so they leased some ships to La Tour.

D'Aulnay had the upper hand, however, receiving from France five ships and about five hundred men. They arrived at the Saint John River fort, ready to attack. It was obvious to La Tour that his men wouldn't stand a chance. I guess he figured he had nowhere else to turn for help except his trading buddies in New England and so, along with his wife, he quickly sailed off in search of assistance.

La Tour and his wife glided into Boston harbour looking for help and one might wonder why on earth the New Englanders would want to get involved in this feud between Frenchmen. Well, the Bostonian merchants knew of d'Aulnay and felt that if he became too powerful he might be a threat to them. Also, Charles de La Tour's father, Claude, had actually become a Knight Baronet of Nova Scotia back when William Alexander was carving up Nova Scotia. Are you confused yet? Perhaps most logical was the fact that La Tour owed a lot of money to the Boston merchants from whom he had previously purchased supplies. Bostonians knew that if La Tour lost out against the well-armed d'Aulnay, they'd never see a cent for their goods. So they graciously contributed 140 men willing to fight and four ships to float them back to Saint John.

It's not clear why d'Aulnay had not already simply trashed and destroyed Fort La Tour. Maybe he wanted a good fight as well as the spoils and he was waiting for the despised "enemy of France," La Tour, to return. If so, he miscalculated his opponent's advantage. La Tour and his Yanks were able to send d'Aulnay scuttling back across the big bay.

Threats from d'Aulnay continued, however, and La Tour sent his wife on a ship to France with a load of goods to help firm up relations there. The captain of the ship, unfortunately, didn't seem to like taking orders from a woman and, instead of sailing straight to France, he went fishing near Newfoundland and then, tiring of La Tour's wife's complaints, dropped her off in Boston. Undaunted and indignant, Françoise Marie Jacquelin took her complaint to the primitive American legal system, sued the pants off the disrespectful captain, and won. She used the money to buy supplies and, after two years, returned to her husband at Fort La Tour.

In the spring of 1645, it was Charles who was away in Boston when the dogged d'Aulnay attacked again. Françoise Marie Jacquelin was not a woman to give up easily. Bolstered by her success in an American legal battle, she was ready and willing to deal with whatever adversity lay in her path. With only forty-five men she kept up a defence against a large battalion of d'Aulnay's men for three days and three nights. One of her sentries, a Swiss soldier, allowed a breach in the perimeter and d'Aulnay's men began to scale the walls as she bravely stood at the forefront of her men to fight back.

D'Aulnay now knew that he was fighting against a woman and the thought of being defeated by her was a humiliation that he could not bear. He got a message to her that if she were to surrender, he would not kill her men. La Tour's wife saw some glimmer of hope for the survival of her people and she surrendered.

While it is not exactly fair to pick out the good guys from the bad in this one, one can certainly admire the courage and stamina of this brave woman. D'Aulnay on the other hand, comes off as a bastard. Realizing at the end of the battle that he had been up against only a small band of hard-nosed fighters led by a woman, he felt dishonoured. So he went against his oath and hanged a good portion of her men, while Marie watched with a rope fitted around her own neck. She was spared the death sentence on that day, but died three weeks later while imprisoned.

To the winner goes the spoils and so King Louis of France named d'Aulnay master of all of Acadia, while Charles de La Tour, his wife dead and his fort lost, went to hide in the governor's chateau at Quebec. He may have fallen out of favour with the king, but he was not without friends and had not given up hope.

Drowning in Debt

D'Aulnay's Acadia now stretched beyond the old boundaries to include everything to the mouth of the St. Lawrence River. For good measure he seized Cape Breton Island, which had been under the control of the One Hundred Associates. Nicholas Denys, who also held land grants from the

French king, had settled into fishing and trading from Miscou Island in the Gulf of St. Lawrence. He too was forced out by the greedy d'Aulnay, who wanted a true monopoly of the region. In one of history's gentle ironies, it appears that d'Aulnay, having eliminated all of his allies who might have helped him truly develop Acadia, found himself unable to replace those men he had driven away. His ambitions were thwarted. In 1650 he fell out of a canoe and drowned. Some say he was "allowed to drown" by disgruntled Mi'kmaq men who were with him at the time.

La Tour must have been elated to hear of d'Aulnay's watery demise, and he was bold enough to sail back to France to reassert his rights in America. Unfortunately, La Tour's debts, which had once proven to be an asset in getting help from the Bostonians, came back to haunt him. He was thrown into prison for not being able to repay his loans in his own country. He was, however, later absolved of all debts and accusations by Louis XIV and even declared lieutenant-governor over all of d'Aulnay's Acadia.

Ironically, d'Aulnay had drowned with his own set of debts, and a man named Emmanuel Le Borgne claimed *he* should be the rightful heir to Acadia. Jeanne Motin, d'Aulnay's widow, who had been fortunate enough to have kept her power-hungry husband at some distance through much of their marriage, claimed the right to half of what her husband had "owned" but was willing to give the other half to someone who would support her claim. Undoubtedly, these claims kept many scribes and legal professionals hard at work until in 1653 a compromise was worked out. Jeanne Motin, with eight children, agreed to marry La Tour—a very bizarre twist, indeed. Twenty years of bad blood would be forgotten and the dowry was the fort on the Saint John River, which had been snatched from La Tour by Jeanne's husband at the expense of many men and La Tour's own wife.

A Very British French Colony

Around this time, the English were getting nervous again about the growth of non-English settlements in the Americas. The king commissioned Major Robert Sedgwick to attack New Holland, but when peace was arranged between the English and the Dutch, he turned his animosity toward Acadia. The English had many potential enemies and if one was lost, another could always be found. New England was prospering—especially the fishing industry. England wanted to protect her interests there and Acadia was just too close for comfort.

La Tour realized he was up against a formidable enemy—although one that could potentially be an ally. Sedgwick had three ships and 170 men when he arrived in Acadia. La Tour gave up without a fight and, instead of cowering as a loser in the affair, La Tour reasserted his baronial status as granted by William Alexander to the Frenchman's dead father. Charles even travelled with Sedgwick to England, where this point was affirmed. The English were then willing to recognize La Tour's authority over the south and east of Acadia, while the rest of Acadia would remain under separate English control. Undaunted and still very much enamoured with Acadian life, La Tour returned with his family to live at Cape Sable. After all the many years of wrangling over the territory, he simply sold his rights to almost everything and stayed out of any future politics or feuding. "Happily ever after" would probably be stretching the point, but La Tour had certainly proven himself to be a resilient survivor.

The One Hundred Associates had backed Emmanuel Le Borgne as the new man in charge of much of Acadia and granted him everything that had not been in La Tour's possession. By 1657, Le Borgne was, for all intents, the governor of that region, but he had been obliged to capitulate to the English, since he had no claims to being a baronet as La Tour had. The terms of the deal, however, allowed the French inhabitants to stay where they were and they were allowed to keep their lands. British governors were more or less uninterested in this region. The Acadians were left alone for some time and no new English settlement was encouraged.

As France and French political interest faded, however, the Acadians grew comfortable in dealing with the English. Many became bilingual and, in general, they had more contact with the British than with the French.

Chapter Ten

Acadia: More Than a Bargaining Chip

Engraving of an early fish-drying station set up by Europeans in the New World in the late 17th century.

Idyllic Rural Life

T he population of early Acadia was never substantial. Like the Scots and English, few average French citizens were eager to leave the safety and relative comfort of home to seek a new life in this region. Nor was the French government overly zealous to populate Acadia. Razilly had brought more than three hundred men in 1632. The first birth to a French couple took place in 1636, although there is little mention of women in the records. A passenger list to Acadia from 1636 still exists and it logs seventy-seven men and one woman on board. Many settlers soon decided they were happier in France and returned of their own free will on ships headed home. Others dispersed to tiny settlements such as Canso and no real records were kept to report on life there.

Both d'Aulnay and La Tour recruited "engagés" who went to Acadia under contract to maintain the outposts and help in the fur trade. In 1644 d'Aulnay claimed to have had a complement of 200 men, but he too does not mention women.

The French population of Acadia in 1641 is estimated to have been a mere 120 souls. In 1643 it had more than tripled to 400, but by 1671 the number was roughly the same. By 1666, French government policy had declared outright that it would not be a bright move to send more emigrants abroad and *depopulate* France merely to help develop this terrain of questionable value. In short, France was wondering if Acadia was simply more trouble than it was worth.

New England, on the other hand, was growing by leaps and bounds and certainly the 60,000 colonists in Massachusetts had little to fear from the 400 Acadians to the north who were of little interest even to their own French king.

Acadia was a fairly small item in the list of continuing grievances and negotiations between France and England, but it was often a bargaining chip to be tossed on the table at the various summits between the two countries. In the 1667 Treaty of Breda, England gave Acadia back to France. Grandfontaine, the new French governor, would have a tough time reasserting French authority over the nearly autonomous Acadians who had settled into their own unique way of life under the disinterested British. Acadians were now mostly farmers and fishermen, people who made a living but not a profit from the resources. Without profit for French businesses back on the continent, there was little of value in such a colony, one would argue, in the polished dining rooms of Paris. The new region drew a communal sigh of apathy in France. New Englanders, as a result, fished as freely off the shores of Acadia when it was French as when it was English.

Acadian life and livelihood had shifted from fur trading to agriculture.

Acadians were becoming truly rooted in the place they lived. Many knew they could sustain themselves through farming and trade and they were becoming more and more independent of France. By the time Robert Sedgwick sailed from Boston to capture Port Royal as part of the French and English war, the rivalry had relatively little impact on the daily lives of the farming families. And as Charles de La Tour had once accepted the British authority, it was clear that "citizenship" issues were no big deal to most Acadians. The issue of who was in charge was almost a moot point, because there was almost no influx of British settlers. There simply weren't many folks in England who wanted to live in Nova Scotia. Maybe that's partly why the Treaty of Breda gave Acadia back to the French. Whatever bloodshed and violence had occurred in the name of loyalty or empire had been a waste, as much larger forces of political concerns were at work on the continent.

Between 1671 and 1672, however, as squabbles erupted between English and French, some Acadians tried to extricate themselves from the problem by moving to the isthmus of Chignecto under the leadership of Jacques Beaubassin. Here was an area of beautiful, fertile salt marshes. Naming the area for their leader, the homesteaders would almost succeed in establishing a kind of autonomy and, with a population of about two hundred, the community might have become a happily-ever-after tale if it hadn't been for the fact that such a level of independence would eventually rile both the French and English authorities.

Grand Pré, on Fundy's Minas Basin, also became a prospering farming community. This idyllic, rural, family-centred village would one day become the site of one of history's most notorious deportation exercises.

The Acadians were never very good at playing by the rules, especially when the rules were issued by distant, arrogant and ill-informed government officials. So they saw the obvious advantages of trading with whoever wanted to do business with them. This meant New England, where grain and furs could be traded for manufactured things like dishes, needles, knives, as well as rum and sugar from the Caribbean. On paper, this trade was illegal, but no one seemed to worry, since it was mutually rewarding. Slowly but surely, Acadia became integrated into the New England economy.

Because of their tiny population, they were not a threat to anyone English, French or Mi'kmaq. They blended in, they adapted and they carried out equitable trade. For a while, both the French and the English were happy to simply ignore them. Yet New Englanders, including many of the merchants who were profiting from the deals that went down, never fully trusted the Acadians. They were, after all, French and they had suspiciously good relations with the Native people. It was also feared that the French government would some day restrict fishing off the Nova Scotia coast. Business was good with the Acadian neighbours, but paranoia lurked in the shadows.

Easy Targets for Revenge

Compared to much of the history of Nova Scotia—a story of power strug-gles, greed, exploitation and even genocide—the Acadian legacy is fairly benign. An alternate time-line may have allowed for this culture of farmers, dyke builders, family men and women to have evolved into an agrarian utopia. They wanted to be out of the French/English wranglings. And if only they had been left alone, Nova Scotia would have evolved very differently. But the politics of Europe hovered like a dangerous thunderhead always above them.

In 1686 another treaty was signed, one of neutrality between the French and English. England acknowledged France's sole right to the inshore fishing along Acadia. ("Inshore" implies fishing that is coastal as opposed to fishing on the Grand Banks, which is much further offshore.) So now the New Englanders had something tangible to hate the Acadians for. Ships from Boston and the other New England ports had been harvesting fish along Acadian shores for years and turning great profits. But by 1689, problems in Europe again intruded into their lives. Yet another war had broken out between the English and the French. In America it was known as "King William's War" or, in Europe, the "Wars of the League of Augsburg." In a bizarre twist of logic, Quebec attacked New Englanders and the New Englanders retaliated by attacking the Acadians—presumably because they were French, nearby and easy to whip. There was also the possibility of expanding the boundaries of New England to include these lands to the north. Whatever good trading relations had developed over the previous decades were quickly dismissed by New Englanders whose heightened hatred of the French was driving them to retaliate against the wrong "enemy."

The raids from New England began in 1689 and continued into 1690 as Sir William Phipps attacked Port Royal and abducted Governor de Meneval, taking him to Boston. When Joseph Villebon, a military man from France, arrived later that year, he found Port Royal had been plundered. The French soldiers there had been taken away as prisoners. Villebon took con-trol of Acadia—or at least he decided that there was no one else available for the job, so it was up to him. Described as "domineering but dissolute," Villebon moved the settlement to Jemseg, where the English tracked him down, plundered his small community and took his men as prisoners. Villebon went on to build good relations with the Native population in New Brunswick and may have incited them to set off on raids of New England. Although at least one peace treaty was signed between the Natives of Maine and the New Englanders, Villebon used gifts of brandy, tobacco and arms to help inspire French and Native attacks on Maine and New Hampshire.

Villebon's military ambitions were nothing but bad news for the Acadians, the great majority of whom had remained home on the farm, tending fields, fine-tuning their dykes and hoping for further peace and tranquillity. William Phipps, now governor of Massachusetts, ordered Benjamin Church and his soldiers to go to Acadia and destroy everything they could find. This was presumably easier than trying to track down Villebon or fight it out with Natives who were now quite hostile to the New England cause. The Chignecto community was not spared and Acadian villages elsewhere were easy targets for revenge.

Handing Over the Keys

Soon after the turn of the century, yet another power struggle in Europe erupted into a war. In 1702 the War of Spanish Succession had begun. By the end of that conflict France would lose Acadia, Newfoundland and Hudson Bay. King Louis XIV would be left holding onto Cape Breton, however, and the right to dry fish along certain parts of Newfoundland shores.

Meanwhile, hostilities continued to heat up between the French and the New Englanders. The year 1704 saw a legendary raid by two hundred Indians and fifty Frenchmen who trekked more than three hundred miles on snowshoes through the wilderness to attack the people of Deerfield, Massachusetts. The governor, in response, mounted a major expedition to get back at the French, but apparently it was again of little concern *which* French would be punished. Benjamin Church, famous as a ruthless Indian fighter and a veteran at savaging near-defenceless communities, sailed with five hundred men to Acadia, burned twenty houses at Chignecto, broke down the dykes, and killed most of the cattle and sheep. His troops despoiled the village at Minas as well. Many families were forced to flee into the forests, where they endured a harsh winter of cold and hunger. Acadians were again scapegoats and victims, but back in France these raids on the small communities seemed of minuscule concern in the larger picture.

The fate of Acadia was not a high priority in France. In 1706, Daniel D'Auger de Subercasé was appointed as the new governor and he would be the last. The French were losing the war in Europe and were not prepared to send much military aid to protect the Acadians. In Port Royal, Subercasé found it necessary to get supplies from French West Indian privateers and the nervous merchants of Boston were soon aware that Port Royal was a haven for this illegal activity. Boston merchant Samuel Vetch travelled to London to persuade the Board of Trade that something must be done about the Acadians and their privateer friends. He hoped to persuade the British to take over all of Acadia, and Vetch himself had high hopes of winning the job as governor of those unruly lands.

The arguments concerning loss of revenue to the French privateers did not fall on deaf ears in London. Capturing Port Royal, it was argued, just might help solve the French problem in America and offset low morale over

English military losses in Europe, while at the same time giving the Scottish nationalists a new focus to distract their energies. The board approved the plan, but the all-out attack by General Francis Nicholson did not happen until 1710. Subercasé was well aware it was coming, but there was not much to be done. He had fewer than 300 men, some of whom deserted before or during the invasion. After all, Nicholson had an estimated 3,400 men on thirty-six vessels. The fort was besieged for two weeks with bombardment from two sides.

On October 2nd the destitute and ragged French were permitted to march out of Port Royal with some dignity, carrying their guns, luggage, drums and flags. Acadians in the region would be allowed to stay for two years as subjects of the British, although most military men were deported to Rochelle, France. Subercasé handed over the keys to the front door of the fort and Port Royal became Fort Anne.

To Swear an Oath

The Treaty of Utrecht was signed in 1713, again turning over Acadia and Newfoundland to Britain, while Île Saint-Jean (later to be known as Prince Edward Island) and Île Royale (Cape Breton) stayed with France. Acadians would be encouraged to move to Cape Breton, but they had heard the farming wasn't so great there and most preferred to stay put. Loyalty to one monarch or another had never been a big issue, but food and farming were a different matter.

Acadia would henceforward be known as Nova Scotia. France could still have a strong fishing base, as it held on to Cape Breton and their interest in the fish stocks remained strong. The French had been fishing off this coast since the 1500s. Cod had become a big part of French trade. To hang on to these fishing rights, a major fortress would be built on Île Royale at Louisbourg, fostering yet more English anxiety about the French.

Acadians left in Nova Scotia would retain religious freedom and their lands, but they would have to swear an oath of allegiance to Britain and promise to fight against whatever enemy presented itself—including the French, if need be. This was cause for some obvious discomfort for the Acadians, and it wasn't until much later, in 1730, that the English governor, Richard Philipps, would allow Acadians to simply swear obedience and neutrality, not armed support. This oath may have sufficed had Britain and France been able to forgo the habit of falling into war with one another. But such was not to be the case.

Chapter Eleven

Louisbourg: A Fortress City

View of Louisbourg from the harbour, 1731.

A Rough Passage But a "Pleasant Prospect"

Sieur de Diereville was born in France around 1670 and sailed for Acadia as a surgeon in 1699. When he returned to France, he published an account of his voyage, originally in verse, and later with additions in prose, which gives us a unique glimpse of the Halifax area fifty years before the British began to build the city. Like so many of his contemporaries he had a rough passage. One gets the impression that no matter how much planning went into an Atlantic crossing during this time, the ships were never fully prepared. Perhaps an easy, uneventful crossing was simply impossible.

Diereville's ship met with bad weather and suffered a shortage of water and supplies. The captain was off course and decided to go with the wind that was driving him toward "Chibouctou"—later known as Chebucto and now Halifax Harbour. He figured there was a fishing outport there that might be of some help. An English translation of part of Diereville's verse describing the harbour goes as follows:

> This Harbour is of great extent.
> And Nature has, herself, formed there
> A splendid Basin, and around about
> Green Fir-trees, which afford the eye
> A pleasant prospect; at the edge
> A Building used for drying Cod;
> That such construction is not known
> To Mansard, is quite possible.

Having had a chance to blast his rifle at small animals, he begins to worry that he might stir up the Native inhabitants who could "ambush" him. His fears are soon offset, however, and he notes that "The Indians have not such cruel hearts." He sees two Mi'kmaq armed with "Musket & Hatchet," but they are friendly to the sailors they meet and to the others, once they learn that the men are French. So the relations between the cod fishers and the Mi'kmaq must have already been well established and amicable. Diereville is a little taken aback that they are so civilized but unable to speak French. Europeans held stubbornly onto the notion that if Native North Americans could not speak a European language then they must still be barbaric. Ironically, it was the civility of the Native population that was all too often met with the barbarism of the so-called civilized.

Diereville and his shipmates, however, got along quite well despite the language barrier "and parted as best of friends." That soft phrasing stands in sharp contrast to the attitude of the military Englishmen who would one day found Nova Scotia's largest city upon the same grounds.

One day three Mi'kmaq chiefs in a birch-bark canoe came to visit. Diereville put on a friendly face, fed them and offered up brandy, which they imbibed with "relish & less moderation than we do; they have craving for it & I think that they would have emptied my Cellar without becoming intoxicated." While this seems a trifle condescending, it's interesting to note that the good Frenchmen had sailed across the Atlantic with plenty of liquor left in the "Cellar" but not quite enough water or food to meet other needs of all aboard. I guess it was just a matter of priorities.

The Mi'kmaq of that day appear to have already been converted to Christianity. They said prayers and made the sign of the cross before eating and they wore rosaries given to them by a priest who had died on their shores.

Frost Heaves, Cost Over-runs and Countless Setbacks

Île Royale (Cape Breton) was a good location to offer protection for the vital French fishing interests off the coast but it would also be a good place to provide protection for Quebec from English naval attacks coming from across the Atlantic. Early French fishermen had found the shoreline here to be a good place to dry fish, but attempts to actually settle Acadians there had not gone very far. The Acadians loved their mainland farms and wanted to stay put. Now, with the loss of most of Nova Scotia, the powers in France realized it was time to get serious about settlement and military protection. Louisbourg harbour was chosen as the site for a more permanent community, because it was close to the fishing grounds and did not freeze in winter; it was relatively unaffected by the spring ice packs coming out of the Gulf of St. Lawrence and it looked like an easy place to defend against attack. About 150 French settlers from Placentia in Newfoundland were shipped in to get things underway.

Louisbourg began as an unruly town with problems of excess drinking, gambling and rowdiness among the soldiers. The early inhabitants were in sharp contrast to the agrarian, family-centred Acadian farmers settling into what was now British-controlled Acadia.

By January of 1715, the civilian population of Louisbourg had grown to seven hundred. Entrepreneurs had set up shops and trade had begun, but there was not enough enthusiasm in France for this outpost to keep it well supplied with provisions, building supplies and other necessities for growth. There were dreams of making Louisbourg into a great port, not necessarily a fortress but a trading capital linking trade between North America, France and the West Indies. Louisbourg's Governor Pontchartrain, however, believed that if the town were to survive, it was going to need more than the soldiers stationed there. It would need walls and major armaments. In his letter to the controller general at Versailles he wrote:

I will not expand, sir, on the urgent indispensable necessity of solidly fortifying this new establishment since you understand its importance... If France were to lose this island, it would be irreparable; and, as a result, it would be necessary to abandon the rest of North America.

The governor's request did not fall on deaf ears. Jean-François du Verger de Verville was sent to Louisbourg as chief engineer for a mighty fort, and so began the task of building a structure made of "mortared walls" with moats all around, two great bastions and additional smaller ones within the framework. The project was plagued with unforeseen problems. Fog, high humidity and rain caused the mortar to set improperly or sometimes even wash away. Walls would not stay in place because of frost heaves and loose soil. Skilled builders, as well as financing, were a long way off. It was, after all, a massive undertaking for France to stake so much of its hopes of defence on this one fort. Within the fortress, government buildings were constructed, as were warehouses and a hospital. On the shorelines, wharves were built and a lighthouse was erected.

Corruption, Drunkenness and Smallpox

Chateau St. Louis at the centre of Louisbourg would be home to the governor and his council chamber. A number of spectacular and splendid rooms in one wing would almost make leaders feel they were home in the wealthy comforts of France. A second wing would provide only the most fundamental basics of life as barracks for the soldier population. These soldiers were from the "Compagnies Détachées" established for colonial work. Stationed here would be between six and twenty-four companies, each made up of fifty to seventy men. Quite a few soldiers were allowed to bring their wives, and others married from the local civilian population while stationed at the fortress. Louisbourg was by then a growing community of not just soldiers but families. Yet family life here inside the great walls of stone and earth was radically different from that of the Acadian farmers.

It was common for soldiers to moonlight with some sort of sideline, often one that involved selling booze. Louisbourg was a fortress city that nearly floated on alcohol. Drunkenness, it was said, was a greater problem here than anywhere in Europe. All kinds of fines and other punishments were decreed in an attempt to keep the men sober and industrious during the day, but these measures proved to be unsuccessful.

There was legal trade going in and out from the wharves, but also a lucrative and extensive illicit trading with New England and the Acadians living on English soil. It started with cod but grew to include all manner of goods until Louisbourg was a de facto free port. If it was profitable, you could get away with it at Louisbourg, where everyone, even the governor, felt so distant and cut off from the traditional rules of the game in France. Aside from sheer profit, trade was good for minimizing hostilities between the North American French and English. Even privateering, the "legal" hijacking of ships flying the flag of a rival nation, was discouraged for fear it would curtail the profits of shipping goods back and forth.

But unfortunately, corruption was to be found at the highest levels in Louisbourg. Money was skimmed off in various ways to line the pockets of officials, thus weakening the finances of the fort.

Even before the battles, the town endured several major crises that went beyond corruption and perennial drunkenness. In 1732, for example, the *Ruby* arrived bringing smallpox that killed off a fair chunk of the townspeople. That same year also saw a kind of famine, a dramatic shortage of food that required shipments from New England, at a profit to the Boston merchants, of course.

Attack on Canso

According to the census of 1737, Louisbourg was a town of 1,500 civilians and 600 military men. It included the core group of settlers from Placentia and a colourful mix of people from France, Quebec, Acadia and the West Indies. Along with the soldiers, officials and tradespeople were fishermen, domestics, convicts, slaves and salt smugglers. Nearly 150 ships a year arrived, making the port at least four times busier than Quebec. Outside of Louisbourg itself were more than 2,500 colonists, almost all fishermen, since the land nearby was too rocky and untamed for serious farming.

The years between 1713 and 1744 were relatively peaceful ones between the great rivals of England and France. In 1739 a trade war had flared in the Caribbean, bringing about a closer alliance between France and Spain (in opposition to England). When Hapsburg King Charles VI died suddenly in 1740, there was no male heir to the throne and this created an imbalance of power in far-away Europe. Frederick II of Prussia attacked Silesia and the War of the Austrian Succession began. As you might guess, this would eventually spill over into the lives of nearly everyone living in Nova Scotia and on Île Royale. France already controlled the St. Lawrence and Mississippi rivers, which were vital to expanding and settling the continent. As international tension heated up, the French minister of marine, Comte de Maurepas, warned Île Royale's Governor Du Quesnel that Louisbourg should be prepared for the worst—attacks from New England or England itself. Du Quesnel was ready and waiting, as were the people of Louisbourg, for attack. Many felt Louisbourg, because of its design and geography, was nearly invulnerable. Others were not so sure.

News of out-and-out war reached Du Quesnel in 1744 and the governor began to work on a strategy that would put the French to best advantage. Strangely, one of the first elements of that military strategy involved the church. He wrote to Abbé Jean-Louis Le Loutre, who was a missionary at Baie Verte. His job would be to encourage the Mi'kmaq to attack English settlements in Nova Scotia—a kind of pre-emptive strike policy—and the Abbé was to accompany such raids as chaplain. It would be okay to kill with God on your side.

Du Quesnel also ordered several companies of soldiers under Joseph Du Vivier to storm and occupy the fishing village of Canso, one of the closest major English settlements on the mainland of Nova Scotia. If Canso could be captured, then the English would have no easy port from which to mount attacks upon Louisbourg. Three hundred and fifty soldiers in seventeen fishing vessels set off under Du Vivier to do their damage. As it turned out, the French must have had the advantage of better communication with Europe, because when the ships arrived in Canso, the troops stationed there had not heard the news that another war had broken out. They were unprepared and Canso was taken easily. The French confiscated what was of value to them and torched the tiny town that had had such a hard-luck existence from the beginning.

English soldiers were taken back to Louisbourg but were generally considered a nuisance, consuming food supplies which were already limited and taking up space. They were later set free, or traded for French prisoners, and were able to report back to the English about the structure of the fort from the inside and tell of the low morale among French troops and the general lack of discipline.

Undoubtedly encouraged by such easy success at Canso, Du Quesnel sent a second expedition under Du Vivier to recapture old Port Royal. Du Vivier set off with a mere thirty men and along the way enlisted a couple of hundred Mi'kmaq to help out. When they arrived at the renamed Fort Anne, the Native people were instructed to "harass" the garrison, while the French sent back for reinforcements. It doesn't sound like such a smart military manoeuvre and one wonders how it could have been so poorly planned. Incorrectly anticipating that French ships would soon arrive to bolster his assault team, Du Vivier jumped the gun and asked the British soldier in charge, Paul Mascarene, to surrender. Mascarene refused, not at all certain what he was up against, and perhaps concluding that Du Vivier was merely posturing. Du Vivier and his Native allies kept up the harassment, while back in Louisbourg the ships were detained as they prepared for the assault. Three vessels finally arrived in October but Du Vivier and his men were nowhere to be found. Another French officer had appeared on the scene and ordered the men on elsewhere. Mascarene had toughed out the ill-prepared attack and called Du Vivier's bluff. The French ships simply turned around and headed back to Louisbourg without a fight.

Chapter Twelve

A Fortress for the Taking

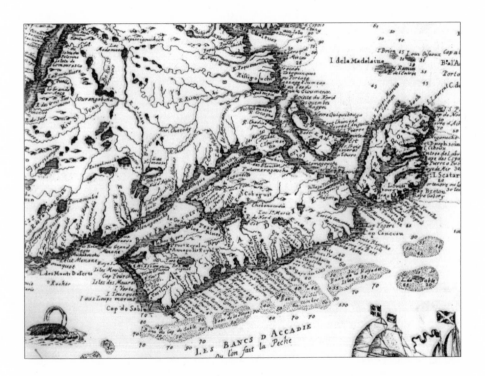

Fragment from a French map depicting Acadia and rich offshore fishing banks, 1755.

"Attack and Distress the Enemy"

The English now had good reason to be nervous about the French presence. The French Navy began attacking New England merchant ships and everything else afloat. François Bauchet de Saint-Marin, for example, became notorious for capturing small unarmed fishing boats. While this sounds like little cause to celebrate, it did encourage other privateers into the act and the French government actively supported privateering. Privateers grew more daring and eventually attacked ships not far off the coast of Massachusetts.

By the late summer of that year, 1744, British privateers were wreaking revenge and reaping their own profits from raids on the high seas. They pursued French ships right back to the shores of Cape Breton and this raised tensions on both sides.

Back in Massachusetts, the business community was getting pretty upset about all the illegal French activity. Governor William Shirley, it is safe to say, hated the French and wanted them out of Cape Breton. The French occupation of the old British fishing community of Canso really angered Shirley and the New England merchants as well. It was a matter of pride, but it was also a paramount matter of business. Something had to be done about Louisbourg. A successful siege of the fort would ensure Americans a monopoly on North Atlantic fish. A takeover of Île Royale would also open up the entrance to the St. Lawrence and leave Quebec vulnerable to an English naval attack. Governor Shirley appealed to England to "attack and distress the Enemy in their Settlements, and annoy their Fishery and Commerce." Attack, distress and annoy would be the order of the day. These were three words that big businessmen such as William Vaughan could applaud. Vaughan and John Bradstreet tried to convince the good government of Massachusetts to forge ahead with an American attack on Louisbourg, fearing that the English would be too slow to respond.

At first, the government of Massachusetts turned down the proposal and Vaughan went to the New England fishermen, where he found more than a little support. These were the men who had lost the most and now had much to gain by the ouster of the French from the lucrative fishing grounds. Support from the fishermen led to the approval of an attack by a narrow margin at the next meeting of the legislature. So in March of 1745 an invasion force gathered in Boston with men from Massachusetts, Rhode Island, Connecticut and New Hampshire. The leader was William Pepperell, a successful merchant and popular citizen who happened to have almost no military experience.

Pepperell had 4,300 men under his command and they set off in ninety ships escorted by a dozen or so privateers. Nasty storms, terrifyingly rough seas and snow made for a treacherous crossing for many men who had previously spent little or no time aboard sailing ships. When they arrived, they found the coast of Cape Breton blocked with ice. (You may recall that the French had established Louisbourg to be an ice-free port.) Pepperell decided to land at Canso and, making the best of a bad situation, drill his amateur army to prepare for the assault. Because of the ice, French vessels could not sail out of Louisbourg, so the people inside the fortress never knew of the nearby English presence. While waiting for the ice to clear in Cape Breton, four British warships under the control of Commodore Peter Warren arrived to assist in the attack, even though news of the invasion had not arrived in Britain.

Death Goes to the Victor

Louisbourg was not the impenetrable fort the French had hoped it to be. Bad design and poor materials had made it vulnerable on the northern and southern flanks. Inside the weak walls was even weaker morale. Everything was in short supply, except for booze and bad attitude. Soldiers were rightfully unhappy in their dark, damp quarters overrun with rats and mice. There were not even enough mattresses and blankets to go around. By mid-May of that year, Louisbourg was already on the verge of starvation, although one might wonder why there was not at least enough fish to feed them.

On May 11 when Pepperell's troops arrived, Louisbourg was defended by 560 regular soldiers and 800 not-so-regular militiamen. The first one hundred men sent to the beach to fight the British did little to halt the invasion and by nightfall 2,000 men of the invading force were camped on the shoreline of Gabarus Bay. The French holding down the outlying Royal Battery gave up and fled for the safety of the main fortress. When the New England invaders checked out the empty battery, they found weaponry intact and used the big guns to blast away at Louisbourg itself. Other advantageous attack points were set up around Louisbourg, although the low, wet ground made transporting the big weapons difficult. Nonetheless, the siege of Louisbourg was underway.

The Americans pillaged the nearby settlements, finding prodigious quantities of alcoholic refreshment. As they drank to the extreme, Pepperell watched with disgust and despair as his army staggered about on the conquered soil. He was disappointed at the obnoxious behaviour of his countrymen, but he was unable to effectively sober up his troops.

Nonetheless, each day the walls of Louisbourg were hammered by artillery. It would only be a matter of time. Conditions inside the fortress continued to deteriorate. French ships arrived with reinforcements but they were too late. First the *Renommé* turned back as soon as it saw the British warships. Next the *Vigilant* was captured and all hopes of Louisbourg surviving were dashed.

The siege would not end without significant American losses, however. If the island battery emplacement in the harbour could be captured, then the battle would be won. The British warships could then come in close enough to finish off the town inside the fortress. On a night in June, 400 men landed in heavy seas and indiscreetly made a lot of noise cheering themselves on to victory. This alerted the French and when the English tried to climb the ladders they had placed against the walls, they were shot or stabbed with bayonets. The attack was a disaster and nearly 200 men died in the ill-planned assault.

Plan B for the attackers was to set up another battery station a half-mile away at Lighthouse Point. It was a daunting task to haul the heavy artillery up the cliffs and drag it over the rocky ground, but eventually the deed was done; the Island Battery was demolished and the British ships could now fire directly on Louisbourg itself.

Holes were pounded through the walls by cannon balls and nearly every building within the fort was pummelled as well. The French troops inside, along with anyone who could fight, including young boys, tried to hold back the invasion but they were overrun. Forty-nine days after the assault had begun, Pepperell's ragtag American army marched into the fort. Pepperell forbade his men to ransack the town but they grew unruly and did it anyway—looting and rioting and taking further advantage of the great supply of liquor on hand in the great French fort.

For weeks, the French flags were left to fly over the fort, luring more than twenty French ships to port. One vessel was filled with gold and silver—several million dollars' worth, hidden under a façade of cocoa bags. Feeling on the generous side, Commodore Warren gave each of his sailors a reward of about a thousand dollars of the new-found wealth. The citizens and soldiers of Louisbourg who had survived were put on eleven transport ships and sent back to France on July 4.

The American men wanted desperately to go home to their families, their farms and their livelihood. The men had to stay on, however, until a permanent garrison of "professional" soldiers arrived and took control. There was a near mutiny over this and Governor Shirley back in Massachusetts agreed to raise the salaries of the soldiers and begged them to hang on through the winter. Conditions were insufferable in the war-ravaged fort. The Americans drank so much of the captured French rum that many died from the booze, as well as from the unsanitary conditions. By spring, nearly a thousand had perished. Eight to fourteen soldiers were dying each day. More died that winter than in the battles leading up to the victory. Fear of French attack also gnawed at the morale of the gloomy troop of victors. If the French had simply turned over the squalid town along with the plentiful supply of booze, they could have avoided the siege altogether and eventually returned to recapture the place once the Americans fell prey to the rum and disease.

Scurvy, Smallpox and Squalid Quarters

The French were predictably hurting from the loss of Louisbourg and a plan was drawn up in France to send sixty-five warships under the command of Duc D'Anville to Chebucto Bay (Halifax Harbour), where he would link up with friendly Mi'kmaq to help fight against the British. Once the news got out about the humiliation at Louisbourg, it was hoped that a general uprising of Acadians could be incited. The plan was obviously being developed in a vacuum without knowledge of the true state of Acadian attitudes. In fact, the entire venture was ill-conceived and disastrous. A grandiose expedition for recapturing Acadia, restoring the French in Louisbourg and going on to attack Boston and New England was being mounted by a leader with little experience in a campaign of this size. Worst of all, the sea and disease would conspire to be D'Anville's greatest enemies.

On the trip across the Atlantic in 1746, storms separated the ships and made for a rough passage. Along with the plague of scurvy, fevers broke out from smallpox in the squalid quarters and many men died before ever having a chance to reach Nova Scotia and inflict revenge on the English. Not far from Sable Island, D'Anville and his ships ran into a ferocious storm that they were not at all prepared for. Most probably it was a tropical storm pushing up the Gulf Stream from the south. Some vessels went to the bottom to join the graveyard of Sable Island wreckage. Others were damaged by high winds and monster waves. At least one ship got hit by a bolt of lightning. Afterwards, several ships' captains lost their bearings in fog and remained cut off from the main flotilla.

It was a very unhappy and unlucky venture all around. On September 10 of that year, D'Anville's own ship, the *Northumberland*, made it to Chebucto Harbour, expecting to meet up with other French ships as well as some of his own that he had lost track of. There was one transport ship waiting for him and some allies—Mi'kmaq men who lived along Chebucto Bay arrived in their canoes. The unlucky D'Anville, plagued by bad timing and bad luck, learned that other French ships had arrived to meet him but had given up because of the delays and returned to France.

D'Anville went ashore near Birch Cove along Bedford Basin, with a lot of sick men dying from diseases. As some of the rest of his fleet arrived, D'Anville discovered they too were manned by sailors and soldiers who were dying and they carried a cargo of those who had not survived the crossing. D'Anville himself died near the end of the month. A new commander, Vice-Admiral D'Estournel, had the sad duty of trying to pull things back together with his own five ships and the survivors of D'Anville's troops. Apparently he saw two options: either return to France or attack Annapolis Royal. He personally favoured returning to France and cutting losses all around, but there was stiff opposition to the idea while enthusiasm for revenge against the British still ran high. So he put it to a vote. And lost. The loss must have been seen as overwhelming damage to his honour, so he committed suicide by impaling himself on a sword.

The unhappy duties of leadership now fell to a man named La Jonquière, who had been appointed as the governor of what was left of New France. He sent out word to the Acadian farmers of Minas Basin that the French soldiers were desperately in need of food and supplies. Local Mi'kmaq people had remained loyal to their French friends and helped out as best they could. Tragically, the Mi'kmaq were given the clothing of dead soldiers and, as a result, disease spread into their own communities, devastating the population.

Six thousand in all had left France to try to recapture Louisbourg and reassert a French presence in this part of the world. When the remainder of the fleet sailed out of Chebucto Harbour on October 13, only 600 were left alive and of that number at least 250 were extremely ill. Two shiploads of men doggedly persevered on to the Annapolis Basin with high hopes of restoring dignity by capturing Annapolis Royal. Unfortunately, they saw that it was substantially defended by the British and finally accepting the notion that discretion is the better part of valour, the commander gave the word to return to France.

A second group of French soldiers under Jean-Baptiste-Nicolas-Roch de Ramezay sailed to the Minas Basin to try and muster support from the Acadians to attack Fort Anne, but most Acadians just wanted to be left alone and stay out of the way of warring empires.

With more French military showing up in Nova Scotia, Paul Mascarene figured it was time to go on the offensive again with support from Massachusetts troops. In January of 1747, the French attacked American forces near Grand Pré and caused a setback for them that was only to be short-lived because William Shirley sent up more troops. By the spring of that year, de Ramezay was ready to admit that the French didn't stand a chance. He and his men said farewell to Nova Scotia.

Command of fortress Louisbourg was delivered to Peregrine Hopson in September of 1747. He controlled what was left of the fortress for just a year, until decisions an ocean away would take the problem of Louisbourg off his hands. The 1748 Treaty of Aix-la-Chapelle gave Louisbourg back to France. It was as simple as the swipe of the pen. New Englanders were furious over this decision and it's easy to see why.

Warriors from both sides must have wondered at the cruel irony that led to the loss of so many lives—all for what? England and France, for the time being, simply seemed to be tired of fighting. So England was willing to take one step back. Maybe the loss of one single fort was no catastrophe after all. What had happened on the ground and at sea as the military men struggled for victory, died from bullets, booze and disease, sank to despair because of their personal losses and their distance from their families, the lousy conditions and the lack of food—all this had very little to do with the decision-making of monarchs and bureaucrats who had never set foot upon North American shores.

And so Louisbourg was back with the French under the control of a new governor, Charles Desherbiers.

Treaties Made To Be Broken

But the story was not over. Treaties after all are made to be broken. When William Pitt became prime minister of England in 1756, he felt that it was worth heating up the war with France to secure America for the English. Louisbourg would just have to be captured again in order to have naval access from the sea for an assault on Quebec. Admiral Edward Boscawen and Colonel Jeffrey Amherst would be the military masters of the endeavours and there would be at least 14,000 men at their disposal.

Louisbourg, back in French control, had actually flourished between 1750 and 1755—mostly because of illegal trade with New England. New Englanders were royally mad at the British for returning Louisbourg where so much New England blood had been shed. But now that it was back with France, it was illegal business as usual, and merchants on both sides saw the profit in it. If European powers had stayed out of it, quite probably, a wonderful trade alliance would have sprung up to weld together Boston and Louisbourg as sister cities. But it was not to be that simple.

As trade grew, the French undertook repairs to the fortress. Some walls were collapsing and there was still a problem with crumbling mortar made with sea sand. The French were well aware of what was going on and they were stocking up Louisbourg, readying themselves as best they could for the blockade that would begin in March of 1758.

Chapter Thirteen

An Acadian Way of Life

A traditional Acadian farm and dyke in the Annapolis Valley; 19th-century etching by Stephen Parrish.

The Strength of Acadian Women

The story of the Acadian people is inevitably linked to the events of Louisbourg, but their way of life was fundamentally different from that of the French soldiers, sailors, merchants and government men who lived in and around that ill-fated fortress. At the time of their deportation, Acadians had lived for several generations in Nova Scotia. Most of them had little connection with France, French politics or contemporary French culture. They had evolved a unique way of life that was suited to the land they loved.

With limited numbers of immigrants coming to the New World from France, there had been an intermarriage of families to such a degree that, after three generations, most Acadians in any given community were related in some way. These blood ties created a positive system of mutual help and interdependence where those who had were more than generous in sharing with those who had not. Ultimately, an extended Acadian family would be formed that was protective and resistant to outside hostilities.

Acadian men appear somewhat noble, family-centred and hard-working in contrast to the English or French soldiers and the adventurous but belligerent New Englanders of this era who arrived in Nova Scotia.

To suggest that women are often overlooked in the records of history is a mild understatement. Men fight wars, and find a multitude of other methods to colourfully act out their aggression or greed while women remain home to raise a family and help repair the wounds. Acadian women, however, were vital to the success of the early settlements and some records survive about the role of a few prominent women of these times.

The first women to arrive in Acadia may have come with Razilly in 1633 or later in 1636, when a woman is first recorded on a passenger list of a ship sailing over from France. Early notables like Jeanne Motin and Françoise Marie Jacquelin undoubtedly saw themselves as French and not Acadian, but they clearly helped to shape the identity of Acadia.

As time passed and reliance on France diminished, Acadian communities relied for their survival on the hard work of both men and women. Men would hunt, fish, prepare the land for agriculture and build houses and barns. Women would take care of the house, raise children and animals. Both would work in the fields.

While Acadian women might have been characterized by their steadfast family orientation, the adversity of attacks from the New Englanders and the aftermath of deportation led to a unique strength of character that comes from the survival over such hardship.

One such example of that spirit can be seen in the story of Madeleine Leblanc who returned to St. Mary's Bay by boat after being deported.

Discouraged by the long journey home, the hardship and the discovery that they would have to clear land and begin all over again at this new site, many returning with Madeleine sat down in despair and cried. Madeleine, only nineteen at the time, was undaunted. She picked up an axe, cut down the first tree and provided enough encouragement so that others took up the challenge. A small settlement eventually developed around the site and Madeleine lived there to the ripe old age of ninety-eight.

It has been argued that Acadians managed to retain their unique cultural identity because women valued the importance of family kinship lines and because *family* had been so central to Acadian culture. Clearly, Acadian women had more responsibility than their English counterparts in Nova Scotia during these times. Much of North America's knowledge of Acadia is probably based on the most famous of Acadian women, the central character of Longfellow's epic poem *Evangeline*, published in 1847. Here was the sad tale of a young woman of indomitable spirit. Although Evangeline was a fictional character, Longfellow used her to convey the love of the Acadians for their land and community. During the deportation of nearly 3,000 Acadians by the British, Evangeline, like a number of women from Grand Pré, was separated from the man she loved. Taken far away in a British warship, she struggled to survive against the imposed hardships of exile. Although the long poem is a sentimental tale, it has captured the imagination of generations of readers with its infusion of the Acadian spirit.

A Community of Happily Married People

Unlike the early English settlers, Acadian men and women had readily developed an intimate kinship to the land they lived on and they were willing to work in harmony with the tides of the sea. At the heart of their farming strategy was the creation of dykes, which required co-operation and countless hours of manual labour. Whereas a British farmer might clear his own land and farm his own small patch, many Acadian families would be reliant upon the communal dyke which allowed for farming in the valley soil. The fertility of the soil was the result of generous rich sediment left by the sweeping ebb and flow of the tides of Fundy.

The seigneurial system intended by the French government simply never worked very well. It was based on European notions of dividing land and providing title to it according to the decisions of a seigneur. Attempts at establishing this system in Port Royal and Beaubassin only produced squabbles, indifference and so much paperwork. While rejection of this system must have certainly enraged authorities back in France, it set the pattern for a spirited but gentle anarchy that suited the Acadians well in adapting to Nova Scotia.

The French settlers sought out and settled meadow land that could be farmed. Their settlements were scattered in accordance with where they found the sort of land they desired. Unlike the British, they did not feel the need to cluster together in garrison towns, fearful of the wilderness. Instead, small villages and pockets of a spread-out population were the norm. For the most part, Acadians had little contact with British or French authorities—and happily so, as long as history would allow. Priests, elder family figures and older women became counsellors and decision makers as needed.

Compared to the English in Nova Scotia who were so absorbed in their mistrust of the land, fear of the French and Mi'kmaq, the Acadians seemed to live an idyllic life. They farmed, fished, traded, created sawmills and grist mills yet lacked what the English would have called "ambition," because they did not exploit the land or waters for significant profit. Certainly, they were a great disappointment to the French investors and colonizers. What good were they if they could not produce wealth for investors back in Paris?

Records indicate the Acadians were physically fit and prone to fewer diseases than the English soldiers at Halifax or French soldiers of Louisbourg. Without a doubt their diet was much healthier. There was a low child mortality rate, women married quite young and older women acted as midwives for the birth of the children. Marriage was strongly encouraged and very few men or women lived without a spouse.

Priests, when available, performed official ceremonies like marriages, baptisms and funerals. Often these clergy were the only literate persons around as well, so they took on certain legal duties. However, there were not enough priests to get around to the scattered villages and many Acadians might encounter a priest only once or twice a year. Hence, even the traditional European domineering influence of the Church was of less significance here in the daily lives of the people. In fact, religious freedom did not lawfully exist for the Acadians while under British rule. The Treaty of Utrecht had guaranteed Catholics the right to worship within the British domain, but English law had forbidden Catholicism. Fortunately for the Acadians, this law was simply not upheld in Nova Scotia. Acadians were left to worship as they desired and French missionaries converted many Mi'kmaq as well.

A Rich Harvest from Land and Sea

The Acadians were not at all fond of chopping down forests to create fields for grazing and farming. Instead, they preferred a somewhat gentler technique of altering the landscape for their purposes, something that had been in use in France and Holland for a very long time. A system of dykes would keep back the high tides of coastal waters and free up rich low-lying pasture lands for farming. Building up the long earth walls of the dykes sounds like hard manual labour, but once complete, and after the rains have had a chance to wash excess salt out of the soil, the rewards can be significant in terms of food and hay.

A very simple mechanism known as an "aboiteau" allows excess water from the land to spill back into the sea. The aboiteau is made up of a wooden conduit at the bottom of the dyke with a swinging door or "clapet" that closes as the tides rise. The whole system was so simple yet so effective that it created envy on the part of the New England farmers who saw Acadians pro-ducing a rich harvest from, ultimately, very little work. As a result, New England farmers were prone to call the Acadians lazy or "slothful."

Many Acadian settlers had chosen the fertile marshlands around the Bay of Fundy for farming. Fundy has some of the highest tide changes in the world—seven to twelve metres, requiring significant dyking. Yet around Fundy's Minas, Cumberland and Annapolis basins were wide meadows free of trees. These fertile meadows looked almost too good to be true to the early Acadian farmers. The first dykes were built around 1640 and by 1710, the Acadians had dykes in almost all the marshlands bordering the Bay of Fundy. The natural fertility of the lands resulted from rich clay soil built up with sediments left by the tides over thousands of years.

Not all Acadian farmers cultivated exclusively for their own needs. The more entrepreneurial farmers were shipping the results of their labour to Louisbourg and to New England. Of course, this trade was illegal, so there were probably no records kept of these activities.

Unlike the English who failed to respect or trust the Mi'kmaq, the Acadians had, from the start, been ready to learn every available trick of sur-vival from the Native people. Weirs or *nijagan* made of brush and nets were used to take advantage of the receding Fundy tides to catch fish. Built near the mouth of rivers and streams, wooden poles are pounded into place to form a corral of sorts and then saplings and smaller branches or string nets are fashioned into a fence that allows water to pass through but not the larger of the fish. When the tide goes down, it is merely a matter of walking out into the shallows and collecting the day's catch. Once again, the Acadians had succeeded in the lazy man's approach to harvesting food.

Friendly and mutually advantageous relations with the Mi'kmaq allevi-ated the fears felt by many French settlers in the early days. There are census records showing marriages between Mi'kmaq women and Acadian men. One notable marriage was that of the French nobleman Baron de Saint-Castin, who came over as a soldier in 1670 and married the daughter of an Abenaki chief. The baron himself eventually became a chief who led raids against the British in defence of the homelands.

Marriages and conversion of the Mi'kmaq to Catholicism helped strengthen the bond between these two peoples. The Native people did not feel threatened by loss of hunting grounds, as the Acadians lived in small communities and settled mostly along the shores. Illustrations dating back to the seventeenth century show Acadian men wearing Mi'kmaq clothing. The French also learned from the Mi'kmaq the craft of making birch-bark canoes and the skills of harvesting edible wild plants. In return, the French traded the Native people iron pots, rifles and ammunition.

Chapter Fourteen

The Founding of Halifax

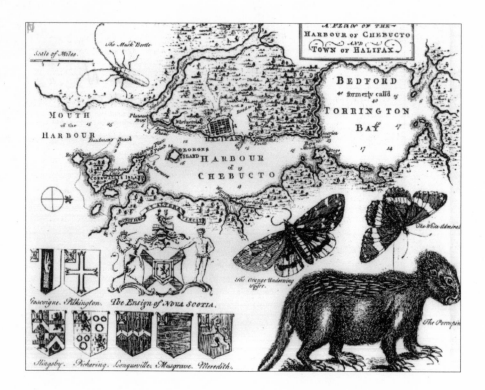

Early map showing plan for development of Halifax.

The Rasp of Cornwallis

By 1749, six years before the expulsion of the Grand Pré Acadians, Nova Scotia had a population of about 11,000 French and 2,000 English. Estimates as to the Mi'kmaq population vary dramatically, but already European diseases had taken their toll. In fact, disease—smallpox in particular—played a significant role in the early history of this province.

After the Treaty of Utrecht in 1713, the British had made very little effort to settle in Nova Scotia. Between 1745 and 1749, however, New England soldiers and their British regular army replacements occupied Louisbourg, boosting the population. No serious attempt was made to develop farming villages or create permanent fishing communities. They perceived their surroundings to be inhospitable, if not hostile. So the British crowded together, feeling safer in the cramped confines of a garrison community.

While that attitude was slow, very slow, to change, the idea of more fully "colonizing" Nova Scotia was taking root in England. In 1749, *The London Gazette* advertised for people to move to Nova Scotia and try to make a life there. England was bursting at the seams with out-of-work soldiers and sailors since the end of the War of Austrian Succession. Unemployed soldiers on the streets of London could mean trouble and England still didn't know exactly what she wanted to do with Nova Scotia, so here was a plan to kill two birds with one stone. George Montague Dunk, Earl of Halifax, was president of the Board of Trade and Plantations and he masterminded the colonization move.

Men weren't exactly beating down his doors to get permission to move to Nova Scotia. In truth, it was a place that appealed to few. The earl realized that previous incentives to lure settlers to Nova Scotia had not been very successful. So he knew he'd have to sweeten the offer. He also felt that he couldn't just send over ship after ship of paupers. First, he'd go after the military men—or at least those who had already completed their military duty in the war. Every officer under the rank of ensign would receive eighty acres. Ensigns would get 200 acres, lieutenants 300, captains 400 and every rank above that would get a full 600 acres plus thirty extra for each family member. Of course, North American land was plentiful and not of much value at all to the Crown. Many envisioned the entire place to be nothing but trees, bogs and marshes along a cold, foggy coastline far from the comforts of England. Rations were promised for one year and there were assurances of a civil government as well as military protection. Similar offers of land and support were also given to skilled craftsmen like carpenters, shipwrights, masons, brickmakers and bricklayers, surgeons and the like.

The discharged sailors and soldiers, however, had seen too much of life in military quarters, where food and shelter were guaranteed. This new deal was full of considerable uncertainty and they were not quick to jump at the prospect. Many qualified workers in rural areas never even found out about the offer—they failed to get the news by word of mouth and many were illiterate. They could not read what was in the papers or on the posters tacked up in the cities. Contrary to the earl's hopes, large numbers of applications came from the poor of London who found the promise of free food enough of a temptation to send them across the sea and into the wilderness.

For once, the ships were brimming with the necessary supplies as they forged across the Atlantic to create a new town. Four thousand pounds of gold and silver were stacked into the ships. The earl's proposal was indeed one to buy the loyalty and commitment of the settlers. Along with the gold was a healthy supply of official stationery, as if to suggest the wilderness could not be conquered without plenty of paperwork. More practical items such as hospital supplies, fishing gear, seeds, bricks, blankets, clothes, salted meats, biscuits, hatchets and surveying equipment were loaded on as well. Quite a good supply of French Bibles were transported in hopes of converting Catholic Acadians to Protestantism. The ships also carried plentiful gifts to make the newcomers welcome to the Mi'kmaq. These, however, were mostly cheap trinkets, indicative of a false generosity.

Edward Cornwallis, the son of a lord and a man with friends in high places, had been appointed to be Captain General and Governor-in-Chief. There were delays at first as the number of Cockney passengers, well beyond expectations, filed on board. Finally, on May 14, 1749, Cornwallis set sail aboard the *Sphinx*. Thirteen other ships followed soon after from the delightfully named port of Spithead.

The ships arrived by late June in reasonably good time with 1,174 families. Well over one hundred heads of families were retired military men and over 400 were retired from the Royal Navy. A sizeable half of the population were former military men. Of the full complement, there were of course many single men, as well as 440 kids and 420 servants. Many who would settle in Halifax were not all that familiar with the discomforts of carving a garrison town out of the wilderness. Although the vast majority of settlers were white, some of those listed as servants were most probably Black slaves.

With thirty-eight doctors, surgeons and other medical personnel on the voyage, Cornwallis had reckoned that medical care, primitive as it was, would be significant to the success of the new town. This was in sharp contrast to the lack of medical concern afforded the English troops at Annapolis Royal up to this time. Some brilliant innovator had even determined that more people would survive the crossing with minimal diseases if the holds of the ships were *ventilated*. Each ship was well stocked with medical supplies and the *Roehampton* was sailing along as a hospital ship.

Nova Scotian author Thomas Raddall, whose passion for the history of this province was of the highest order, describes Cornwallis as a good-looking bachelor of thirty-six who had seen battle and even commanded troops against Prince Charlie in the Highlands. Raddall says he had a pleasant voice and cool demeanour, although he was known to lose his temper on occasion. In *Halifax, Warden of the North*, Raddall notes, "Later on his voice acquired a rasp, and so did his pen, as troubles mounted and the harsh winters of the new colony destroyed his health." All the best-laid medical preparations could not stave off the ravages of the Nova Scotia winters, even for the most privileged.

Aiding Cornwallis was Richard Bulkeley—tall, Irish, rich and handsome—who was not exactly planning on roughing it. He brought along three good horses, a mountain of personal belongings, a valet, a groom and a butler. Horatio Gates, a captain, was also a close associate of Cornwallis. The illegitimate son of the Duke of Leeds, he proved to be a capable young officer. In fact, most of the officers and military men were young by modern standards. Halifax would be a city of people in their mid-thirties and younger.

The Amazing Shrinking Town

When the Halifax settlers arrived on the twenty-first of June, they saw signs of plentiful fish, which should have been a good omen that food, at least, would be available in the new town. The cod would have been closer in to the coast at that time of year, pollack and haddock would have been schooling and salmon would be heading upstream, through the harbour toward Bedford Basin and the river beyond. Everyone aboard was on the lookout for some great navigable river but none really existed here in Chebucto Bay. The harbour opened up into a wide and ultimately very useful basin with some small rivers emptying into it.

The first government would be both military and civilian, with Cornwallis in charge. He was supported by Captain Edward How, Captain John Gorham and civilians Benjamin Green, John Salisbury and Hugh Davidson, who would act as councillors. Paul Mascarene would also be on hand after his stint at Fort Anne. He was considered to have a solid knowledge of the French and the local Native population, but undoubtedly he knew of each as enemy and not ally and there was a significant degree of prejudice to his knowledge.

Gorham had with him his rangers, mostly New England descendants, but some were Native people from tribes who were enemies to the Mi'kmaq. Although Gorham has often been portrayed as a great defender of white settlers, this may well be a misreading of history. Mi'kmaq historian Dan Paul describes the rangers as "some of the most blood-thirsty individuals ever assembled." French Father Maillard, who had been living among the Mi'kmaq before the arrival of the Halifax settlers, recorded that he had observed Gorham and his men wantonly murder three pregnant Mi'kmaq women and two small children. Such actions attest to the magnitude of the brutality of the so-called civilized people who were in control of Nova Scotia at the time.

There was considerable debate as to the precise location for the new town but a compromise was reached. Halifax would be carved from the forested hillside just west of George's Island. A brook, long since erased by urban development, flowed down to the harbour in those days and it provided fresh drinking water. It existed where George Street runs today. There was a big hardwood tree at the landing site and this became the town's first gallows. In future years, the death of criminals by hanging would prove to be a popular form of entertainment to Haligonians.

Along the shores of the harbour, it is said that settlers found the skeletal remains of D'Anville's men, some holding rusting muskets, some still in tattered French uniforms, some propped against trees.

The location of the new settlement was not all it had been touted to be by the enthusiastic advertisements. Settlers were only allowed a small parcel of land within the defences of the new town. There had been promises of deep, rich soil for farming but, of course, all of this desirable farming terrain was far away on the Fundy side of Nova Scotia where the Acadians had been cultivating for several generations. Realizing the bad deal that it was, many took off for New England on ships within a month of arrival. There were jobs there, real soil for farming, and more established communities. The original passenger lists to Halifax reported 158 heads of families who had jobs related to animal husbandry, but by the end of July another census suggested only sixty-nine settlers with that skill. Most of the men must have quickly decided that the Halifax site wasn't a good place to establish a herd of anything.

Fear of attack by the French and the Mi'kmaq, who had already suffered serious harassment by the English, made everybody nervous. For the first two weeks the new arrivals felt vulnerable, until soldiers under Hopson and Warburton were transferred from Louisbourg to protect them. During those first two months, most settlers actually stayed on the transport ships. After a long voyage in cramped quarters, fear of this new land was still strong enough to make most hang back in their familiar confines rather than camp ashore in the Nova Scotia summer. To ease the fears, Cornwallis sent for Mascarene's regiment to come up from Annapolis to ensure protection of the civilians. As soon as Mascarene and his troops arrived in July, the first Council meeting was convened, after which Cornwallis wrote a letter of frustration to the Lords of Trade in London. He noted that his population had dwindled to 1,400 from the initial 2,547 who had arrived not more than a month earlier. Halifax was a diminishing city even before it had taken root.

In his complaint, Cornwallis wrote that many soldiers "only wanted a passage to New England. Many [of the passengers] have come as into a Hospital, to be cured, some of veneral [sic] disorders, some even incurables. I do all I can to make them useful, but I shall be obliged, I believe, to send some of them away. I published a proclamation in the terms advised by your Lordships with regard to such as should [anyone]…be absent two days together without permission, forfeiture of all rights and privileges of settlers. Eight fellows that had gone off to Canada and were brought back, I punished [them] by striking their names out of the Mess Books, and out of your Lordships Lists, and ordered them to leave the province."

Well, orders to leave the province were probably not such great punishment if it meant a chance to move on to New England. In fact, Cornwallis's meagre threats didn't stem the flow of un-settlers. Nearly a thousand people departed in July. Transportation to New England was not hard to come by. Raddall speculates that some may have left because they were Catholic and, therefore, were not permitted to own land. Many of the Catholics were here as workers or servants and they soon realized that more freedom could be had in New England or elsewhere. At least 191 families were not granted land as promised when it was handed out in August.

The Bottom Line

There was nothing fancy about the layout of the town. The settlement was set out in blocks, each 98 metres by 37 metres with sixteen house lots per block, each measuring 18 metres by 12 metres. There were only twelve streets in all. A rectangular "square" was created as the official centre of activity. A church, St. Paul's, would be built at the north end and the first courthouse was built at the south. (St. Paul's later moved to the south end.) The Parade Ground which exists today along Barrington Street was not at all flat, but sloping, as it had been set up on the side of a hill leading up to the Citadel. It would not be levelled off until the turn of the century. The streets were named in honour of notables back home, many of whom were responsible for sending the English settlers to this place. Holles Street (later changed to Hollis) was named for Prime Minister Henry Pelham's mother, Bedford Row for the Duke of Bedford, Granville for the Rt. Hon. George Granville, Barrington for Viscount Barrington of Ardglass, Argyle for the Duke of Argyle and so on. George Street was named for the King; Prince and Duke streets were thrown in for good measure as generic names for anyone who might have been missed.

Cornwallis wanted to get the town underway. Realizing he couldn't rely solely upon those who had come with him, he brought in builders from Annapolis and elsewhere and even hired Acadians from the Minas area. For the first winter, however, only temporary barricades of logs and branches were in place. Yet in a letter from a new citizen of Halifax to *Gentleman's Magazine and Historical Chronicle* dated December 7, 1749, the writer asserts, "there are already about four hundred habitable houses within the fortifications and not less than 200 without." That was probably putting a good spin on a bad situation. Two hundred and thirty-seven people died that first winter—at least that was the number recorded. The true total was probably much higher.

The hospital wasn't established until March of 1750 and by then it was long overdue. This hospital, nonetheless, predates those in Philadelphia and New York. The ever-vigilant Lords of Trade were concerned that the cost of the hospital—as well as the cost of the whole colony—was simply too high. They were afraid that Cornwallis was not being lean and mean enough so they let him know it. As a result, in February he got rid of some of the hospital staff to cut overhead. The Lords were more concerned with the bottom line than with lives lost, although this probably came back to haunt them since it was so expensive and time-consuming to find new settlers.

Hugh Davidson, treasurer for the colony, was called on the carpet back in London to explain why the tab had run up to nearly 77,000 pounds instead of the 40,000 allotted. Halifax was just proving itself to be more expensive than it was worth.

A Botched Opportunity for Peace

Gorham's Rangers proved themselves to be the "best" defence to the town. They were cruel and ruthless and some of their company, of Mohawk descent, knew how to track down, harass and murder the Mi'kmaq whose homeland had been invaded. Cornwallis admitted to his confidantes that he thought the Rangers were barbaric and he was happy to see them out of town—sent on missions to kill the Mi'kmaq. He knew that the Mi'kmaq who gathered along the harbour had come from the interior, probably paddling their canoes down the Sackville River. So he sent the bloodthirsty Gorham and his crew to build a fort near where the river emptied into the basin. The Mi'kmaq, however, had an alternate route, a traditional avenue down the lakes through Dartmouth. Cornwallis and his men had not really made a thorough exploration of both sides of the harbour where the English had settled so, quite often, the Mi'kmaq arrived near Halifax undetected.

Thomas Raddall believes Cornwallis to have been a diligent leader with good intentions who really wanted peace. He ordered Captain How to various Native communities to ask the chiefs to come to Halifax to work out a treaty. Three did come—from the Fundy area, from the Saint John River area and from Passamaquoddy. Most of the Mi'kmaq from around Halifax, or Chebucto as they called it, had already wisely moved away after the ravages of European diseases had taken their toll. Cornwallis could not seem to draw them back into the treaty process. After the murderous acts of Gorham's Rangers, this should have surprised no one.

The three chiefs and their nine warriors were greeted aboard the *Beaufort* with a seventeen-gun salute. The interpreter was a Frenchman named André who may or may not have been providing a legitimate interpretation. Foolishly, the English had not spent any great effort in training their own interpreters for such important business but instead were willing to rely on a man who may have had allegiances to their enemy.

Cornwallis tried to get the point across that His Majesty wanted friendship with the Native people (despite how things had appeared in the past), and he was even willing to provide them with protection. *Protection from whom?* they must have wondered. Native leaders probably saw the redcoats themselves as a bit of a joke. They had little understanding of the wilderness and were so poorly prepared for survival in Nova Scotia. How could they protect even themselves? And what had the English done to prove their friendship? Certainly the presence of Gorham and his rangers would appear to run counter to any attempts at friendship.

If these Mi'kmaq and Maliseet leaders showed any sign of amusement, it was interpreted by the English as drunkenness. The chiefs, however, signed the document (not necessarily cognizant of what they were signing) and left with presents accompanied by another seventeen-gun salute. Cornwallis had probably missed his best opportunity to establish communication and goodwill. Both Gorham and How should have been worldly-wise enough to see the sham of the event, but then not everyone wanted peace with the Native people.

To make a treaty official from the Mi'kmaq point of view, there should have been a ritual of washing away war paint, and burying the hatchet. Apparently Native leaders had gone so far as to perform a war dance right on the deck of the *Sphinx*, but Cornwallis had interpreted this as another act of drunkenness. And so, like many treaties to follow, this one would be a sham and within months, the English and Native people would be killing each other again.

Salt Meat and Hard Tack

Cornwallis was hoping for peace with everyone but even in his own front yard, he was having trouble keeping all the new troops in some kind of order. Along with the garrison of men from Louisbourg came the riff-raff who followed the troops to sell them rum. Drinking establishments (well, huts) blossomed on the waterfront area that would evolve into Water Street. The buildings would become more permanent, but the commodity of consumption would remain the same for well over a century.

Booze led to violence and the record of the first murder of an Englishman by an Englishman took place on the *Beaufort* itself, which was the veritable centre of Nova Scotia government. A man killed the boatswain's mate and wounded two others. The criminal was promptly hanged.

Discipline was slack everywhere in the new colony and especially among military men. Cornwallis saw problems both close to home and farther afield. He sent stern orders to the regiment leaders in the Annapolis Valley to get things under control. Dissidents were promptly shot or hanged and that worked well enough in quieting those individuals but, in Halifax and elsewhere, it didn't seem to improve the overall problem.

History is wont to record the cheery times, the moments of bliss or sense of accomplishment felt by the new settlers. Suffice it to say that there were plenty of bad decisions and a general lack of understanding of the new environment and the Native people. That first winter in Halifax set a bad precedent. Despite what had seemed to be elaborate planning, it was a tough season for the human spirit. Most people lived in crude wooden huts or remained on the ships in the claustrophobic quarters. Salt meat and hard tack was the menu for existence. Why hadn't they harvested at least a good supply of edible wild fish, meat and vegetation during the summer? you might wonder. In those first two years, maybe a thousand died of typhus, taking a big bite out of the colony. Raddall suggests that the epidemic may have been a positive way of weeding out "the unclean, the drunken, the shiftless, the physical dregs." That would certainly be putting a positive spin on a pretty bad situation.

The arrival of "hard-working" New Englanders helped to eventually improve life in Halifax as many of them signed on to the rations list to accept the hand-outs of food previously allocated to those who were now dead.

A Question of Savages

Near the end of 1749, a Mi'kmaq "war party" came down through the Dartmouth lakes waterway and killed four men at a sawmill in Dartmouth. Other problems with the Mi'kmaq convinced Cornwallis that maybe the treaty wasn't working out after all. His council would not commit itself to an outright war with the Mi'kmaq, "as that would be to own them a free people, whereas they ought to be looked upon as rebels to H.M. Government or as banditti ruffians." An order went out then to take Mi'kmaq prisoners and/or kill them wherever they were to be found. It was a heartless decree of genocide and there was no concern for retribution against specific individuals who may have committed grievances against any Englishman. Instead, ten guineas was offered for every Native person, living or dead, or for his scalp. As money was paid for the scalps, it was rarely questioned whether it came from man, woman, child or possibly even a Frenchman or an Acadian. Cornwallis and his council had unleashed an irrevocable horror on the new land that they hoped to settle. As Mi'kmaq historian Dan Paul rightfully questions, "Who exactly were the savages here?"

In the summer of 1750, 795 more settlers arrived on three ships and by the fall of that year the population had grown to 3,200 souls. Not all of the arriving ships had been modernized with ventilation. The *Ann*, arriving from Rotterdam, was one of them, bringing many more sick and dying immigrants to add to the health problems of the town. Between August of 1750 and March of 1751 an average of forty-two people a month died. Winter was a particularly "popular" time to die in the early days of Halifax.

The summer of 1750, however, also saw the arrival of the *Alderney* with more than 350 passengers who set up house on the Dartmouth side of the harbour to create another community. Conflict arose with the Mi'kmaq more often there. Nearly twenty were killed or taken by the Native population, but the official records don't document what English grievances and murders/scalpings may have prompted these acts of self-defence. Dartmouth, in its earliest days, was a town of fear. When the *Speedwell* arrived in July with 212 passengers, Cornwallis had work begun to build a picket fortification wall along the wilderness side of the Dartmouth. The *Speedwell* and three other ships brought new immigrants and new blood—nearly 1,000 Protestants from Switzerland and Germany who were supposed to set up in Dartmouth (probably in hopes that the Mi'kmaq would attack them first instead of the English in Halifax). The new arrivals, however, ended up in Halifax anyway due to the fears of what lay in wait on the other side of the harbour.

Chapter Fifteen

The Rowdy Town
on the Harbour

Halifax Harbour, with George's Island in foreground.

Built-in Poverty

With so many parents dying of disease in Halifax, Cornwallis had to figure out what to do with all the orphaned children, so on June 8, 1752, an orphanage opened and the lucky woman to get the job of head matron was Mrs. Ann Wenman, who was paid three pence per day per orphan. Cornwallis optimistically calculated that the kids could be maintained by the public purse until they were old enough to work for local fishermen and earn their own keep.

In 1752 Mrs. Wenman had fifty-five orphans under her guidance, although there most certainly must have been more unattended urchins running around the primitive town. At about the same time, the hospital, never short of patients, had forty-nine citizens under its care and in August it was deemed necessary to open a section for the sickly folks who were prisoners of debt. Halifax was a city born with a kind of built-in poverty and no easy solutions, although there was some small degree of compassion as illustrated by the orphanage and the poorhouse medical care.

More ships arrived in 1752, many with Foreign Protestants. Hopson replaced Cornwallis as governor and by the end of that year the population had swelled to 5,250, of which at least 2,000 were soldiers.

Cornwallis had begged the Lords of Trade to send him more hard-working immigrants. He considered the Cockney settlers to be lazy and not much good for anything. Cornwallis thought highly of the Germans, however, and the Swiss (although these were probably immigrants from the foothills of the French Alps). Together they were referred to as the "Deutsche" or simply and incorrectly, the Dutch. The English had a way of homogenizing foreigners into various groupings and once a label was established, it stuck. So the "Dutch" settled on streets they named Brunswick and Gottingen and were later given some land on the peninsula itself. Blockhouses were set up for their protection. As expected, the Germans proved themselves good farmers, but they couldn't produce enough to support the whole town and food had to continue to be imported from Europe.

Hard Workers and an Assortment of Adventurers

In September of 1752, the Shubenacadie Mi'kmaq signed a peace treaty with the English governor that would allow the establishment of a second colony to be called Lunenburg. Unfortunately, the actual founding of the town was set back by an incident in which two Natives on the Eastern Shore supposedly killed a pair of settlers and captured two men, John Connor and James Grace, who escaped to report back to Halifax with six Mi'kmaq scalps. Dan Paul points out that there is strong evidence to prove that Connor and Grace had probably attempted to plunder a Mi'kmaq set-tlement. They were captured and, in escaping, murdered a woman and a child along with Mi'kmaq warriors before fleeing to Halifax in a canoe.

Early on, a church for Halifax became a priority and timber was shipped in from Boston for this purpose. St. Paul's opened in 1750 with no pews. In many respects, the church was quite liberal for such an uptight garrison town. "Dissenters," Mi'kmaq people and Hessian soldiers were allowed to hold services there in their own languages in the off-peak Sunday hours. Catholics, however, were given no such privilege.

Along with religion came street lights. Money was found for four hundred lanterns to be hung on posts along streets and near the landings. It was a noble effort at "civilizing" the wilderness but, unfortunately, it became a popular pastime for Haligonians to steal or smash the lanterns, so the project turned out to be a failure.

Halifax attracted an odd assortment of settlers, some of them American traders and fishermen. One naval captain by the name of Bloss built a man-sion of sorts in Halifax and kept sixteen Black slaves. Another infamous character was Joshua Mauger, who also had his own personal Black slaves. He made his money in the West Indies slave trade with ships run by slave labour. Mauger had been on hand to pillage Louisbourg in 1745 and then moved with the crowd to Halifax to make it big as an entrepreneur, with a fishing station on McNab's Island. You can still swim at Mauger's Beach on the island today, if you don't mind the pollution. The wily Mauger was ware-housing rum in town as well. He provided food for His Majesty's fleet at a good profit and traded with the Mi'kmaq. Cornwallis was more than a little miffed that Mauger had a healthy smuggling business going on with the French at Louisbourg, but the man was too rich to tamper with.

Burned at the Crossroads

Bartholomew Green set up the first printing press on Grafton Street in 1751 and the next year, his partner, John Bushell, published the first edition of the *Halifax Gazette*—the first newspaper in Canada. The local content was mostly advertisements and it carried old news garnered from month-old English papers.

Raddall envisions early Halifax as a thriving town with hotels, black-smiths, stores, at least one "academy," teachers of dance, artisans and every-thing necessary for bringing English civilization to this uncomfortable rustic place. The less-polite side of this city involved things like Mauger's slave trade run out of Major Lockman's store and other fashionable locales where Black men, women and children were bought and sold. The price for a Mi'kmaq scalp had risen as high as thirty pounds in Halifax before the so-called raids diminished along the Halifax and Dartmouth frontier. Even if the French, or possibly even the Mohawk, were responsible for such raids, it would be the Mi'kmaq who paid with their scalps and their lives.

Streets of Stumps, Rocks and Occasional Riots

So what exactly did early Halifax look like? Well, the streets were pretty bumpy with tree stumps and rocks. They were muddy in spring and fall and dusty in the summer. Human waste and garbage pails were emptied into the street gutters or anywhere convenient, which gave the town an aroma that Haligonians learned to adjust to. (Even today, Halifax dumps its human waste untreated into the harbour. In one respect, little has changed.) Those who couldn't adjust to life in town would move into the wilderness or south to New England. For many who stayed on, the filth bred diseases that would kill them.

The rough log walls of early Halifax homes were beginning to shape up with coverings of sawed boards and wood shingles. Some frame houses were now being built and all manner of shops were being set up, mostly in the front of homes.

Probably one of the weirdest days of the year in Halifax was November 5, Gunpowder Plot Day, better known now as Guy Fawkes Day. One group of rowdy effigy-toting Haligonians would set itself up against another band of rivals. They cursed, fought, drank heavily and had a bloody, merry time trying to beat the living daylights out of each other as they attempted to capture the opposition's effigies.

However, authorities did their best to maintain some semblance of order, usually of the military variety. Every male between sixteen and sixty was required to serve in the military. The "regulars" lived in wooden barracks to the south of Citadel Hill and to the north, near today's corner of Brunswick and Cogswell. The road between them, Brunswick Street, was also called Barrack Street and it was well known for its booze dealers, pimps and prostitutes. It would suffice to call it a slum. Its rival slum was on Water Street, another boozy place that catered to the earthly pleasures, vices and the degeneration of sailors, soldiers and anyone else willing to pay the price. Fights and riots spiced up the night life of Water Street and no decree from the Council seemed to greatly alter the character of these two colourful sectors of Halifax.

Chapter Sixteen

The Creation of Lunenburg

English map of Nova Scotia and Cape Breton Island, 1750. Lunenburg is labelled with the Mi'kmaq name, "Mirliguegh."

Wanted: Hard-working Protestants

After the arrival of the *Alderney*, more ships kept coming with European immigrants for the new homeland. The *Speedwell*, the *Gale*, the *Pearl* and the *Murdoch* all arrived, each with two to three hundred passengers hoping to start a new life. For military and political reasons it made sense to get loyal subjects settled into a territory that might once again be in dispute with France. But why so many foreigners? All of these ships, with the exception of the *Alderney*, were arriving from Rotterdam with Foreign Protestants. Englishmen, for the most part, wanted to stay at home during this time. And for good reason. Agriculture was in a golden age and there was no war on the home soil. Those exported to the colonies were generally somewhat undesirable—war veterans who could not easily fit back into civilian life and the unemployed from the cities. The working poor, however, were needed at home to keep industry and agriculture moving, so they were not encouraged to leave.

Cornwallis had long since recognized that the English coming to Halifax were lazy and he pushed for people with a stronger work ethic, no matter where they came from. It was no less than a matter of survival. Young, unmarried men were the most desirable immigrants, or so Cornwallis thought. In truth, they were more likely to head off for more adventure or a better life elsewhere.

Exploiting the Immigrants

The whole business of immigration was rife with exploitation. The British agent in charge of bringing in foreign settlers in 1749 was a merchant named John Dick. A Scotsman from a distinguished family, he had a reputation as a heartless scoundrel. He helped a guy named Count Orloff in a complicated marriage scam that conned for himself a knighthood in Russia. He had decided to call himself Sir John Dick and argued that he was the descendant of good old Sir William, one of the Knight Baronets.

Dick promised other Europeans the same deal as the English in settling, but they had to pay their own way across the Atlantic and Dick often profited in the wheelings and dealings that would get them to Nova Scotia. The journey for the Germans was inevitably more dangerous than for the English. Take, for example, the case of those who came over on the *Ann*. Transportation arranged by John Dick was supposed to be on hand when the emigrants arrived at the Prussian border. However, Dick's competitor, a Mr. Steadman, arrived at the meeting place to persuade the voyagers to come with him. He pretended he was Dick and when Dick's own agents said otherwise, Steadman tried to get revenge by convincing the crowd that

Nova Scotia was a barren, inhospitable land and the Germans were only wanted as soldiers against the French and Indians. The crowd rioted against Steadman and drove him off. Later Steadman returned and entreated some of the poor confused peasants to take passage to Philadelphia. Some were nearly kidnapped and the whole thing was a snarled mess, probably representative of the pure chaos that marked most of these early efforts at immigration. The skirmish also created bad press for Dick on the continent and discouraged some would-be settlers who had concluded that the English were simply insane.

Most of the passengers who did board the *Ann* were "redemptioners"—that is, they couldn't afford the ticket and would have to pay off the bill with their own labour. This system led to further human exploitation as people sold themselves and their families to the agents who actually resold them to the highest bidders upon their arrival. If a debtor tried to run off or in any way refuse servitude, he was put in prison or otherwise punished. The only financial problem here for Dick and his business was that there simply weren't enough people with money in Nova Scotia to buy the immigrants. His best shot was to *sell* them off to the Board of Trade. Then it became the governor's headache to figure out how they would work off the debt—partly by helping to build Halifax. So the redemptioners were sent to work, putting money back in Mr. Dick's pocket and giving Halifax the labour force it so desperately needed.

What was it like for those passengers on the *Ann* with a man like Mr. Dick in charge of their comfort and their fate? The ship was crowded and unventilated to begin with. On their arrival, Cornwallis wrote that the passengers were "very sickly and many dead. They were, in general, old miserable wretches and complain much of their passages not being paid as the Swiss were." He was also much distressed to discover some Roman Catholics and had immediate intentions of having them booted out of Nova Scotia.

When Hopson took over in 1752, he received some complaints about John Dick, who was accused of overcrowding his ships, of making passengers sleep on bare wooden decks and transporting unsuitable immigrants who were old or already infirm. Mr. Dick countered that he would never allow his passengers to be less than comfortable and attributed the many deaths to bad weather. He argued that the elderly were on board because he felt bad about breaking up families. In the end, Dick was given the boot by the Board of Trade and lost his monopoly on human freight and, to a degree, slavery.

But there were other complaints as well and not all of them aimed at Dick. The land-grant arrangement simply wasn't what was promised. The government was also supposed to provide implements for farming and raising animals to help establish the new citizens as farmers and herdsmen. The

Germans, because of a faulty translation, thought they would also get household items like pots, bedding and enough tools to really start off with a household. But this was not to be. They felt cheated and so developed a grudge with a lifespan of several generations.

When all those "foreigners" arrived in Halifax, they went right to work to begin paying off their debts. The government set the wages artificially low. This also meant that pay could be lowered, in the name of "fairness," for those already working in Halifax. You either had to work for low pay or get out of Halifax. It seems that nobody in power figured there could possibly be any complaints. But they figured wrong. The Germans began to protest. They may have been hard workers but they were nobody's fools.

This set Cornwallis thinking about the original plan to establish secondary settlements away from Halifax. The town needed food anyway and it would be a good idea to set up a farming community to provide for her needs. So most of the Foreign Protestants would be sent off, along with about 300 English settlers, to get some farming going. But where to send them? The Fundy area was fertile but there were still those nagging worries about the French influence and, of course, fears about the Mi'kmaq, who were friendly with the Acadians and therefore considered dangerous.

Well, something had to be done with Dartmouth on the other side of the harbour, so the immigrants from the *Speedwell* would put up the picket wall over there and build up the settlement that had been abandoned after the previous hostilities with the Mi'kmaq. Immigrants from the *Gale* would settle further up on Bedford Basin. Cornwallis eventually handed the worrisome matters of settlement over to Hopson who didn't like the idea of granting *any* land around Halifax Harbour to these foreigners. Still, the problem lingered as to where to put them all. England was continuing to foot the bill for their food and that was draining the purse. Such headaches.

Some of the foreigners saw the bad deal that was going down and left to live with the French. Many of these deserters were returned, although the Catholics stayed on with the French. The Germans were getting more and more uncomfortable with the situation in Halifax. Hopson tried to import a Lutheran minister in hopes that a little religion would act as a pacifier but that proved unsuccessful.

The Foreign Protestants organized their own religious activity anyway and, by 1752, many had worked off their debts and achieved the freedom to work for personal wages. Hopson decided to extend the free food—these immigrants, after all, had dramatically improved the colony with their labour.

An Uneasy Settlement

Hopson sent word off to London that he needed money and supplies for the Foreign Protestants to get on with establishing Lunenburg. Even before he received approval, he decided to go forward with the plan. His cheap labour pool, however, had grown exceedingly restless and he didn't want an uprising on his hands. Food and other provisions would be needed for at least another year to keep these people alive until they could fully provide for themselves—and, of course, for Halifax. Hopson could only hope that the Board of Trade would see his desperation and come through.

Mirliguegh was the Mi'kmaq name of the location and it would be renamed Lunenburg. The soil was not as good as in the Fundy area but it was reported to be fertile. The settlement would be on a defensible peninsula of 6,000 acres. Fishing, if considered at all, was of secondary importance here. So on Monday, May 21, at 7 a.m., the Foreign Protestants each drew a card from a pack—in St. Paul's Church. The card had a number representing the plot of land that the settler could build on and farm. Charles Lawrence would be in charge of things to begin with and Patrick Sutherland would take over if Lawrence were needed elsewhere—and Hopson knew he would be. Hopson also hired English and foreign overseers to make sure that the immigrants would live up to their bargain and provide food for Halifax. Lawrence and Sutherland mustered 500 men and boys for a militia to ward off (or incite) hostilities as was deemed appropriate.

The Mi'kmaq had already had enough of the haughty English coming in and running them off their own land. Word reached Hopson that 300 Native people were ready to fight to save Mirliguegh against an English invasion. The wily Hopson sent a courier to the South Shore with a false message that the settlement would be delayed. The Mi'kmaq either intercepted the messenger or changed their minds about an immediate confrontation, because the expected battle never took place upon the arrival of the settlers.

Colonel Lawrence thought he had a neat, organized plan as to how things should proceed, but the Germans had had enough of being pushed around by the English. They cut trees for shelter at their own discretion and went walking in the woods without regard for the dangers. Lawrence could not tolerate this lack of discipline, so he issued orders to cut off provisions to anyone who didn't follow his instructions. Worse still, those who could not follow orders would be sent back to Halifax. Point made.

The Germans didn't exactly cower at his command. They insisted on having Sunday off to rest. Many refused to cut trees for the picket wall that would help defend the peninsula. Lawrence was very paranoid that an Indian raid was imminent. He wanted more control of what he called the "turbulent" Germans, insisting they begin work at 4:30 in the morning. He also delayed doling out the lots of land until he realized that their "turbulence" was reaching the boiling point. Finally, Lawrence agreed to give out the land if the settlers promised to act more orderly.

Blockhouses, palisades and a wharf were successfully built. During that first short, wet summer, progress was delayed time and again by chronic diarrhoea. With everyone building and clearing land, not enough effort was put into catching and preserving fish which could have helped sustain them through the winter. Rations were low. Some people simply gave up and left—or deserted, as the English would call it. If you were caught, you'd be put in the brig aboard the *Albany*.

Lawrence offered up a shilling a day for work on the necessary "public" projects. Nonetheless, the food rations were really slim and people did not have time to do the necessary clearing and gardening which would have helped them to be self-sufficient. The Foreign Protestants really wished the English could have just left them alone to fend for themselves and get on with their lives. Lawrence viewed this independent spirit as lawlessness. At one point he genuinely wished for a Mi'kmaq attack in order to reinstil a recognition of the need to be protected. Had the English slipped back to Halifax and left the settlers alone, it's possible they would have made friends with the local Native population, but this would be impossible with Lawrence and his soldiers in control.

Eventually, Lawrence could report (without stretching the lie too far) that the settlement was going well—at least the people were too busy for open rebellion. When they asked for livestock to further their self-sufficiency, their request was granted by Halifax. However, on December 17, 1753, a message arrived in Halifax from Patrick Sutherland saying that the Foreign Protestants were in armed rebellion against the British. Council sent 200 soldiers under Lieutenant Colonel Monckton to use any means necessary to put down the uprising.

The man who stirred things up has been described as a "nervous illiterate" named John Petrequin, but he may only have been illiterate in English and he may also have had good reason to be agitated over the way the English were treating his friends and neighbours. Petrequin had supposedly received a letter suggesting that the settlers should be receiving a great bounty of food, housing supplies and farming equipment. But this was, of course, not the case. Word got out about this letter and people began to get angry. Unfortunately, Petrequin could not produce the letter. It was lost or destroyed. Everyone got mad at Petrequin and he was locked up in the blockhouse. The English released him, but he was seized again by the townspeople who confined and tortured him to try and make him produce the letter.

As this convoluted tale of a missing letter proceeded, paranoia grew over the fact that the English must have destroyed the letter to hide evidence of the supposed supplies for the colonists. The eventual result was an outright riot which brought to boil the hostility the settlers were feeling toward the English. Word was sent to Halifax for troops, but Sutherland also tried to convince the settlers that they were about to be attacked by the Mi'kmaq and that he ought to mount big guns on the barricades. The settlers didn't buy this. New demands were being made of Sutherland. Were the people of Lunenburg being cheated out of what was rightfully theirs? After all, they had been promised so much more than the English had provided.

Monckton and his men arrived and the settlers gave up the blockhouse. Things began to quieten down and Petrequin admitted that maybe there had never been a letter and he had lied about a few other things as well. Various individuals on both sides were charged with treason, conspiracy, high crimes and misdemeanours. It all sounds a bit like a comedy of errors except for the fact that it illustrates how deeply angry these immigrants were about their treatment by the English and the promises that had been broken.

Farmers, Not Fighters

The settlers of Lunenburg came to North America to be farmers—not fighters, not slaves for the British or enemies of the Native North Americans. Now they finally had some land and they would proceed to farm it. Unfortunately, since they had come from parts of Europe away from the coast, they had little interest in fishing, despite the fact that they were now living with this tremendous resource at their doorstep. Lawrence thought it would be a good idea to stimulate something of a fishing industry, so he encouraged a company from New York to set up fishing stations in nearby Mahone Bay in 1754. However, it wasn't until the 1790s that fishing really began to develop in the area.

Lunenburg became a major source of firewood for Halifax probably because there was more hardwood available there. Small boats would carry the wood along the coast to the city. In 1757, French privateers started to interrupt these shipments and spirit the cargo away to Louisbourg. A quick glimpse at the map of the coast suggests that such pirating would require a lot of time and effort for a very few logs. Certainly firewood would be more readily available from Cape Breton. The firewood pirates themselves probably quickly realized all the trouble they were going to for a few sticks and soon learned it was better to capture the ships headed the other way from Halifax to Lunenburg. This prompted Lawrence to instruct his navy to chase them down and to provide protection for Lunenburg cargoes as well.

By 1758, hostilities between the Mi'kmaq and the English in Lunenburg had increased. The growing community seemed more of a threat than it had first appeared and the Native people were loath to lose more of their adopted homeland. Provoked and unprovoked raids took place. Reports show that thirty-two people from the settlement were killed and others were taken prisoner, but Mi'kmaq losses remain undocumented.

While traditional history books have reported aggressive actions by the Mi'kmaq, it is clear that they also made significant efforts at establishing peace. In 1757, four Mi'kmaq men went to Annapolis Royal on behalf of their father, the Chief of Panook. Two stayed on as hostages (a kind of guarantee that the effort was a serious one) while their two brothers, the father and two other chiefs went to Lunenburg to speak with the English and eventually to Halifax for a peace summit. Word had not reached Lunenburg of their plan, however, and the party was shot at by the Lunenburg sentries. Despite their best efforts, the peace party was not allowed past the picket barricade at Lunenburg. Annapolis and Lunenburg never did communicate clearly over what the intentions were here, so the English in Annapolis decided the whole thing was a trick. The two Mi'kmaq brothers left behind were sent to a prison in Halifax and the Mi'kmaq interpreted the whole thing as treacherous.

Mi'kmaq efforts at peace had been so badly misinterpreted that by September an English detachment of a hundred men was sent off to hunt down the Mi'kmaq around Lunenburg. Fortunately, they couldn't find any, only traces of those who had moved on to deeper, safer forests. There were a few Mi'kmaq attacks on Lunenburg in 1759 but by 1760 things began to grow quiet again. Farmers were getting on with their farming and the town was well established if not exactly thriving.

Chapter Seventeen

Empires at Odds

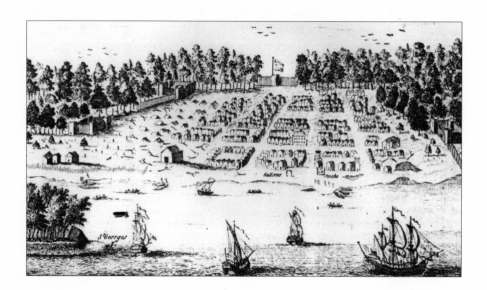

A view of Halifax from "Ye Topmasthead." Note gallows and stocks conveniently located at edge of harbour.

Shocked and Appalled

You might say peace existed between the French and English between 1713 and 1744, although many wounds were left unhealed. During this time, the French dramatically increased trade by water routes—much of it with the Spanish empire. France supplied coffee and sugar to continental Europe and had a booming fish business going as they harvested on the Grand Banks and in the Gulf of St. Lawrence. The story was not the same for the English who were hunkering down, just trying to get solid military footing. Let's face it, while France was getting on with actually exploiting their position in this part of North America, the English were obsessed with just hanging onto what they had and the design was almost purely a military one.

There was some illegal trade (smuggling, that is) going on between certain entrepreneurial Englishmen and the Spanish. Spain tried to keep this activity to a minimum and that annoyed the English. England knew that if things kept going so well for the French, as well as the Spanish, the English stake in the new land would be diminished. War ensued in 1739 with the Spanish and in 1744 (again) with the French. Louisbourg, as we've seen, had been taken in 1745, and by 1747 France was pretty well cut off from the colonies here. Then came the Treaty of Aix-la-Chapelle and Louisbourg went back to France but, naturally, the English political and military engineers were not satisfied. In their view, France had to be whipped and whipped good, sooner or later.

The French wanted no more of war. For them, fish and trade were the tickets to colonial success. By 1754 more than 400 French ships were actively hauling up fish in these North Atlantic waters and they employed a whopping 14,000 men along with a host of families who worked ashore in the fishing ports and camps along Cape Breton, Îles de la Madeleine and the Gaspé. Clearly, the French were firmly established here. Nonetheless, the French decision makers couldn't entirely forget about the strategic importance of Louisbourg and that passageway to the Gulf and the St. Lawrence River.

Louisbourg would once again be a base for a naval fleet to protect those 400 fishing boats and keep a clear eye on the British fleet in these waters.

This next war began far away but soon caught up with the people of Nova Scotia. American speculators were moving on a scheme to push into the Ohio River Valley. This threatened the French hold on the centre of the continent and eventually led to a military clash at Fort Duquesne (Pittsburgh) and further violent escalation from there.

King Louis XV of France had his share of weaknesses. He laboured over trivial matters and had a hard time making up his mind about important things. He was prone to appoint inadequate ministers who soon were overworked, resulting in a high turnover of ministers of war, marine and foreign affairs. As with most royal courts of the day, Louis's was rife with intrigue practised by various sycophants, political climbers and self-serving schemers who succeeded in interfering with sensible decision-making.

Locked into a defence mentality, the French military officers still favoured the impossible ideal of an invulnerable fortress. Unlike in the days of Louis XIV, the French Army was now weakened and staffed with incompetent officers. Commissions were granted through money and connections. The military arms were primarily muskets and bayonets, adequate for close range but not much else. The navy was in somewhat better shape than the poorly organized army. Their ships might even have been superior to the English but there were fewer of them and few sailors to man them. To bolster their navy for war, France commandeered 800 merchant ships with their 3,000 seamen. This must have taken its toll on public support from the merchants as well as lowering the overall morale of those hustled into war. Epidemics were raging in various French ports where the navy docked and some men went AWOL just to avoid disease. Then the naval officers had to settle for whatever landlubbers they could press into service to help sail ships they were totally unfamiliar with.

In May of 1755, a fleet of French ships with more than 4,000 men left France for Louisbourg and would prepare to fight the English at Halifax if necessary. Governor Lawrence found out about this and reckoned that Halifax was unprepared and undermanned with only 3,000 men at its disposal to stave off an attack. British Admiral Boscawen met some French ships off the coast of Newfoundland and captured two of them. This seemed to discourage the French from an outright attack on Halifax. The *Alcide* and the *Lys* were ushered into Halifax Harbour with 1,200 soldiers and sailors as prisoners to be jailed on George's Island. The English also had the good luck of having captured a French war chest worth about 30,000 pounds. What scared them, however, was a shipment on board of 500 scalping knives that were to be distributed to the Mi'kmaq and the Acadians. While the English had themselves employed the barbaric technique of scalping for their own colonial purposes, they were shocked and appalled to think that the French were planning to use the same tactic to run the English out of Nova Scotia.

The Privateers of Boomtown

The presence of the French at Beausejour had continued to nag at governors in both Nova Scotia and New England. The French fort was actually in pretty bad structural condition and the governor there, Louis Du Pont Duchambon de Vergor, was less than capable of keeping up a solid military presence. When Massachusetts volunteers and British regulars under Robert Monckton laid siege to Beausejour, the governor tried desperately to rally the Acadians to fight with him but they were loath to get involved in the bloodshed. Many of them abandoned Beausejour for good reason. Those who stayed later regretted the decision and many refused to follow the French commands. Less than two weeks into the siege, Monckton had his men open fire on the fort and by the sixteenth of June, 1755, the governor admitted defeat. The English promptly renamed the place Fort Cumberland.

In July of that year, Lawrence was still panicked about those scalping knives and worried about the loyalty of the Acadians. The incidents at Beausejour had convinced him that these French-speaking farmers and cat-tlemen were not to be trusted. Unwilling to accept the point of view of the Acadians—they just wanted to be left alone and were more than willing to remain neutral—Lawrence called for their expulsion. Next, Halifax prepared for full-scale war. The streets were filled with British redcoats, American bluecoats, all sorts of sailors and New England rangers. Privateering was also on the rise. Anyone willing to take the chance could go capture a French (or any other French-friendly) ship and keep most of the goods, all in the name of the British Crown. This bloodthirsty entrepreneurial opportunity attracted businessman Joshua Mauger. He prepped the *Mosquito* for such work and pro-ceeded to capture a Dutch merchant ship with French supplies.

A greedy lot, the men in Mauger's employ tortured the Dutch seamen, putting thumbscrews to the crew and passengers to find out about possible hidden money. According to Thomas Raddall, Mauger's second mate grabbed one of the screaming victims as he was being tortured with the thumbscrew and danced him around deck while another one of the men played the fiddle. A merry lot they were, these Halifax pirates who hoped to profit all they could from hostilities between the French and English.

At least fifteen privateer ships were using Halifax as home port for their forays, bringing in a great influx of merchandise to be auctioned off to the highest bidder. St. Paul's Church found itself the recipient of an organ des-tined for a Spanish settlement further south.

Halifax was a boom town. Previously with a population of less than 2,000, there were now 3,000 new soldiers and a couple of thousand seamen coming in with the fleet. All this influx of people, prosperity, stolen goods, stolen booze and the like made for a wild and overcrowded town with a plethora of criminal activity—and certainly not enough women to go around to enter-tain the rowdy men.

The Advantage of Allies

When the war began, the French had three forces: colonial regular troops, militia and Indian allies. The colonial regulars were actually in a bit better shape than their counterparts back home on the continent. Commissions on this side of the Atlantic were granted on merit and the training was decent. Twenty of these companies were in Louisbourg and twenty-one in Louisiana.

By the time the Seven Years' War flared up, these men had plenty of fighting experience and they had also learned something of guerrilla-type warfare from their Native American friends. Unlike most British regiments, they could live off the land, strike quickly and then disappear, using the forest as cover and even sanctuary.

On the other hand, the militia men were treated like cheap labour or even cannon fodder. The men were often conscripted from French villages and forced to serve without pay. They didn't particularly like taking orders and especially didn't like waiting for orders when under fire. Sometimes they rudely shot back at the enemy before the command. It was also common for these soldiers to express their displeasure with their situation by fleeing in the midst of battle. While French history may not paint them as heroic, I think it's at least common courtesy to consider them as being sensible in these circumstances.

In battle, the French officers did not always consider their Native allies reliable. Mi'kmaq warriors were not always willing to play war by the stiff etiquette of European warfare. Better to retreat and hide, wait for an advantage to attack on another day, rather than sacrifice one's life in a losing position. The French soldiers soon began to learn from such unconventional notions. As the English became more aware of the combined strengths and uncouth but effective strategies of their opponents, they also became ever more cautious about getting involved in wilderness battles with an enemy that didn't always play by European rules.

Always at home on the land in any part of Nova Scotia, the Mi'kmaq were excellent scouts and good spies, even able to take prisoners from the English camps and gather information from their captives. As a result, the French were usually better informed than the British.

Full-scale Attack

The British had launched into their full-scale attack on New France in 1754 without a formal declaration of war. While the British sent two battalions of regular troops to America, the French reinforced Louisbourg with two battalions from France. Each battalion, it's worth noting, had a grenadier company—a band of élite soldiers who would stand behind the line of attack with bayonets fixed to insure none of their own men would retreat once the battle had begun. The military liked to look after its own.

Most of the French forts in America, like the one at Beausejour, were really not prepared for a full-on assault from the British Army. Louisbourg was more substantial but still plagued by structural and organizational problems. In charge at Louisbourg was Augustin de Boschenry de Drucour. Baron Jean-Armand de Dieskau was in command of all battalions in the vicinity. At the top was Governor-General François-Pierre de Rigaud, Marquis de Vaudreuil. In 1756 the Marquis de Montcalm replaced Dieskau.

The French regular troops were paid much better than the colonial fight-ers who were defending their homeland. Any new soldiers coming from France obviously wanted to join the ranks of the higher-paid. All this led to tension between the two factions who would be fighting side by side for unequal pay. The French regulars, however, despite the financial perks, weren't fond of garrison life. They were plagued by mosquitoes and black flies as well and were often depressed at being away from France for so long. News from home was rare and they had a hard time adjusting to the alliance that had been struck between the colonials and the Mi'kmaq. War on the continent had been so much more civilized. There they had grown accus-tomed to comfortable transportation to the front as well as the regular atten-dance of hospital and baggage wagons. Back home there had been cosy war encampments with servants, wine, clean linen and good food. Now they were in the wilderness with no amenities whatsoever. They had to carry their own food, consort with "savages," swim rivers and fight side by side with the crude colonials. And on top of that, the rules of war were not being adhered to. All this amounted to a total affront to their continental dignity.

The French militiamen saw the better-paid élite soldiers as wimps and the French regulars looked down on their colonial counterparts as crude and unkempt. The locals also recognized that the overall defensive strategy adhered to by the bigwigs wasn't going to work, but they had no power or plan to change it.

Vaudreuil complained to Paris that the French regulars were reluctant to leave the relative comfort of camp and actually fight. With good reason, he saw a personnel crisis looming. As soon as the present fighting stopped, he wanted all French regular troops back in France and out of his territory.

The French were far outnumbered by the British troops, but that may not be what lost them the war. Historians argue that it may well have been lead-ership. Montcalm has taken some blame for bad decisions that led to the fall of Quebec. But there were other factors. As the war heated up, the British troops actually improved while the French deteriorated, perhaps as a result of the morale issues brought on by the French regulars. The war was popular in England—nothing like a good war to revitalize the old empire. Short-term enlistment was introduced, which was not really such a bad deal if you were lucky enough to survive and return home. The British had also hired skilful mercenaries, the Swiss in particular, who were good at adapting to the North American wilderness.

French reinforcements were less prepared, many of them hauled off the streets and sent without enough training into battle. Mutinies and looting among the rabble were common. They also brought disease, along with the discipline problems. Sickness, however, haunted both sides of the war almost constantly. It has been estimated that in Quebec in 1759, at least a quarter of Wolfe's army was sick with scurvy and dysentery.

Chapter Eighteen

The Deportation of the Acadians: "Into Utter Misery"

Acadians being forced to leave their homes at Grand Pré; 1893 engraving by F.O.C. Darley.

"A Mild and Tranquil Government"

In 1744 before the first siege of Louisbourg, the French had attacked Fort Anne at Annapolis Royal not once but twice. This was a patriotic effort to restore French honour by recapturing a landmark of early French colonization. Typically, the Acadians living in the vicinity tried to avoid involvement but from experience they knew they would be punished for whatever harm befell the British. The British commander Paul Mascarene, who recognized the Acadians' neutrality, said of them: "The inhabitants, though French, have however kept in their Fidelity much beyond what was expected notwithstanding all the entreaties of the French officers from Louisbourg who could not prevail on them to take up arms against us."

It sounds as if there was at least one clear-headed English military man who could see that the enemy was not necessarily everyone who spoke the French language. The Acadians themselves, not fearing to be called traitors by the French, asked simply to be left out of other people's quarrels. One resident of Grand Pré had written to the English to say, "We live under a mild and tranquil government…and have all good reason to be faithful to it. We hope therefore, that you will have the goodness not to separate us from it, and that you will grant us the favour not to plunge us into utter misery." Unfortunately, he and his fellow citizens would indeed be plunged "into utter misery" as the years unfolded. That phrase could not have been more apt.

The governing council of Nova Scotia and the meddling Massachusetts governor, William Shirley, suspected the Acadians of ill will. New Englanders were making suggestions to the British that the so-called "nest of traitors" should be somehow removed.

After the English captured Louisbourg in 1745, the French counterattacked the next year by trying again to recapture Fort Anne. This attack and a subsequent one in 1747 failed and while these were actions undertaken by French military men, the peaceful Acadians were once again under suspicion. In 1748 some British troops were killed in the Grand Pré region. Acadians were blamed, though the evidence of their involvement was slim. In that year the war was over, Île Royale was again returned to France and the mainland Acadians were quite willing to continue their lives under British rule. This created an odd predicament for the British, for now Nova Scotia was officially English but predominantly populated by people of French descent.

Herded Like Cattle

The building of Halifax in 1749 under the direction of Governor Cornwallis signalled a shift of British attitudes; it was not just an effort to create a city but also to create a powerful military presence. Hundreds of Acadians began to take the hint and a few migrated to Cape Breton (the poor farming there notwithstanding) and several hundred to Île Saint-Jean. Cornwallis now demanded a full oath of allegiance and the Acadians refused to accept the terms, raising the ire of Cornwallis. He responded by establishing new military posts in Acadian areas. The next Halifax governor, Peregrine Hopson, softened the hard line and was willing to accept an oath of allegiance that would not require Acadians to fight against the French, but he left Halifax by 1753 and the next year Charles Lawrence (for whom my own community of East Lawrencetown is named) was appointed lieutenant-governor.

Lawrence was more than leery of the Acadian population. There were too many of them and they were too settled, too entrenched and, to his mind, too dangerous. Lawrence saw the threat of the French all around him—Quebec, Louisbourg and the loyalty of the Natives to the French. France also had control of the Mississippi and Ohio River valleys. Lawrence felt that he had inherited a vulnerable and weak position and he wanted to do whatever he could to strengthen the English position.

There were 10,000 Acadians under Lawrence's jurisdiction in Nova Scotia and this number weighed heavily on his mind. He was also fearful of a possible attack from the French to the west. So with the support of nearly 2,500 troops sent up by Governor Shirley, the British attacked Fort Beausejour in the Tantramar Marsh at the head of the Bay of Fundy. More than 300 Acadians were found inside, some had been coerced into fighting against the British. This fact would help seal the fate of a broad sweep of Acadians. Many claimed they were threatened and forced into fighting the English by the French, but this was not enough to quell the growing mistrust of all Acadians and it gave the impetus to Lawrence to take stronger measures against these "traitors from within."

The New England troops went further and seized guns from the Acadians in the entire Fort Beausejour area. The Acadians thought this was going too far—guns were necessary for hunting—so a group of delegates went to Halifax to try to sort things out. Once again they were asked to sign a very strong oath of allegiance to the British. They refused and were imprisoned on George's Island in Halifax Harbour. Later, in July, 1755, a second group of Acadians came to Halifax and again the issue of the oath was put before them. Like their predecessors, they refused to agree with the British definition of allegiance and the possibility they would be forced to fight against the French. Undoubtedly, the threat of expulsion had been put before them but they felt certain the British would not follow through. They had been living with this threat since the first time it had been put forward in 1713.

From a pragmatic point of view, one wonders why the Acadian leaders did not simply swear the oath and go back to their farms—after all, they had no desire to become embroiled in anybody's battles. They wanted to be left alone. Alas, the concept of being obliged to *fight* against the French must have seemed too much. The British, on the other hand, would have been foolish to send Acadians into battle against the French, as they would no doubt turn out to be very poor opponents of their own countrymen.

Undoubtedly the business of the oath was really part of a larger agenda which had already been set. Fear had been growing among British leaders since the Mississippi River valley had recently been lost to the French. So on July 28 the Halifax governing council, which included Lieutenant-Governor Charles Lawrence, Admiral Boscawen and Chief Justice Belcher, called for the deportation of the "French Inhabitants." Later the British government in London would claim that it did not know of Lawrence's decision on expulsion and if it had, it would have quashed such a measure. If Lawrence is the man most damned with the guilt of having caused such monumental grief, it's worth noting that British colonial leaders were in a new sort of panic about the prospect of the French conquering much of North America. Powerful Boston leaders like Phipps and Shirley were also urging Lawrence to offset any potential attacks against New England from the French in the New Brunswick region.

Orders went out to Chignecto, Pisiquid (near Windsor), Beausejour and Fort Anne. Livestock and land would be turned over to the Crown. Families could take only what they could carry with them, as they would be sent off on ships brought in from the colonies along the Atlantic Coast from Massachusetts to Georgia. By August 11, the operation had begun at Fort Beausejour. The men were held in custody until the ships arrived. It is reported that some men tunnelled out of the fort, collected their families and escaped to freedom in the wilderness.

The most populated settlement, Grand Pré, heard the deportation orders in early September of that year. It came as a complete shock. Despite events at Beausejour, no one in Grand Pré expected the deportation of a group of families whose lives were entirely dedicated to agriculture. They had been out working in the fields just the day before. But in Grand Pré and nearby Pisiquid, the men were brought together and told that they were about to lose their land and their livestock.

At Grand Pré, Colonel John Winslow was the officer in charge of the expulsion. His diary reveals that he felt badly over the fate of the Acadians. He knew that he did not have enough men to forcibly remove everyone from their homes without bloodshed and he wanted to avoid a confrontation. Before the Grand Pré villagers were aware of what was about to happen, Winslow installed himself in the priest's house and asked the people to take all the religious ornaments out of the church. He intended the church to become a temporary military prison and did not want religious fervour over sacred objects to further complicate his already difficult task. More than 400 men and boys aged ten and older were ordered to gather inside the church, where they learned they were now prisoners and that soon they would be deported, along with their families. It would be a long, tense wait for the necessary ships to arrive. Each day twenty men were allowed to go back into the community and bring back food. However, if they did not return, the other prisoners would be shot.

Winslow, hoping to reduce the possibility of an uprising, ordered the young men to leave on the first five ships. With some refusing to leave without their fathers, soldiers marched them at bayonet-point to the boats as mothers and sisters stood by and watched in tears.

Before more ships could arrive, twenty-four men did escape. Winslow decreed that if they did not return, the entire village would be burned immediately. Twenty-two men did return, while the other two were shot in pursuit. Within a few months, everyone was herded onto ships and the Acadian community of Grand Pré had been depopulated. By December of 1755 more than 2,200 Acadians were shipped away from their homes in and around Grand Pré alone. British troops burned barns and houses so there would be nothing for the Acadians to return to. They knew how strongly these people felt about their land and they wanted to do the utmost to discourage them from coming back.

The Tragedy of Exile

Families were separated in many cases—not so much out of cruelty but more a result of the bureaucratic nightmare of orchestrating the loading and dispersal of so many unhappy souls. Some of those families would of course never be able to find their way back together. In all, about 6,000 Acadians were ripped away from the homes they loved and scattered to Massachusetts, New York, Connecticut, Pennsylvania, Maryland, Virginia and the Carolinas. Conditions aboard the Boston ships were unhealthy and many died on the voyage.

Many Acadians accepted their fate and adapted to the ways of Anglo-American life. A new language was learned and names were changed. But hundreds of others refused to give up on their cherished homeland and did whatever they could to find their way back to Nova Scotia. Still others moved on to Louisiana, French territory, to begin a new life. Not all of the colonies were hospitable toward the destitute immigrants who were to arrive. Virginia refused to accept the 1,500 Acadians deposited there and had them shipped to England as prisoners of war. After the Treaty of Paris in 1763, those who were still alive were sent on to St. Malo and Morlaix in France.

Not all Acadians were deported. It was a massive and complex task that could never fully succeed. Acadians from Cape Sable were imprisoned in Halifax and finally shipped off to France. Even as late as 1762, more than fifty Acadian families were imprisoned at Fort Edward in Windsor.

Others were luckier and escaped to the Restigouche, Miramichi and Bay of Chaleur areas of New Brunswick. Still others made their way to the Gaspé Peninsula of Quebec and to the islands of St. Pierre and Miquelon.

In 1760, after the fall of Montreal, France lost control of North America and the British fear of the Acadians abated. By 1764 they were permitted to return—yet still they were required to take the loathed oath of allegiance. They were also instructed to settle in the more remote areas of the region. The move was not entirely altruistic. Acadians were needed for labour in the fishing industry and their farming and fur-trapping skills would also be greatly in demand. On top of that, the Acadians had a good working relationship with the Mi'kmaq, which might also be profitable in the trade of furs.

British law asserted that only Protestants could purchase or own land. It was a tough policy to uphold but it kept the Catholics at a severe disadvantage. They might be permitted to hold land, even live on it without title, but only if the land was not in demand by a Protestant and in particular an Englishman. As the Acadians found their way back to the Annapolis Valley and elsewhere, they discovered that many of their farms had been given to New England colonists known as Planters, who were not nearly as skilled in working the land. A few families were permitted to return to their own land in Pubnico in southwest Nova Scotia and on Île Madame off the coast of Cape Breton.

The growth of the fishery led to Acadians being encouraged to settle in Argyle, Clare, Cheticamp, Havre-Boucher, Île Madame, Minudie, Nappan, Maccan, Pomquet, Tracadie and Chezzetcook. French culture and language would survive most strongly in Clare and Cheticamp, while other areas experienced a gradual assimilation into English culture. Prejudice against the Acadians would continue, however, and the tragedy of the exile could not be easily forgotten by those families that had suffered severe hardship and personal loss. It's been estimated that, despite the deportation, by the early nineteenth century, seventy per cent of all surviving Acadians (23,000 of them) had returned to live in the north—in the Maritimes or in Quebec.

Chapter Nineteen

The Fall of Louisbourg

Louisbourg falls to the British.

Of Cabbages and Kings

The belief in empire-building may have been more the inspiration for the Seven Years' War than any real desire for control of more land. Underlying that notion was the fact that England and France each wanted the entire North American continent for its own. The war lasted officially from 1756 to 1763, but fighting had started in Ohio in 1754. By 1755, the British had already captured Fort Beausejour and expelled the Acadians. France knew that the fall of Louisbourg and Quebec would mean the end of French power in North America and they were prepared to fight. The English, however, were determined to capture Louisbourg again.

Lord Loudon came to Halifax in 1757 and drilled his soldiers for battle. To avoid scurvy, the men ate vegetables that they had grown themselves. As a result, Loudon's contingent became known as the "cabbage planting expedition." His men camped near the base of the Citadel, along with the American rangers on hand for the battle for Louisbourg. Loudon himself was not well liked (some thought of him as all pomp and no circumstance). On two occasions he was nearly killed by "accidental" misfiring of American muskets. He also had a habit of complaining about the quality of Halifax rum, which all too often made his troops sick.

Admiral Holbourne had arrived from England with eleven warships to blockade Louisbourg, but something happened to stall the plan of attack. Loudon's troops were on their way to attack Louisbourg when the French ship *La Parole* was captured. On the ship, hidden in a fish barrel, were fake letters addressed to the French government indicating that Louisbourg had twenty-two warships, other small craft and more than enough French troops to stave off the English. Loudon, believing that his men were outnumbered by French ships and soldiers at Louisbourg, refused to send them off to what he believed would be certain slaughter. Loudon decided to sail his men back to England but first returned to Halifax where they were responsible for spreading a smallpox epidemic that would kill 700 Haligonians that winter, a high casualty rate for a battle that never happened.

Holbourne wasn't as readily dissuaded from the attack but he had a stroke of bad luck as gale force winds lashed his fleet, smashing up some of his ships along the coast of Cape Breton. By the time they had regrouped, it was too late in the season to attack.

In England, Loudon's refusal to move on Louisbourg was considered an outrage, so by the spring of 1758, a larger military force was sent over for battle. General Jeffrey Amherst controlled 12,000 men and Admiral Boscawen commanded more than forty ships. Together they were prepared to attack Louisbourg by the end of May. Amherst had previously held only administrative jobs, most recently in charge of providing supplies for Hessian troops, but back in England his superiors had decided that Amherst was the man for the job. Boscawen, on the other hand, had fought in Spain, Panama and India. Nicknamed "Wry-necked Dick" or more affectionately, "Old Dreadnought," he was famous for hauling poor sods off the streets and pressing them into naval service. He had been to Nova Scotia previously with a crew of men dying of typhoid and had helped in the dirty work of "removing" Acadians from their homes. Louisbourg was not one of his favoured sailing destinations and he worried considerably about "the dismal prospect of floating islands of ice sufficient to terrifie [sic] the most daring seaman."

Instead of overindulging on cabbages to fight scurvy, the soldiers now drank a palatable spruce beer made from boiled spruce, molasses and yeast. By the time everyone was crowded into Halifax, the city was even rowdier, drunker and more crime-infested than before. A semblance of order was maintained by severe punishment: floggings, hangings, execution by musket, all attended by considerable crowds for their entertainment value. A less drastic but somewhat painful and humiliating punishment was "riding the wooden horse," which, as close as I can figure, involved being strapped naked onto a sharp wooden rail for hours at a time with weights attached to your legs and feet. Pirates (privateers on the wrong side) were hanged and their bodies left to swing in the breeze for all to see.

Nobody knew what to do with the poor and the insane, so a poorhouse— a kind of a prison really—was built where the library on Spring Garden Road stands today. The inhabitants there also received considerable floggings—in hopes of what? one might wonder. Reforming them? Improving their attitude? When they died, they were buried in shallow graves, so that the smell of rotting human flesh wafted up and down lovely Spring Garden Road where now fashionable shops sell overpriced items of fashion.

Most colonists in Halifax were not at all eager to get involved in the battle for Louisbourg. In fact, there would be no provincial regiments and relatively few Americans in the attack. The provincial units served mostly as labourers, not actual fighters. In Halifax, the red-coated Brits looked down their noses at their blue-jacketed American counterparts, but the British desperately needed the forest-fighting skills of some of the American Rangers. One of these Ranger units was made up almost entirely of Mohicans. Along with some other First Nations warriors, they were armed, paid and fed by the British in the fighting at Louisbourg and later at Quebec.

Amherst and Boscawen hoped that they could get the job done quickly at Louisbourg and then move on to attack the French stronghold in Quebec. That didn't happen. Difficult winds made for a slow crossing from Britain for Boscawen's ships. Once all the troops and ships were gathered in Halifax and ready to go, General James Wolfe complained that the men were not yet ready for battle, partly because they were poorly attired. It wasn't just a matter of fashion but the fact that the men were fitted for a summer war on the continent, not a cooler war in rough Nova Scotian terrain. He noticed that the English troops and seamen were not in top-notch physical condition as a result of surviving only on salt-meat and rum—not exactly an ideal, nourishing diet. He also argued that they were too well paid to be good soldiers. As a leader, he had serious doubts about a lot of things. Nonetheless, the plan went ahead.

The Seven-week Siege

Governor Drucour had been expecting the attack and his men were prepared. They had an ally in the sea and the weather as well. On June 2, 1758, when the British Navy sailed into Gabarus Bay, thick fog and high waves made a landing impossible. The French knew what was going on and were prepared to defend the fortress when the British troops finally did land at White Point, Flat Point and Kennington Cove. French gunfire was so intense that General Wolfe was ready to tell his men to retreat to the ships but he saw many of the boats were already smashed on the rocks along the shore. So the British fought on.

Once a beachhead was established, the British didn't have an easy time rolling the big guns ashore and making a roadway to get them closer to the fort. It was tough going along the rocky shore and through the swamps beyond. Eventually, however, General Amherst had landed a thousand of his men and Wolfe was hunkering down to create a battery at Lighthouse Point.

Inside Louisbourg, Drucour had 8,000 men and at least 800 guns. The fort itself was stronger than it had been in 1745, but it took a heavy pounding from the massive British weapons. The walls were breached and buildings inside were smashed. Men, women and children helped serve the guns inside Louisbourg. Even Madame Drucour was seen firing back at the British. Every day she would fire three guns at the British to bolster the spirits of the bedraggled French defence. Fires raged in the town. Eventually, citizens inside what was left of the walls pleaded with the governor to surrender.

English shells had fallen on everything inside, including the hospital. Drucour felt that this had overstepped the bounds of decency and actually implored Amherst to allow for a zone for the sick and wounded that would be protected from the shelling. Amherst told Drucour to put them on a boat, but Drucour figured he couldn't afford to spare a ship. While this round of "negotiations" brought little success, it did establish a communication link between the two leaders and gifts were exchanged. Drucour sent Amherst two bottles of champagne (the French were always well stocked under all circumstances with decent refreshments) and some butter. Amherst sent Madame Drucour two pineapples, one of which was rotten.

Seven weeks of siege had gone by. Massive holes gaped in the walls. The town was in ruins. Women and children were out in the streets without protection. Fires raged. French ships in the harbour had been captured. There was not much hope for Louisbourg. Finally, the British leaders stood inside on the parade ground. It would be a defeat without "the honours of war." Many of the French were outraged. Better to die than be humiliated. Drucour, however, handed his sword to Admiral Boscawen and surrendered. While Drucour was stinging from the agony of the defeat, he knew, however, that it was now too late in the year for the British to mount another attack on Quebec, so he had at least saved that bastion of the French Empire for a while. Apparently both Boscawen and Amherst were charmed by Madame Drucour and granted her every wish for comfort as a prisoner.

By the time of surrender, Drucour himself was not a healthy man. He was also broke, having borrowed heavily to keep himself in office. Madame Drucour returned first to France with her husband's journals. She hoped to convince the public back home that Drucour had done the best he could to preserve Louisbourg against impossible odds. When Drucour himself finally returned to France, however, he was a shattered man without enough money to pay his own passage.

As news of the fall of Louisbourg spread, celebrations broke out in Boston and in Halifax, where bells rang and bonfires were lit. As the soldiers returned, people danced in the streets and Governor Charles Lawrence, who had been an officer in the battle, held a grand ball in his official residence.

The fall of Louisbourg meant an end to French control in Cape Breton and Île Saint-Jean. The British sent 500 men under Lord Rollo to Port la Joie to root out the Acadians, many of whom had fled there to avoid expulsion. Once again, the Acadians wanted only to be left alone and allowed to work their recently established farms. They begged to be permitted to stay, but to no avail. Before being loaded on the boats, most single men were married in hasty ceremonies in order to avoid conscription when they arrived back in France. They were then shipped off to Louisbourg as prisoners or sent back to France. Some would end up in English prisons. Some escaped and stayed behind but were eventually forced to swear the loathed oath of allegiance.

It was a sad and rugged crossing back to France for those Acadians who were driven out of their homeland. France would not feel at all like home to them and they would endure the bitterness of losing their farms and livelihood. One of those ships, the *Violet*, sank with all aboard. Another one of the ships was leaking badly and then something set off an explosion. At least 700 died in this and other disasters. On the *Duke of William* a kindly priest gave the last rites to 300 Acadians who were about to drown on the sinking ship. As the vessel sank, he himself jumped into an English lifeboat and found his way safely to England.

The following year, 1759, would see the British defeat the French on the

Plains of Abraham. Both British General Wolfe and French Lieutenant-General Montcalm would be killed in the battle.

The War Against No One

In 1760, British soldiers continued to attack Louisbourg even though the battle had long since been won. What was the occasion? The British decided it wasn't worth saving what was left of the elaborate fortress, for fear that the French might try to wangle a way to regain her territory and repair the fort. For months, the war without enemies continued as the remains of Louisbourg were smashed even further into rubble. Some stones from the Louisbourg walls and houses, however, were salvaged to build homes in Halifax.

Since the fortress of Louisbourg was demolished, the remaining English soldiers had to find shelter elsewhere. Many returned to Halifax and lived in tents where quite a few died from disease and drinking. Halifax was just not a good place to settle in for the winter with a tent and a nearly unlimited supply of cheap liquor.

The first General Assembly of Nova Scotia got underway in October of 1758. Although it had limited power, it was a big step toward some kind of representational government here. The Halifax Dockyard began to take shape and a lighthouse was built at Sambro, although its actual use was fairly haphazard for some time.

Most Mi'kmaq realized that their alliance with the French was over and further resistance to the English would be futile. Argimault, chief of the Monguash Mi'kmaq, signed a treaty in Halifax, attended by Father Maillard, a French missionary who had lived among the Mi'kmaq for twenty-five years. Father Maillard, who had once translated the Catholic liturgy into Mi'kmaq, now acted as translator in the peace proceedings where Argimault buried the hatchet in the garden of the colonial governor on Spring Garden Road.

The war with France was pretty well over in this part of the world. More immigrants began to pour into Halifax. King George refused Halifax's request to incorporate in 1759, believing that the town was merely a military outpost. Halifax was, alas, still a pretty primitive place. Slaves were advertised in the papers and auctioned off before the public. Because there were more soldiers and sailors here than civilians, the city remained a ruffian's town, often on the verge of getting out of control. With the excessive drinking and indulgence in other worldly temptations, the city's reputation as one of the most wicked in North America grew.

In 1762, after the British fleet captured Havana, they brought their booty to Halifax for sale and distribution. The new merchandise from the exotic Spanish south amazed the people of the town.

Fear of another French invasion spread in 1762 and Halifax again prepared itself for war, but nothing came of it. The Treaty of Paris in 1763 gave Britain control of all lands that had once been held by the French in North America. France held on to St. Pierre and Miquelon and some fishing rights in the North Atlantic. As terms of the agreement, Britain would grant a very limited degree of religious freedom for the first time in Nova Scotia. George III, who had recently succeeded his father, George II, issued a royal proclamation which established a set of rights and freedoms for First Nations people in Canada. Today, this proclamation is still part of the debate on the fundamental issues of fishing and land claims such as the one in Oka. It did, however, establish English dominance over what had once been Native land.

All of the Maritime provinces were then known as Nova Scotia, but the English settlers of the renamed St. John's Island (PEI) petitioned to become a separate province and succeeded. They had successfully complained that it just took too damn long to get word back and forth from Halifax. Even after the breakaway, the first governor, Walter Patterson, started up a birch-bark canoe mail service between his island and the mainland to try to improve communication between the two provinces.

Chapter Twenty

The Land of Exile and Immigrants

View of farmland settled by Scots in Pictou area not far from where the
Hector landed.

The Return of the Acadians

In 1764, after it was decreed that Acadians would be permitted to return to Nova Scotia, the battered refugees trickled back slowly. It was a difficult journey home from the American colonies along the seaboard to the south and many came on foot or undertook a harrowing journey in cramped quarters on sailing ships.

The government in Halifax was pushing to populate more of the land in Nova Scotia and now that the French had been defeated, the Acadians were not considered to be of any significant danger. In 1768, the British asserted that non-Protestants could now own land, but the law wasn't officially applied until the last decade of the century. Meanwhile, ownership of land by Catholic Acadians would be tenuous at best, making it difficult for a family to feel settled. All the best Acadian lands had been commandeered, given away to British and New England settlers. Acadians returned to Pubnico and Île Madame and then settled other communities where the fishing and farming could be developed: Digby, various Yarmouth County harbours, Minudie, Nappan, Maccan, Cheticamp, Pomquet, Tracadie, Havre-Boucher and Chezzetcook. The return from exile continued slowly until the 1820s.

Not Quite New England

Up until 1758, New Englanders generally didn't see Nova Scotia as a particularly desirable place. Halifax was considered a rather degenerate little seaport town. Representational government—democracy—was coming along very slowly, hostilities between English and Mi'kmaq continued and it was anyone's guess when the power struggle with France might flare up again. The climate was harsher, the farming in general was not nearly as good as in the New England river valleys and the black flies were debilitating in summer. So why would any New Englander in his right mind want to give up the family homestead and set off north for a new life there?

Well, after Louisbourg was captured, the immediate French threat diminished and a token *near*-democratic government was set up in Halifax. These two factors still would not have been enough to attract New Englanders. Governor Lawrence, however, was giving away the rich farmlands stolen from the Acadians and throwing in some further incentives as well. There would be freedom of religion—for all Protestants anyway. Dissenters would be excused from paying taxes collected by the Church of England. The English were promising protection from the French or the Mi'kmaq or anyone else a settler might consider threatening. After all, the place was crawling with under-utilized military men with nothing but time on their hands.

Lawrence also claimed that the government and legal systems were pretty much like what they were used to at home.

At first, only a handful of New Englanders went north to check things out. They indeed saw the fertile Acadian dyked farmlands and the attractive possibilities, but all the other negative firsthand reports delayed immigration. From 1760 to 1763, however, at least 5,000 people had been persuaded to give up New England for Nova Scotia. Known as the Planters, the settlers were not only farmers, but some were fishermen. Many had come from Massachusetts, Rhode Island and Connecticut where conflicts were arising over the use of "common" ground. The idea of private, available land for the asking was a great temptation. Many were Congregationalists and they saw the move as an opportunity to spread their brand of religion.

While the farmers came mostly from Connecticut and Rhode Island, the fishermen came from coastal Massachusetts. Some of the latter may still have held a grudge against the Nova Scotian British for not having given Massachusetts credit for the part her people had played in defeating the French at Louisbourg. New Englanders had also suffered at the hands of the French military. Fishing schooners had been captured by French privateers during the Seven Years' War and New England fishing ports had, in many cases, been destroyed. On the more positive side, many coastal New Englanders would feel at home in villages along the shores of Nova Scotia and were happy to make a fresh start. This was not unfamiliar territory to them; many had sailed here to fish during the summers. Now they were closer to the Grand Banks as well, which gave them at least one advantage over the fishermen they left behind in New England. Yarmouth, Barrington, Liverpool and Chester became home to many of the arrivals.

Not everyone who came to Nova Scotia, however, stayed on. They discovered it wasn't all as grand as Lawrence had proclaimed. Nonetheless, there were other settlers from elsewhere ready to be lured to Nova Scotia.

McNutt's Grand Scheme

After the 1763 Treaty of Paris, George III thought it wise to "reward" the Highland Scots for their help in the war with France. Handing out land grants wasn't exactly taxing on the Empire. It was still considerably difficult to persuade people to leave their homes and undertake the arduous journey across the Atlantic to a rough and rugged land.

Five hundred more families came to Nova Scotia in the spring of 1760, including Scots and Ulstermen who eventually settled in Onslow, Londonderry and the Pictou Harbour area. Land was being readily doled out and a kind of land boom was underway as the new influx of settlers continued. American speculators, who had already found ways of cashing in on land grabs in the new territories opening in the west, saw a chance to profit in Nova Scotia as well. Land companies were formed and big tracts of land were bought up. The ambitious and bold Virginian Colonel Alexander McNutt had a grand scheme to establish a city called Jerusalem where Shelburne now stands on the South Shore. He proposed to the Board of Trade the importation of 8,000 Ulstermen, thus creating instant civilization in an undeveloped part of Nova Scotia. The Board of Trade saw problems with schemes like this. They worried that if the scheme worked, McNutt and other entrepreneurs like him might well succeed in depopulating Great Britain. Cheap labour was needed at home for farming as well as industry and it would be unwise to let everyone skip off to start a new life across the Atlantic.

The board members need not have worried. McNutt only succeeded in getting 400 immigrants onto a boat and settling them in Truro and the Minas Basin area. He was a great schemer but a bad planner, more interested in profit than in the survival of the folks he deposited on the shores of Nova Scotia. His passengers suffered food shortages and destitution as they tried to settle in and McNutt was unwilling to help. Nova Scotian Governor Belcher, hearing of the problem, sent some seed grain, but by 1762 tough times were still hampering residents of the Onslow area. Things in Truro and Londonderry, however, started to improve.

Despite his lack of concern for the client immigrants whom he had deposited here, McNutt continued to exploit the potential for profit in Nova Scotia. Through the Philadelphia Company, he established himself as landholder of a big chunk of property around Pictou Harbour. The company took control of the land in 1766 and was obliged (to the Halifax government) to plant 250 settlers there within a year. Here was an early example of government privatization of a job it would rather not undertake. The company leased a ship called the *Betsey* but had a difficult time enticing wary Philadelphians into believing that there was a better life to be had so far to the north. Only six families signed on and there were forty passengers in all.

The captain figured he'd sail to Halifax and then ask for directions to this Pictou Harbour that he'd never seen. He was a bit off course and headed toward Newfoundland when another sailing ship's captain pointed the *Betsey* in the right direction to Pictou. Lo and behold, when they pulled into the harbour at night, they saw bonfires on the shore, which conjured up scary pictures in their minds of wild savages waiting to devour them. The *Betsey* waited offshore until morning to have a good look and when the captain decided the coast was clear, they came ashore to find that the wild savages were only a bunch of friendly souls from Truro, trying to welcome them and guide their ship in. Once everyone was safely ashore, the *Betsey* surreptitiously slipped away under cover of night so that no ship would be there to carry the immigrants back to Pennsylvania should they decide that the deal wasn't as sweet as the ignoble Philadelphia Company had let on. This was, after all, another one of those false Nova Scotia promises. For there was no rich, cleared farmland and no organized community with a democratic government. Nonetheless, by now there were nearly 700 settlers in the Cobequid townships with other growing communities in Amherst to the west and on the Canso peninsula isolated far to the east.

The nearby Pictou Mi'kmaq were known as the Pectougwac. The word "Pectou" itself probably derived from the Mi'kmaq term for the gas bubbles that arose in ponds and streams—methane gases that would later suggest the richness of coal deposits beneath. In one of the treaties, the Pectougwac had been promised a return of their lands along the Northumberland Strait, promises which the Halifax government had withdrawn. For good reason, the Pectougwac wanted to stem the flow of more white settlers into their homelands. There were uneasy feelings but the Mi'kmaq were not openly hostile. On occasion, hunters might show up at a settler's doorstep asking for food but often they were willing to help the newcomers in return with their own hunting skills.

The Highlanders of the Hector

The Philadelphia Company had not succeeded in getting nearly enough settlers for Pictou. One of the original six families had already left. They shipped in nine more families in 1769 but couldn't muster more interest than that and it seemed like a losing proposition all around. Shopping about for people less fortunate and more willing to take chances, they commissioned the *Hector* to sail with a shipload of Scots from Loch Broom. The passengers were poor people who could barely pay the price of passage, but the Philadelphia Company willingly took the cash. These were Scots fleeing poverty, unfair rent increases by their landlords, famine and various kinds of trouble with the law. They were a desperate lot, eager for a chance to make a go of it in some place where the dream of owning their own land would become a reality.

The *Hector* was not terribly fit for sea duty. She had rot that the passengers might poke through with their fingers or pick apart with their fingernails. But the wily American had put a good paint job on it, making it look like a warship that could ward off pirates. Aboard were 200 passengers, mostly Gaelic-speaking Highlanders.

The voyage started out smoothly enough. Passengers cooked food in fires contained in sandboxes on deck and if an oatcake or two looked mouldy it would be tossed out. With such smooth sailing, days could be spent in the warm fresh air up on deck. Everyone but Hugh MacLeod, it seemed, was expecting an easy voyage. MacLeod predicted trouble ahead but was laughed at for hoarding away all the unwanted food scraps he could get his hands on. He had plans for a rainy day.

And plenty of rainy days were to come. The seas grew stormy, the fog thickened and almost everyone succumbed to seasickness. Navigation became mere guesswork, as seasickness gave way to smallpox and eighteen children and a few adults died. Less than two weeks away from arriving in Pictou, a storm hit that drove them far off course; many thought the frail ship was being driven back to Scotland. Food was now at a premium. Some salt meat was left but the fresh water was nearly gone and the bread supply had been drenched and ruined. The story goes that it was then that Hugh MacLeod hauled out his stash of hoarded food scraps to share, saving them all from starvation.

The *Hector* arrived in the destined harbour on September 15, 1773, where the beleaguered passengers and crew put a good face on a bad voyage with a display of plaids, broadswords and the playing of bagpipes. Unfortunately, the Pictou settlers who greeted them said the new arrivals had missed the harvest and that there wasn't really much food to feed the whole lot of them. Nonetheless, they would all make the best of life ashore until the *Hector*, still rotting but afloat, returned in the spring with more supplies.

The new Scots were afraid of the Pectougwac and some Mi'kmaq had themselves reason to fear the Scots after seeing them at Louisbourg in battle as the enemy. Communication and relations between the two peoples were not good. This was unfortunate, since the Mi'kmaq could have been of great assistance. Instead, most in the Pictou community were unwilling to ask for advice from those so close by who had such masterful skills at surviving off the land.

Apparently most new settlers had been given the line that all the land was clear—a lie that must have become a staple for anyone trying to lure farmers to Nova Scotia. Instead of cleared land, the Scots saw forests with trees as tall as 200 feet. This was a totally unfamiliar, and seemingly hostile, landscape. They had no idea how to cut the trees to clear land or to build log houses. They preferred to stay near the harbour where they could at least fish and sustain themselves. In the fall of 1793, they were still refusing to settle the lands further from the harbour and squabbles were breaking out with the Yankee settlers who had preceded them. The Highland men were forced to go to work as labourers in Truro and the women and children became indentured servants to those already established. Some moved on to Onslow and Londonderry. The *Hector* returned in the fall with more sup-plies, but the American agents argued that the Scots were not living up to their end of the bargain. They would be given no more food until they set-tled those properties away from the harbour or paid cash. Times were des-perate and some people were forced to sell everything they owned in order to buy food.

Unfortunately, the Scots had never warmed to the Pectougwac people enough to learn the necessary skills of survival here without dependence on food from outside. Certainly the Mi'kmaq had a healthy diet, living off the land and sea around them. Once again, a perverse and unyielding focus on dependency from a distant provider created undue hardship for these settlers living in a bountiful corner of Nova Scotia.

Two of the settlers, Colin Douglas and Donald MacDonald, decided that they were tired of being pushed around by the Americans. They seized the food they needed from the stores of the Philadelphia Company but insisted on recording an account with the agents for what they took. They would pay the company back when they were able. Thus, urgency and decency were married in the event. The agents, however, sent news off to Halifax that a "rebellion" was underway. Halifax sent word to officers in Truro to handle the situation, but the citizens of Truro knew the truth of the matter and refused to intervene.

After that event, most families abandoned Pictou to spend the winter in Truro where they could at least count on some sympathy. Those who stayed behind barely survived. The local Mi'kmaq again took pity on their white neighbours and provided food, instructed them in hunting and taught them to make snowshoes to get around in the winter. But when local rations of wild meat were not enough to sustain the fledgling hunters, they used their snowshoes to hike to Truro to retrieve flour and other staples.

The Highlanders were not quick to adapt to the land or the lifestyle of their new home. One newcomer, with a deathly fear of bears, shot a porcupine at close range with nine bullets, thinking it to be his dreaded nemesis. Other settlers who had tapped the flowing sap of maple trees were discouraged to find the sap ceased to flow and tied thick bands around the trees in an attempt to squeeze out more of the nutritious fluid.

For those who stayed on and some who later returned, Pictou would become home. Crops were planted and there were fish to be landed. Dependence on outside providers diminished, but trade with other towns increased until Pictou grew into a rather respectable community.

Chapter Twenty-one

Coastline of Conflict

Pastoral view of Fort Needham, not far from the centre of Halifax; engraving by G.T. Parkins.

1776 and All That

By 1776 and the outbreak of the American Revolution, the population of Nova Scotia was nearing 20,000. Along with the Mi'kmaq, and all the early European settlers who had stayed on (or whose children had been able to survive here), there had been the recent immigration of Ulstermen, Yorkshiremen, Scottish Highlanders and an assortment of destitute and persecuted Roman Catholics. Nonetheless, nearly half of the Nova Scotian population had originated in New England. There were still strong family, social and political ties to the Americans as well as economic and religious links. Since these settlers had moved north before the abrasive Stamp Act, the Nova Scotian New Englanders had gripes and grudges against the British Empire but they didn't have the revolutionary fervour that had been fomented in the south *after* they left.

Massachusetts still had certain economic powers over Nova Scotia, controlling much of the fishing business here. But almost no one in New England thought of Nova Scotia as any kind of competition in the race to develop and prosper. Compared to other settlements along the seaboard, Halifax was a still a tiny seaport.

The Fourteenth Colony

If we go back and look at the Halifax census of 1767 (nine years before the American Revolution) we find 302 English, 52 Scots, 853 Irish, 264 "Foreign Protestants," 200 Acadians and 1,351 Americans. With only a short stretch of the imagination you could almost have called Halifax just another American seaport. Trade was increasing with New England, helping somewhat to diminish commerce with and dependency on England. The Assembly which purported to be democratic was made up mostly of upper-class merchants who were looking out for their own interests. Laws were decreed and enforced by the military. The Stamp Act of 1765, for example, enforced taxation on the colonies and boiled the blood of many an American. Haligonians, as well, were not without concern.

The *Halifax Gazette* was so bold as to publish editorials against the act as well as a sort of political cartoon from *The Pennsylvania Journal*. The *Gazette* became even more brazen when a printer's apprentice refused to include the required taxation "stamps." This act of protest was, of course, an outright crime under the act. Nor was the protest condoned by the paper's editor, Richard Bulkeley, who fired the printer and his apprentice. The apprentice was asked to leave Halifax after that.

Other forms of protest, too, were visible in Halifax. An effigy of the stamp master was burned at Citadel Hill and an old boot was hung from a gallows as an intended insult against King George's unpopular cohort, Lord Bute. The governor at this time was Lord William Campbell, a Loyalist. Nervous about these signs of discontent, he stationed guards around the stamp master's house. The governor and his high-society wife were less interested in politics than personal social activities. Horse-racing, for example, was high on the good governor's agenda and so he was instrumental in the promotion of gambling in the colonial capital.

The ever-unpopular Stamp Act was repealed in 1768, but unwilling to let the colonies off the hook, the English demanded a new form of revenue from a tax on tea. Nothing could possibly have been more insulting to colonists. In America, the Boston Tea Party resulted in elevating new levels of animosity toward the Crown. General Gage in Boston called for help, and soldiers from throughout Nova Scotia were summoned to the scene. Outposts were abandoned and Halifax was suddenly left with only a handful of soldiers.

Pamphlets and propaganda from the Americans began to flow into Halifax. In 1773, Campbell was transferred to become governor of South Carolina and replaced by Major Francis Legge who was jealous of the well-liked Michael Francklin. Legge also was troubled with fears of conspiracies and espionage.

Legge had good reason to worry. Most Nova Scotians had no great love for the king. After all, two-thirds of the population was from New England or had parents from there. The foot soldiers and the sailors were, however, under the employ of the king and most weren't about to question which side they should be on. A plan evolved in 1775 in Machias, Maine, to invade Nova Scotia, and with the assistance of disgruntled Halifax residents, overthrow the British. George Washington, chief of the revolutionary army, however, called it off. He saw it as an offensive move likely to cause more harm than good. On the practical side, he was also afraid the Americans didn't have enough ammunition to successfully pull off the invasion. Thomas Raddall suggests that the attack, if it had gone ahead, might well have succeeded. Nova Scotia would have become the fourteenth colony at that point. And Canada might never have become Canada.

Rebels Without a Roar

Jonathan Eddy was one of those unsettled New Englanders who had moved north to Nova Scotia. John Allan was a Scotsman who had been educated in New England and later settled here as well. They both felt it unfair when they learned that there would be yet another new tax levied to pay for the militia to defend Nova Scotia against the American Revolution. Eddy and Allan found it easy to muster support from the angry citizenry around the Cumberland area, but Governor Legge, who got wind of the potential uprising, decided to defuse it by calling off the tax.

Eddy and Allan were so fired up that they tried to get a good revolution going anyway in January of 1776. The only problem was that almost nobody was much interested any more now that the tax was gone. The two rabble-rousers also discovered it was impossible to get a good war going without an army. Those Nova Scotians sympathetic to the cause of revolution were thinking that maybe if they sat back, the American revolution would come north to "liberate" them from British rule. It would be an easy way to win without risk or bloodshed. Restless to get things moving, however, Eddy and Allan went to talk to George Washington to persuade him that Nova Scotia was ripe for a revolution if he could help get one going here. Again, Washington thought he might be stretching his army a bit thin and indeed there were a dozen good reasons to ignore Nova Scotia and worry about the Thirteen Colonies.

Legge knew what Eddy and Allan were up to and sent Francklin (a good talker and charming to boot) to cool things off in Cumberland. Nothing much happened and so in June John Gorham and 200 of his men were sent there to offer rewards for the ringleaders. Eddy was in Massachusetts, failing again to get support for an invasion. All he could get from that colony was some ammunition and a little pork to take home. But on his way back he had gathered together a small (well, very small) contingent of eighty men ready to take over Nova Scotia. John Allan tried to convince Eddy that it wasn't going to work, but Eddy was all fired up for a good revolution. He said he was sure that if he could just light the match the whole damn thing would blow.

He mustered seventy or so Cumberland Chignecto Yankees to his cause and he now had a small army of about 180. At least he had more than doubled his force. Eddy succeeded in taking control of the Chignecto area since no one offered any real opposition. What was the point? At the same time, he didn't get many new recruits. The revolutionary fervour just wasn't there. Most people wanted to hang onto their land and be left alone to live their lives. Eddy seemed incoherent sometimes, so they didn't want to mess with him or get in his way. When Gorham's men finally turned on the rebels, they didn't last long. Most ran for the woods and all hopes of a Nova Scotia revolution disappeared with them.

"Nova Scarcity"

Back in Halifax, Michael Francklin sent a delegation to London to convince the British government to have Governor Legge shipped back. Legge was disliked by so many Nova Scotians that Francklin feared this hostility directed at one man might help unify any movement afoot toward independence. Francklin's delegates succeeded in proving their point and Legge left town, boarding a ship as he shook his fists and screamed at a crowd on the

Halifax waterfront, cheering his dismissal there. Francklin lost his own job as lieutenant-governor, possibly to diffuse the rift that had developed over booting Legge out of office. He hung around, however, to support the Loyalist cause and did a pretty good job of it. Legge was replaced by Marriot Arbuthnot, a gentleman of high social standing.

In the spring of 1776, the British pulled out of Boston and, along with a great number of new Loyalist refugees, who dubbed their new home "Nova Scarcity," landed in Halifax. Once again, an ill-prepared Halifax was over-run with military men. By summer, however, the redcoats were off to attack New York and Halifax was emptied of men. Less than a hundred soldiers were left to defend the town should anyone want to attack. Those civilians who stayed behind were mostly poor and without means of sustenance.

From 1778 to 1781, a brigade of Scottish troops made Halifax home base for their attacks on New England. A corps of mercenary Hessian soldiers was also stationed there. When the fleet came to port, press gangs roamed the streets kidnapping "recruits," putting them immediately to service on the warships. The Halifax government heartily supported this as a means of ridding the city of the poor, the homeless and the criminals.

Cruise the Seas for American Gold

Privateering was on the upswing on both sides of the war. New England looters jumped aboard British ships and grabbed everything they could, including the ship. They were brazen enough to come ashore at Liverpool, Louisbourg, Charlottetown and Annapolis Royal as well. This roused the ire of even the Nova Scotian New Englanders, who retaliated by making raids against the coast of New England—for profit, of course, from the booty taken. It was a dangerous business, but there was good money in it. The Americans who got caught on this side of the line ended up in prisons in Halifax, but as the supervision there was lax many of them escaped.

Privateering was obviously a profession that attracted men who were less than fond of following rules. Washington didn't always have the means to enforce maritime legal measures and there was a multitude of abuses. But there were some rules of the game that distinguished privateers from the even less ethical and more bloodthirsty pirates who didn't follow anybody's rules. Pirates stole for themselves, split the booty, and tried to evade the laws of any land. Here was the ultimate free-enterprise system. Privateers, on the other hand, were legitimate in the eyes of the government (Washington's or England's). They received a "letter of marque" which was their licence and calling card to capture ships.

Privateering was a sanctioned and well-established tradition in New England and Nova Scotia before the American Revolution. The licence would occasionally switch as to *whom* you could plunder, but the business was the same. It was a very attractive career for some because it included freedom to do violent deeds without fear of punishment, coupled with a chance to reap great financial gain. It was adventurous, daring and brought a degree of macho glory. For the investor, it was an opportunity to make a fortune from an investment in a ship or two. If, as an investor or a privateer, you had any moral twinge over the dealings, that was easily allayed by the political overtones. You were performing a patriotic service by distressing the no-good enemy. In short, the business, whether it was in Boston or Halifax, attracted primarily the scummiest of both the upper class and the lower class.

Stan Rogers immortalized the life of the privateer for my generation in his a cappella song, "Barrett's Privateers," telling the tale of one poor sod from Sherbrooke lured to serve on a privateer sailing ship to "cruise the seas for American gold" in 1778. Rogers, who had scoured the provincial archives in Nova Scotia for such stories, had himself found gold when he used his research to conjure up the narrator of this tale of the man who puts to sea from Halifax on the king's birthday in the *Antelope* and ninety-six days later finds an American ship heavy in the water with riches. The attempt to take her is a disaster. Barrett is "smashed like a bowl of eggs" and our sad hero returns to Halifax, having lost both his legs in the battle—all before he's twenty-three years old.

Part-history and part-fiction, Rogers' song captures the story of the lure of easy wealth for a young man not grounded in the realities of war, who then suffers the consequences.

Although American privateering reached new heights during the Revolution, George Washington had given privateers a stern warning not to plunder Nova Scotian ships or harm Nova Scotians unless they were obviously part of the British war effort against America. His decree could have been a sensible act of goodwill and he may have also been looking forward to the day when Nova Scotians themselves might take up arms against the British and become one with the other colonies along the seaboard. Privateers were forbidden to steal private property or ransom prisoners. Washington also insisted that torture was out of the question.

The larger American privateer vessels followed Washington's ethical code to some degree, while the smaller New England privateers had little regard for it. Some had also simply forged their letters of marque. So in the end, the line between pirate and privateer became quite blurred, because of the nature of the work and those who were attracted to it. In the early part of the revolution the New England coast was downright crowded with privateer ships trying to get in on the action. Sometimes they got in each other's way and had to fight for the right to board a vessel that was about to be a victim. It was a messy business, driven by greed and bloodlust, but still glorified both in its day and in history books to follow.

The owner of the privateers did not need to get his hands dirty, except to collect his due—one-half of all that could be seized. The officers and crew divided the other half. The business arrangement was a veritable template for other seemingly more dignified enterprises to follow in the American industrial revolution. For those new American patriot investors looking to profit from the war, it was tough to evade the enticement of such easy money. And all for a good cause.

Supposedly, the American admiralty courts would decide (after the fact) what goods could be legally kept according to the rules of the game and what couldn't. Sometimes Nova Scotians even appealed through proper legal channels to have their stolen goods returned. But Washington and his military enforcers had more important things on their minds. Rarely did a Nova Scotian appeal actually succeed in gaining the return of stolen property.

One of the more daring privateer attacks took place not at sea but on land. On November 17, 1775, the American schooners *Hancock* and *Franklin* arrived in Charlottetown where they kidnapped Governor Callbeck and looted his house. They plundered the storehouses and threatened to cut the throat of the governor's pregnant wife, but she couldn't be found. They kidnapped the surveyor and other hostages and took off after two days, loaded down with stolen goods.

So much of everything was being stolen as raids increased in 1776 that food prices soared as did the cost of all manner of basic goods. Fishing boats were stolen or wrecked or simply taken for a joyride and left abandoned. Communication and trade between ports was being severed by the extent of this harassment and, since many communities still weren't self-sufficient, this brought on new hardships.

The smallest of fishing communities were not spared and as privateers became more brazen, they even made their way into the Northwest Arm of Halifax Harbour. Sometimes they left their victims stripped of clothes—either out of greed to steal absolutely everything they could get their hands on or for sheer sadistic amusement or possibly both.

Liverpool was particularly hard hit but, when American Captain Benjamin Cole arrived with two schooners in Liverpool Harbour he met serious resistance. His crew came ashore and captured the town's fort, taking hostages. The Liverpool militia, however, succeeded in overtaking Cole's men and captured the captain. Cole, realizing he was in a tough spot, suggested a prisoner exchange, but his men were greedy to acquire the ammunition and other supplies at Liverpool. After a stand-off, the militia finally released Cole and the privateers fled without the booty they had been hoping for.

Raiders of the Resolution
Dreams of stealing gold and costly jewels proved more often than not to be

unrealized. Therefore, privateers stole ammunition, food, furniture...whatever they could lay their hands on and haul off. Take Captain Amos Potter, for example. A Yankee privateer captain cruising off the coast of Nova Scotia, he and his crew aboard the *Resolution* had just seized a schooner full of dry goods and were on their way back to New England. Potter was sailing past Halifax Harbour, feeling pleased with having done well for himself, when he encountered an English military vessel. The captain of the British ship figured the *Resolution* to be a friend, not a foe. As they drew nearer, he hailed Potter and invited him over to his ship for a drink. Potter, not wanting to show his hand and not wanting to pass up a little free swill, said he'd oblige. He also hoped that he could use the element of surprise to capture this vessel as a prize. Before he boarded, he passed the word to his men to prepare to board the British ship and to wait for his signal.

The British boatswain had somehow heard Potter talking to his men but clammed up until the privateer captain was aboard, at which point he shouted out, "A traitor!" The English sailors grabbed Potter and pulled away from the *Resolution*.

Now the men on the *Resolution* felt as if they had been cheated out of an easy capture of a good ship. Their captain had been taken and they felt humiliated. A shipload of dry goods was not enough to assuage their privateering machismo. For revenge, they decided to attack Annapolis—a little town that forever seemed to be an easy target for revenge involving injuries that had nothing to do with them. Potter's men figured they would kidnap some Loyalists and bargain for their captain's release. On August 19, 1781, eighty men took over the blockhouse from three sleeping soldiers. The lusty lads promptly got drunk and accidentally shot their own ship's pilot. The sober raiders, however, rounded up the poor citizens of the town and took their weapons. Houses and buildings were properly looted and the scoundrels made off with a prominent citizen as a hostage.

Still smarting from the defeat at Louisbourg and the loss of territories, the French were more than happy to aid the Americans in their efforts toward independence. In 1780, the French Navy began to provide assistance to the American privateers, making life even more difficult for the already disadvantaged Nova Scotians who were so dependent on outside supplies. Supply lines were virtually cut off and some communities such as Pictou couldn't even get essential ingredients like the salt necessary for preserving food.

Privateers began increasing their raids between 1781 and 1783, capturing even poverty-stricken fishermen and holding them for ransom. Privateer ships assaulted small communities as well as sailing vessels, ransoming ships and cargo.

In July of 1782, some American ships arrived in Lunenburg to loot and plunder. As the invaders came ashore, a woman named Mrs. Schwartz was going out to milk her cow. When she saw the hoodlums coming, she alerted her husband who ran a full mile into the town screaming, "The Yankees are coming!" At that point, everybody began to hide their money and jewellery by dropping them down wells or burying their valuables in their gardens. Only three men manned the blockhouse to attempt a defence, but they didn't stand a chance against the big guns the Americans had brought ashore. So the invaders took control and began to search the houses, stealing what they wanted or simply trashing the residences and stores. The kids in town apparently had a wonderful time of it. They followed the looters around and every now and then an American would give them some stolen candy, knives or trinkets. When the looters were tired of their fun, they threatened to level Lunenburg to the ground unless 1,000 pounds (in the form of a promissory note) was paid. Three hostages were held as insurance that they'd get their way.

It wasn't until the spring of 1783 that the raids let up and Nova Scotians along the coast could sleep a little sounder at night.

Chapter Twenty-two

Loyalists: The White and the Black

"New Settlement" on Cape Breton Island, 1785; painting by William Booth.

"Inexpressibly Rugged"

Jacob Bailey was an Anglican priest from Maine who, as a Loyalist, decided to move to Nova Scotia to keep out of harm's way during the American Revolution. He arrived in Halifax in 1779 to serve as a parish priest at Cornwallis and later at Annapolis Royal. Bailey provides us with an intimate and opinionated glimpse of Halifax and beyond with notes from his *Journal of a Voyage from Pownalboro to Halifax, with Notices of Some Events in the Latter Place*.

On June 21, 1779, Bailey sails into the harbour after a truly rotten twelve-day trip at sea. Halifax is a bit of a disappointment. Bailey was expecting to see "lofty buildings rising in conspicuous glory" and a "respectable part of the Royal Navy" at anchor in the harbour. Instead he sees only the blunt rocky fortress of the Citadel, a few scattered, primitive-looking homes and a handful of battered ships in the harbour. Not a shred of conspicuous glory to be found anywhere.

Bailey's ship is greeted by a large congregation of Mi'kmaq in their canoes, cruising along the harbour. This image, for Bailey, is actually a bit more positive as he refers to them as "copper-faced sons of liberty." Once anchored at George's Island, Bailey is pleased to see more ships and more buildings of the town that ascends from the harbour up the hill toward the Citadel. There is no commodore to greet the passengers as expected, so they go directly to the Halifax wharf where crowds gather around them and throw them into "some confusion." Bailey records himself as having shouted out, "Gentlemen, we are a company of fugitives from Kennebeck, in New England, driven by famine and persecution to take refuge among you, and therefore I must entreat your candour and compassion to excuse the meanness and singularity of our dress."

I doubt if such an oration would have gone over all that well with the rabble on the wharf but fortunately an old neighbour of Bailey's is on hand to recognize the preacher's oratorical tone and to provide a safe haven for him as he becomes acquainted with life in Nova Scotia.

Despite Bailey's misgivings about his new home, he went on to become a prominent citizen of Annapolis Royal where he served as a diligent minister for the town and surrounding rural community. In his journals he wrote accounts of undertaking long, difficult journeys through rain and snow to perform a wedding or a funeral. He viewed himself as a kind of frontier missionary and even turned some of his experiences into satirical verse.

Overcrowded and Unsanitary

The influx of the more well-to-do New England Loyalists into Nova Scotia also meant the arrival of a number of slaves. Slaves were advertised for sale in the papers and notices were posted offering rewards for escaped slaves and indentured servants.

As the American war progressed, it brought new money into Halifax and the town grew. In 1781, Joseph Howe printed the first edition of his *Halifax Journal* which stayed in business until 1870. Also in 1781, Cornwallis surrendered at Yorktown and it became obvious that the Americans would have their way. Those citizens left in the colonies who wanted to remain under British rule would have to move north to do so.

Until 1783, New Brunswick remained, for all intents and purposes, under the control of First Nations people. Both American and British agents tried to get the Mi'kmaq and Maliseet people to become allies without great success. Michael Francklin, however, had made significant inroads with his language abilities and efforts at goodwill. He died in 1782, but the following year the New Brunswick Native people turned down George Washington's proposals for alliance by returning his gifts. Instead, they accepted the so-called "peace agreement" with England. That same year, Loyalist refugees flooded into the Saint John River Valley.

Twenty-five thousand more Loyalists arrived in Nova Scotia, at least half of them in Halifax. The remains of the British army and fleet also packed into the city, jamming it again with military men, this time defeated military men. While the wealthier Loyalists tore down old houses and built themselves new mansions, the poor built shacks with leftover lumber. The soldiers, however, were back to living in tents. Halifax was overcrowded, unsanitary and disease was rampant.

Runaway Black slaves from New England also arrived as well as those set free because their American masters were too poor to keep them. Black communities grew in Halifax and in outlying areas. There was also such an influx of Roman Catholics among Loyalists and discharged soldiers that the government finally decided they could now own their own land and build churches.

The Price of Allegiance

The Loyalists who had not abandoned America were in bad shape after the British gave up the fight. They felt forsaken by the king and hoped they could yet live in peace with their revolutionary neighbours, but this was not to be the case. The new American Congress was looking for some form of restitution from the Loyalists. Despite the ill feelings, many Loyalists who had left during the war wanted to return to their homes in America. Many American revolutionaries were violently opposed to allowing them. Those who had left during the war should stay out, they argued, and those who remained should get out as well.

Nova Scotia was the obvious place to emigrate to but it had a reputation as being a snow-ravaged land of hard times and it was decidedly less than civilized. Nonetheless, it was reasonably close and land would be granted to them when they arrived. Charles Morris was the man who would survey the province and decide where the most suitable settlement sites would be.

In America, a mass exodus took place, led by Sir Guy Carleton. He received little financial support from the British government which was more concerned with protecting the defeated army than the civilian Loyalist population. There simply wasn't enough transportation to go around. Evacuating families were forced to leave behind mountains of personal possessions. Carleton also worried that if the troops moved out too quickly, the refugees would have little protection.

George Washington was getting pushy and urged Carleton to hurry up and get his people out of New York in particular. Washington was anxious to see them leave behind as much of their possessions, including Black slaves, as possible. Carleton was doing the best he could in a tough situation and at least he knew that the Loyalists were, in fact, wanted in Nova Scotia. If not the promised land, at least it was a new home where land could be had and these people could live in peace. Nova Scotia, recently with a population of only 17,000, was about to see the head count double in a very short time.

Loyalists kept coming into Nova Scotia and New Brunswick through late 1783, sometimes under very difficult conditions. Despite the difficulties of travel, the refugees struggled to bring as much of their household possessions as possible. Also arriving were 200 Blacks who had run away from their American masters to the promised freedom and protection of the British government. Washington had opposed this exodus but Carleton had succeeded in allowing the Blacks to join the other Loyalists. Ironically, if you were a Loyalist and owned Black slaves, the slaves would still remain as "property" after they arrived in Nova Scotia.

Cold Comfort for Refugees

Food was in very short supply in Nova Scotia now that everyone had arrived. There just wasn't enough to go around and Britain was unable to ship enough bare essentials into the province to feed all the hungry mouths. Some families had to keep moving from one community to another in hopes of finding enough sustenance to keep them alive. At least 2,000 left Nova Scotia altogether in search of a better life anywhere but here. The Nova Scotia government also decided to help alleviate some of the problems by shipping the sick and the poorest of the refugees back to America.

The majority of the Loyalists stayed, however, adapting to the tough times and learning the ropes of survival in Nova Scotia. Many became cod and whale fishermen. Some built and worked in sawmills where timber was cut into lumber for the West Indies. Most immigrants, however, were more comfortable with a life of farming. Unfortunately for them, most of the really good land had already been taken, so the agrarian life was a struggle. It was not an easy adjustment for these people who once had comfortable houses, plentiful food, access to shops, education and all the amenities of town and city life.

Food shortages remained at the heart of the immigrant crises. There was a virtual famine in British North America by 1789 and this forced Nova Scotians to work at improving their agriculture.

The Colony of Cape Breton

Oddly enough, British colonial policy stood in the way of immigrants settling on Cape Breton Island. At first there was little interest in developing the coal fields there. In 1766, however, a group of Halifax businessmen were granted a lease to Spanish Bay (Sydney) to mine coal and sell it for no more than three dollars per ton to customers in Halifax.

People already living in Cape Breton didn't like this manipulation by distant Halifax. They wanted the right to own and control their own land. They wanted to mine it or farm it as they saw fit. In 1784 Cape Breton was granted its own government, independent from Halifax. Major Joseph Frederick Des Barres was the first governor. He was assisted by a chief justice and a nine-member council. Spanish Bay was the capital and the whole colony had no more than 2,000 people. Land was granted to Loyalist refugees but it was not an extremely popular place to settle. As on the mainland, many who arrived were anxious to move on to greener pastures.

Various factors led to a short-lived history of an autonomous Cape Breton, but paramount was the intrusion of land speculators and battles over land ownership. The government was eventually dissolved in 1820. Expectations of a Loyalist influx leading to the island's prosperity were never realized. Even though Cape Breton was again absorbed into Nova Scotia, there has remained a strong sentiment of independence and a distinct identity that is still rooted in the people of the island.

Black Loyalists in Search of Freedom

Unlike Cape Breton, Shelburne had grown quickly with the tide of refugees. There was a large Black population and many Blacks had been forced to become indentured servants or waged labourers in order to survive. Conflicts arose between the white and Black settlers. While white Loyalists were taking advantage of the Black settlers with very low wages and various sorts of abuse, they shamelessly accused Blacks of lowering the "morality" of the community and taking work from the white population. What was the grievance? Black people, the sober white Loyalists said, danced and sang and were having too much fun. And that just wasn't appropriate for a community that was trying to model itself after a respectable New England town.

Inevitably, tension increased between Blacks and whites, erupting in a riot in 1784 when the homes of twenty Black settlers were destroyed by retired soldiers. Black families were forced to leave Shelburne and move into the segregated community of Birchtown, where other Black families had already settled. The soil there was rocky and the land barren or heavily wooded. Many of the Blacks were from the South and unprepared for the harsh winters. They lived in crude huts or semi-subterranean hovels and some fell dead on the streets from starvation. Others, out of desperation, were forced to kill their dogs or cats for food.

Blacks were a very low priority for the Nova Scotia government and even when they were finally given official title to lands for living and agriculture, these lands were poor for farming—grim fields of boulders and glacial deposits of stones.

In contrast to Birchtown, Shelburne prospered as an economic centre with inns, schools and stores. Fancy New England-style houses were built and it began to look like a proper New England village. While it would have been wise for the people of Shelburne to build a sustainable cod fishery, the men instead opted to go into whaling, a more lucrative business at first, but like the town, an industry doomed to failure.

Shelburne was too isolated to sustain a healthy trade with the larger population in Halifax. Commerce was exclusively by sea and there were no decent roads. Hopes had flourished at one time that Shelburne would become larger and wealthier than Halifax and even become a centre of government and culture. But Shelburne was headed for economic collapse. There were too many merchants and too few buyers. Bad weather, fires and smallpox also crippled the town's development.

By 1788, the town, with a population diminished to merely 300 people, was on a severe economic decline. People were moving away to Halifax or elsewhere for better opportunities. Already there were 360 empty houses and the school teacher, with only eighteen students, gave up and left for Halifax herself.

The decline of the Shelburne white community might have given some satisfaction to those Blacks who had been so poorly treated there but it was small comfort. Nova Scotia surely was not the promised land for most Black Loyalists. Many had sought their freedom by following the British Army and some had fought side by side with them against the Americans. (George Washington himself was an owner of slaves.) Three thousand of these Black Loyalists had come here with promises of freedom but found they were more often than not denied land and the supplies they needed to live. Instead of freedom and a plot of land, they became share-croppers or indentured servants. Like other Loyalists, they started looking for a better place to live.

In May of 1790, the Sierra Leone Company was granted the rights to set up a government in territory in West Africa. They needed settlers and John Clarkson, the company's recruitment officer, encouraged Black Nova Scotians to emigrate yet again.

Thomas Peters was one of those disgruntled Nova Scotian Blacks. He had been a slave in North Carolina and later a Loyalist soldier. In Nova Scotia, he felt cheated out of the freedom and land he was looking for. Peters persuaded many of those around him in Shelburne and Birchtown that a better life could be had away from Nova Scotia. In January of 1792, about 1,200 Blacks left Nova Scotia for Africa. In short order, almost a third of the Black population of Nova Scotia left to start a new life and a new country on the continent of their ancestors.

Still other Black Loyalists remained in Nova Scotia and more would arrive during the War of 1812. However, slavery continued in Nova Scotia. Loyalists with slaves tried to hold onto what they saw as their rights of ownership while their disenfranchised "property" began to take their case for freedom to Nova Scotian courts. It wasn't until the abolition of slavery within the British Empire in 1833 that the buying, selling and ownership of slaves was completely eradicated here. While Nova Scotians sometimes speak proudly of having granted freedom to American slaves, it was a freedom that came grudgingly from those owners and merchants in human misery.

Chapter Twenty-three

From Rags to Royalty:
Halifax Comes of Age

**The Governor's House and St. Mather's Meeting House in a rather orderly
and civilized-looking Halifax.**

A Prince for Nova Scotia

Halifax hit the bottom in its postwar slump around 1788 and after that things began to look up. Prince William, son of King George III, arrived from England with an entourage of fashionable folk and this gave Haligonians an enhanced self-image. William was rich, of course, but he was also used to living a life on the wild side, which allowed him to feel right at home in Halifax where no one would criticize him for being noticeably drunk a good deal of the time.

If the French Revolution had any effect at all on Halifax, it was not in the realm of politics but of fashion. Well-to-do Nova Scotian women shed their hoop skirts, stays, laces and bustles for sexier garb involving low-cut bodices and a reduced arsenal of underclothing. Upper-class men had taken to tight breeches, layered waistcoats, oversized collars, tails, short hair and oversize hats.

The lower classes still wore the same old stuff. Women were attired in bulky, cumbersome dresses and covered their heads with mob caps, while the men of the house wore rustic breeches, puffy shirts of coarse cloth and three-cornered hats.

Governor Parr died and, in 1792, John Wentworth filled his shoes. Thomas Raddall suggests that Wentworth got his job in return for a favour. Mrs. Frances Wentworth had been sleeping with naughty Prince William and her husband, John, had been good enough to look the other way. It was a scandal that rocked the sensibilities of some respectable people in Halifax but life went on as usual.

Governor Wentworth landed his job just as tensions were mounting again with the French, which meant that Halifax would return to full military alert as a naval base. The fleet returned and press gangs went back to the streets and taverns to "enlist" the men needed to fulfil the bloody demands of war. The military man at the top was General Ogilvie, who would take more than his fair share of glory for his expedition against the tiny colony of St. Pierre and Miquelon off the Newfoundland coast. There the French governor, Danseville, surrendered without putting up a fight and he, along with his staff and a couple of hundred fishermen were hauled off to Halifax as prisoners. Ogilvie fancied the bell from the church in St. Pierre and that too was hauled to Halifax for St. Peter's Church. The French prisoners were scattered around Nova Scotia, while Governor Danseville was eventually paroled to live in a fancy estate outside of Dartmouth, thanks to a generous allowance from the British government. Danseville must have been well liked by the enemy. Many of the St. Pierre fishermen stayed on in Nova Scotia as well, some assimilated into Acadian communities.

Another Prince with a Grand Plan

In the spring of 1794, another prince, Edward, had found his way to Halifax after a number of family squabbles with his father, King George III. Halifax was looking like a pretty good place to fob off troublesome members of the royal family. Edward was unlike his brother William in many ways. He wasn't quite as lecherous or raucous and he consumed less alcohol. But he liked to play military games and push people around. Both pompous and vicious at times, he abused the authority accorded by his royal rank. King George had bestowed upon his troublesome son the title of Commander-in-Chief of Nova Scotia.

Edward was certain the French would one day assault Halifax and try to take it over, so he wanted to see the town fortified. Suddenly there was scads of money to be spent on Halifax. Edward had a French "mistress," which of course seems somewhat odd, given his paranoia about French invasions and the fact he was the military leader intending to do battle with the French. Alphonse Thérèse Bernardine Julie de Montgenet de Saint Laurent (Madame St. Laurent, for short) lived with Edward as a kind of common-law wife, and if anyone pondered the indelicacy of this, no comment was made to Edward.

Fortunately for Halifax, Edward wanted to see the town develop into a much grander place. He oversaw the building of roads, public buildings, the great fort of the Citadel and all manner of military structures. He had a fancy for mechanical toys, which led to the building of the clock tower on Citadel Hill in 1803. For his own comfort, he built a big house facing the Commons for Madame St. Laurent and himself. He also called for the reconstruction of the dingy barracks a stone's throw from his new estate.

If you were to visit the Citadel today, you might wonder how the fort fits so snugly on the top of this great drumlin deposited eons ago by the glaciers. Well, Edward had his workers excavate the top of the hill by some fifteen feet. As you might imagine, it was no mean feat to simply give a brush cut to the top of a small mountain. After this extraordinary labour, the new fort was built with massively reinforced bunkers against the worst possible attacks.

The Maroons from Jamaica

One of the factors that made the Citadel construction possible was the arrival of a group known as the "Maroons," a corruption of the Spanish word "Cimaroon" which means wild or untamed. The Maroons (also known as the Trelawny Maroons) were from Jamaica and had been slaves for the Spanish up to the time the British took over in 1655. Upon the departure of the Spanish, the Maroons were given weapons to continue harassing the British even after the exodus of their former masters. This was probably more a move of revenge toward the English rather than goodwill toward the Maroons.

Armed and dangerous, the feisty Maroon population proved to be excellent guerrilla warriors and the British failed to force them back into the cruel harness of slavery. A peace treaty signed in 1739 would allow the British and Maroons to co-exist on the island, but the Maroons, in the bargain, agreed to help capture runaway slaves of the British and also to fight alongside the British if the island was ever invaded. In return, the Maroons were "given" land to live on as well as "Freedom and Liberty."

The Maroons were short-changed on the land deal. There was not enough of it to grow sufficient food. They had many complaints against the plantation owners and the grievances were not settled by the British, so the Maroons took up arms again in 1795–96, only to be tracked down by British dogs and persecuted even further. The British, eager to preserve their slave economy here, feared that co-existing free Blacks among slaves was dangerous, so they came up with a plan to get rid of the Maroons.

Over the years, Halifax had gained a reputation as a place to send people who were unwanted by the authorities so it seemed like a good destination for the Maroons. Through various persuasive techniques, the British actually succeeded in sending the Maroons off to Nova Scotia with the promise they could live here as free people. Late in July of 1796, the *Dover*, the *Mary* and the *Ann* arrived with 568 Maroons and a British commissioner—a general named Quarrell—and his assistant, Ochterloney.

Halifax authorities weren't prepared for this. They made Quarrell keep his ships four miles off shore and refused them permission to dock lest the uncivilized Maroons create havoc in their supposedly well-mannered little city. Quarrell wrote a letter to the government convincing them that the Maroons had displayed excellent manners while aboard ship and that they were willing to help build Prince Edward's Citadel if they could come ashore.

A deal was struck and even the Maroons felt somewhat flattered by being able to help build a fortress for a prince, although clearly they had been manipulated back into a position not far removed from slavery. They moved into barracks and tents and were paid regular soldiers' wages. By September they were asked to move to Preston where Governor Wentworth found them to be a convenient labour pool for his summer home there and so the Maroons were promised clothing, shelter, food and even a judiciary system for resolving grievances and punishing crimes. Their first winter in Preston, however, was said to be one of the worst in Nova Scotia's history. There were shortages of everything and the Maroons were not happy with their new home. They viewed themselves as an independent nation with the right to dictate their own future. One thing became clear to these people who had grown up in a tropical climate: they wanted to move to some place warmer like India or the Cape of Good Hope.

Wentworth wasn't prepared to let them sail off as free people. The Maroons had proven to be good workers and extremely useful to the advancement of Nova Scotia. He thought if they could somehow be assimilated into Nova Scotia society, they would be happier. (It was probably the best thing he could think of; he couldn't alter the climate.) Halifax "society," however, was frightened by the Maroons who worshipped a god named Accompang. They were polygamous and buried their dead at ground level with rocks piled on the bodies and provisions left for their journey into the afterlife. Given the barbarity of the British military practices and the lasciviousness of their nobility, it's ironic that the Maroons would be taken to task for their beliefs or their lifestyle.

The governor thought a little stiff Christian religion coupled with English schooling could fix things up, so he sent an Anglican minister and a teacher to Preston. The Maroons saw no real harm in letting their kids be sent to school and even allowed them to be baptised, but adults would have none of this for themselves. The hypocritical Governor Wentworth, himself having fathered several children by Maroon women, was insisting that polygamy cease and that all Maroons become Christians.

They continued on as workers—cheap labour—constructing roads and buildings in Halifax, but they refused to cultivate the land they were given because they seriously believed they would still be leaving for a home in a warmer climate. All the while, their upkeep was being paid partly by Nova Scotia but primarily by the Jamaican government, which was footing the bill to keep them far away so their own slaves would not be inspired to demand a similar freedom.

One conniving Nova Scotia landowner offered to buy the Maroons from the government as his own labour force for ten pounds each per year. The Maroons were a proud, resolute people who never lost their love of freedom. They insisted they were nobody's slaves and could not be bought. Grievances were sent all the way to London. In 1800 the majority of them followed in the footsteps of the Black Loyalists and sailed on to Sierra Leone, although a number of their descendants remain in Nova Scotia to this day.

A Mediterranean Touch

Along with the Citadel, Prince Edward had other grandiose plans for military development in Halifax. He built a fort in the shape of a star on George's Island and laid a chained boom across the Northwest Arm on the westerly side of Halifax. It was anchored with a ring bolt in Point Pleasant Park, at a location still known as Chain Rock.

Edward liked the look of the round towers made of stone that he had seen in Corsica and thought Halifax needed such a Mediterranean touch. So began the building of Martello towers at Point Pleasant, the eastern Battery and York Redoubt. He also established the first European long-distance telegraph system in North America—a massive undertaking which involved relaying messages from hilltop to hilltop by way of a system of flags, wicker balls and drums (or lanterns at night). In its heyday, this system could convey messages from Halifax to Fort Anne in Annapolis Royal.

With Prince Edward investing so heavily in Halifax building, others followed suit and the city underwent a kind of boom time. Edward and Madame St. Laurent had moved into the summer house owned by the Wentworths along Bedford Basin, displacing that married couple to the aforementioned abode in Preston which was soon to be a centre of the growing Black population in Nova Scotia.

With French prisoners of war being hauled into Halifax, it quickly became obvious there was no place to put them and the government didn't want to have to pay for their keep anyway. Some were set free and allowed to work for their own welfare. More Blacks were also arriving, this time as prisoners of war—soldiers from the colonial regiments of the Caribbean. The incarcerated POWs found themselves either on Melville Island in the Northwest Arm, in Dartmouth or simply on ships used as floating prisons in Bedford Basin and down around the Dockyard. Needless to say, the conditions were less than comfortable and the English weren't really prepared to handle the thousands of prisoners who poured into Halifax.

During this time, privateers once again had a chance to do their good deeds for the Crown and rake in profits as they plundered their victims on the high seas. In fact, privateers and nobility alike were bringing considerable new wealth into Halifax. Wentworth picked up on the spending spree, convincing the Assembly to build a new Government House that is still in use today. Nonetheless, for the have-nots, Halifax was still a pretty desperate place. While the numbers of socialites, merchants and prosperous government appointees had swelled, so too had the population of the poor, few of whom had a chance to share in the relative prosperity of the times before Edward was recalled to England in 1800.

Wealth on the Waterfront

Privateers continued to ply their trade right up to the end of the century and beyond. In Halifax, the latest booty would be "legitimately" split between the owners and crew as well as the co-operating judges and lawyers who would get an appointed chunk of the prize money. Some of the men who sailed and pillaged the ships at sea became wealthy. Still others died in battle or from Caribbean diseases or ended up languishing in foreign prisons. One of the more notable ships in this business was the *Charles Mary Wentworth*, respectfully named after the son of the governor. The ship was built by Simeon Perkins in Liverpool and sailed by Captain Joseph Freeman with sixty-seven men and four boys. In 1798 the *Wentworth* took over a ship which was loaded with cotton and cocoa and flying the Spanish flag. When it sailed into Halifax, it fetched a hefty sum of 9,000 pounds.

The *Wentworth* was a real money-maker for all involved and the stories about her were good enough to lure many a landlubber into signing up for a privateer on the high seas. One of those privateersmen, Enos Collins, made a considerable amount of money in the business and invested it wisely as a merchant on the Halifax waterfront. He died one of the wealthiest men in North America. Some of his stores and warehouse buildings of stone still stand today along a part of Halifax Harbour rightfully developed as "Privateers' Wharf."

Joe Cracker of Herring Cove

The stories of sea wrecks, disasters, heroism and horror abound in Nova Scotia from the fifteenth century right up to today. One that leaves a lasting impression in my mind is the story of *La Tribune*, recounted by Archibald MacMechan in *At the Harbour Mouth*. This French ship had been captured by the British HMS *Unicorn* in 1797 and, now manned by a crew of British sailors, it was making its way to Halifax Harbour unescorted. The captain, a man by the name of Barker, was not all that well qualified as a leader or navigator, it would appear, for he chose the wrong man to steer them into the harbour on November 23. The ship could be seen from York Redoubt cruising along just fine until she ran straight aground on the rocky ledges known as Thrum Cap.

The captain was furious and blamed the man steering the ship, while, ashore, the soldiers at York Redoubt sent word for help. Barker had his men throw some cannons into the sea, hoping that the higher tide would float *La Tribune* free—but with no success. A barge was sent to help out, but Barker seemed insulted that it was an insignificant craft manned by a sailor of low rank. He refused to allow any of his men or his passengers to board the barge. (One writer reports that on board were women and children.) Meanwhile, the gale force wind was growing steadily. All were nervous about the weather as well as the captain's uncompromising attitude.

Night arrived, the storm grew worse and the pounding waves and rocky shelf conspired to rip the rudder from the ship. Now there would be no way to steer it even if they did float free. The captain, it appears, had been stalling on abandoning the ship in hopes that he could yet save his prize booty and his own reputation, which would surely be a tarnished beyond repair if he lost this French vessel.

The ship was leaking badly when it finally lifted free of Thrum Cap at nine o'clock that night and began to drift steadily toward the granite rocks of Herring Cove in a rising southeast gale. The men worked the pumps and some attempt was made to rig the beleaguered sails to nose the ship in toward the calmer harbour waters, for they were still only at the harbour mouth. By nine thirty they were just off the shores of Herring Cove when the ship sank, settling onto a rocky bottom. Many drowned but at least a hundred survivors—this included the men who had boarded from the barge—clung to the rigging that was above the water line. By midnight, the mainmast must have cracked and fallen and most of the crew and passengers were swept to their deaths. By morning, not many more than a dozen remained alive and the citizens of Herring Cove stood on the shores and prepared to watch them die. None of those ashore were willing to attempt a rescue in such dangerous stormy conditions.

There proved, however, to be at least one hero in the crowd along the shoreline; Joe Shortt was thirteen, a fisherman's apprentice without a family, who was said to be "weak in the head." While the whole community watched, Joe rowed his skiff out of the cove and fought the raging waves to make it to those men still clinging to the rigging. He succeeded in bringing one of them, John Galvin, ashore but couldn't manage to get his boat back out past the breakers on a second attempt. Some of the Herring Cove men who were watching, however, were inspired by Joe's lone heroic act and volunteered to put to sea in a jolly-boat. Eleven more were rescued. But that made for only a scant twelve survivors from a shipload of 250.

Joe Shortt, nicknamed Joe Cracker, became a Halifax celebrity, praised by the visiting Duke of York. When asked by the Duke what he wanted for his good deed, Joe replied that he only wanted a pair of corduroy pants. Unfortunately, he was given more than that—a position as a midshipmen on a flagship. He hated the job, was homesick and eventually found his way back to a simple life in the Herring Cove fishing village after having been "punished" with the reward of enduring life in the British Navy, the very same navy that had fostered the bull-headed, autocratic attitudes that had led to the sinking of La Tribune.

Chapter Twenty-four

1812 and After

Captured American frigate Chesapeake *is led into Halifax Harbour by*
HMS Shannon, 1813.

Warships and Brazen Rascals

S hortly after the turn of the century, Halifax had a population of more than 8,500 but there were only 1,000 established homes. Housing would often be a problem in this seaport town whose population exploded during wartime with the influx of the military. In 1801 fires had swept through Halifax, destroying many homes and buildings. The first fire companies were created as a result.

There was a short interlude of peace for Halifax, but hostilities, which were growing again between the British and Americans, would lead to all-out war. Even though the United States had claimed neutrality during the Napoleonic Wars, the British had searched American ships. And when press gangs couldn't find enough men on the streets of Halifax to force into military duty, they boldly advanced ashore into American ports and hauled off unwary Americans to serve aboard British ships. To make things worse, the British warship *Leopard* attacked the American *Chesapeake* in 1807 and seized four crew members, two of whom were British citizens trying to avoid military service. One of the two was flogged to death and the other was hanged.

The naval intrusions helped push the Americans to the point of going to war, but war sentiments were also escalated by the "War Hawks" in the U.S. Congress who wanted to expand American territory. When the U.S. finally declared war on England on June 18, 1812, Halifax was once again to become the military base for much of the activity on the British side. By now Halifax was a town of some 10,000 citizens, most of whom were staunchly loyal to the British government and confident that the British could not possibly be defeated by the upstart Yankees.

Most of the actual fighting took place near the American borders of Upper and Lower Canada. Here was territory that the Americans hoped to capture for expansion purposes, land considered to be more valuable than Nova Scotia. Although Nova Scotia was located far from the main activity of the war, there was, however, some glory for Halifax when the *Shannon* captured the *Chesapeake* and towed her into the harbour to the cheers of onlookers.

Naturally, privateer raids continued on both sides. War was always a good excuse to escalate raids and get away with whatever theft you could. Privateers became more and more brazen. The rascals aboard an American vessel called the *Young Teazer* at one point had nearly all the British fleet from Halifax trying to track them down. The privateer would lay off of Sambro Light, beyond the mouth of Halifax Harbour, and attack British merchant ships when they were vulnerable. Ultimately, though, a British warship spotted the *Young Teazer* and chased her into Lunenburg Harbour.

The privateer captain failed to find a safe exodus to the high seas and the crew rowed with oars in an attempt to hide the ship between two islands. As the British ships drew closer, someone on board the *Teazer* accidentally set off the gunpowder stores and the ship blew up in a tremendous explosion. Only eight of the crew survived to tell the tale.

Today people around the area say you can still sometimes see a strange light moving over Mahone Bay at night, a ghost version of the doomed vessel. The light moves along the water and then disappears in a bright burst. Whatever the true cause of this eerie phenomenon, it is called the "Teazer Light," and is believed by many to be some inexplicable re-enactment of the events leading up to the explosion that took place that night.

A Question of Property

The British Navy was overworked and relied on its own privateers to pester and pillage the Americans. About a third of all the American ships captured during the War of 1812 were hauled in by privateers. The privateers wreaked such havoc on New England during these times that, Nova Scotian historian Phyllis Blakeley reports, "grass grew on many of the wharves of New England." Trade in many ports was at a standstill.

In 1814, British ships sailed from Halifax to Castine, Maine, and took over the docks there, collecting customs money on anything coming into that port. In 1818, these funds would be earmarked for starting Dalhousie College and so this war would prove provident for the emergence of higher learning in Nova Scotia.

The war also brought about another wave of Black immigrants, this time from the Chesapeake Bay area where British ships from Halifax had set up a blockade. While there, the British offered freedom to any Black slave willing to go north with them. This was certainly not entirely an altruistic move, as the British hoped to deprive the Americans of their workforce and at the same time enlist the former slaves into the British military to fight. It was an enticing proposition anyway and many slaves bought their freedom this way.

After the war, 1,200 Black men, women and children were brought to Nova Scotia and settled in Halifax, Dartmouth and Preston but put in a position where they, like the Maroons before them, were dependent upon the state for survival. Most ended up in poverty. After the Treaty of Ghent in 1814, Americans were demanding the return of their property, including Black slaves who had escaped to some semblance of freedom in Canada. The British nobly refused to recognize the new Nova Scotians as "property" and thus the Blacks stayed on.

Smallpox took an extreme toll on the Black population on the Dartmouth side until it was brought under control with vaccinations in 1815. The Americans kept wrangling with the British for the return of their "property" until 1818 when the Czar of Russia acted as an arbitrator on the matter. The British, in the end, agreed to pay $1,000,000 in compensation to the Americans for a total of 3,000 former slaves who were allowed to remain in British North America. It would not be an easy life for the Southern Blacks who had arrived during and after the war. Nonetheless, they had achieved their freedom decades before other Blacks who remained as slaves in the South until the Civil War brought an end to slavery in America.

In Search of the Promised Land

Cape Breton had been sparsely inhabited right up until 1800. It had changed hands back and forth from French to British and appeared to be an unstable island from a political point of view. When Cape Breton was set up as a separate colony from Nova Scotia in 1784, land was granted for settlement. At first, it was not a popular destination for immigrants but that all changed in 1820 when it again became part of Nova Scotia and a new wave of Scottish Highlanders began to arrive. At least 25,000 would sail the Atlantic and settle permanently there by 1850. The earliest settlers were given free lots of land if they agreed to homestead upon the properties.

One of the Scottish immigrants who did *not* make Cape Breton a permanent home was the Reverend Norman McLeod, but he has an interesting tale nonetheless. Along with a band of his devoted religious followers from Scotland, he first arrived in Pictou in 1817 but found it an undesirable place. McLeod was anxious to find his version of the true "promised land," a place untainted by the decadence of civilization. Obviously, he had not heard the stories about Halifax or he would not have wanted his people anywhere in the same province. But even Pictou, rural as it was, seemed tainted. So in 1820, along with 200 followers, he set sail again, this time to head south to another port and then to travel inland to Ohio. Bad weather forced his ship ashore at St. Ann's in Cape Breton, and finding this place to his liking, McLeod decreed that his followers should stay put.

A land grant was easily attained from the government. The families built houses and barns and planted potatoes, barley and oats. Even a grist mill was put into operation. McLeod, a fiery charismatic man, lived in a formidable three-storey house, and convinced his followers to farm for him in return for his labours as minister. He preached on Sundays in both English and Gaelic. McLeod must have been a persuasive man with a dominant control of his community, for he taught school as well and convinced his followers to build boats from the plentiful timber nearby. The first vessels were small, but soon McLeod had encouraged his men to construct larger sailing ships. In 1840, his son Donald sailed one to Glasgow, Scotland, and then went on all the way to Australia, where he wrote to his father saying that he had found a wonderful place to live.

McLeod grew anxious about the encroachment of civilization on his own settlement at St. Ann's and was afraid that his followers might lose their purity and be tainted by North American life, even here on this remote community. The preacher, now seventy, prayed and God told him to move on to the new continent. His dutiful followers built a ship and prepared for the voyage. It took a full year. On October 28, 1851, McLeod moved his people yet again—at least 136 of them followed the holy man who couldn't seem to find the perfect earthly paradise.

Nineteen thousand kilometres away, they reached Adelaide, Australia, only to find that Donald had packed up and moved to Melbourne. Yet when they arrived, they found that Donald had moved on again, this time to New Zealand. Reverend McLeod was tired of chasing his son and tried to settle into Melbourne but found it wanting. When another of his Cape Breton ships, the *Highland Lass*, arrived with 188 more of his people, he boarded ship and directed the captain to sail for New Zealand. When the minister and his followers arrived at Waipu in 1853, they were granted a generous thirty thousand acres of land and began a community much as they had done in Cape Breton years before. The settlement thrived and many people there today trace their roots to families that had once lived on Cape Breton Island. Fortunately for those who had arrived in New Zealand, McLeod was getting on in years and his wanderlust was no longer strong enough to uproot them yet again.

Chapter Twenty-five

The Golden Age of Sail

An impressive shipping pier for coal at Sydney, Cape Breton, built in 1870.

Sun, Sea and Ships Afloat

About five years ago I taught myself to sail a four-metre sailboat with a single sail on the salty waters of Lawrencetown Lake. I proved myself lousy sailor but I did eventually learn the basics, essentially that in order to get from point A to point B, you usually had to point your craft toward some imaginary point C and then change directions. I liked the feel of the wind in my hair and I liked leaning far over the side to keep the boat in trim as I hung onto the rope (or "sheet" as it is called) that controlled my sail. I revelled in staring down into the cool, clear waters as I raced along oblivious to the concerns of the modern world.

Lawrencetown Lake is fairly shallow and sooner or later I'd drive my little sailboat into a sandy shoal. Here I would hoist the centreboard and wrestle the wind-snarled sail until I had realigned my ship and prepared myself to launch again. My shipwrecks were usually minor, the worst being the time I got my foot tangled in the main sheet and the wind whipped up hard to flip my little fibreglass boat on its side. My youngest daughter was with me at the time and I grabbed her as we went flying through the air, splashing down in the rather chilly March waters of the lake. I walked my daughter ashore and then struggled to bring my cursed craft back to home port.

It was all pretty unhappy and uncomfortable and I realized that, like a myriad of sailing men before me, I had learned that sailing was a thing that made you oscillate between love and hate, pleasure and pain. Above all, I grew to respect this principle of sailing: you are never *totally* in control. The wind and waters are full of variables. Nothing is to be completely trusted— wind, sea or wave. You have to always be on your guard. You will continually be forced to conjure up solutions and variations to get you from point A to point B. Therein lies the adventure and therein lies the danger.

Periodically, Halifax Harbour is visited by "tall ships" and the shopping malls empty as the citizenry lines the harbour shorelines by Alderney Drive in Dartmouth and at Privateers' Wharf in Halifax. Nova Scotians stand in awe as they watch the display of restored historic sailing vessels that come from around the world. After the parade of sail, one or two of the big schooners will leave the harbour and turn east.

It will be a cool, decently blue morning without waves when I find myself writing at my computer before a slightly salt-stained plate-glass window. I look up and away, beyond the boring stare of my computer monitor. Not so far out in the blue Atlantic I see the blossom of white sails as a ship navigates past Lawrencetown Beach on its way perhaps to Louisbourg or Sydney. I pull out my binoculars and get a better peek at her, convince myself that this indeed is the *Bluenose II*.

A little over a hundred years ago, it would have been quite common to see such ships plowing the seas beyond Lawrencetown, headed east or west, to or from Halifax. Ships from around the world would have had their sails billowing on the horizon here, just beyond my doorstep.

Nova Scotians rooted in their past will often remind me of the fact that there was a time when no one would have called us a have-not province. It was a prosperous time, sometimes referred to as the Golden Age of Sail, roughly between 1830 and 1880. Sailing ships were being built in a hundred inlets and harbours from Hell Bay to Hawbolt Cove. Historian Phyllis Blakeley speaks of these ships as "the finest sailing vessels afloat," and of the sailing men reared in Nova Scotia during these times as "the best sailors in the world." It was an age that is spoken of with hyperbole.

The Captain's World

Shipbuilding was a formidable industry by the mid-nineteenth century. First a "designer" would create a model or half-model of the ship he would like to build, perhaps carving all the pieces with a very sharp whittling knife. Then real timber was cut from the forest and, along a level stretch of shore, the keel was laid down on blocks not too far from the water's edge. There were usually no sketched-out plans, but instead the carved model would be used as a guide. Careful workmanship went into fitting the keel, the veritable backbone of the ship to be. Frames had to be bent with steam and fastened with hardwood pegs to the keel. Every board had to be fitted as perfectly as possible and then "corked" with oakum to make the ship watertight. Water was pumped *into* the hull and leaks were marked with chalk for repair. If she could hold her water tight, then maybe she could keep afloat once out sailing in the sea.

Then the deckhouses were built and the masts mounted into place. The ship was painted to perfection and a rudder hung in place. When she was ready, she would be launched with some form of celebration for her maiden voyage.

These were good times, heady times. Nova Scotians had mastered the skills of boat-building and of sailing big ships long distances. Their audacity to venture out across vast expanses of ocean to trade at ports around the world was unparalleled. Undeterred by a long legacy of sea disasters, Nova Scotians built bigger ships and faster ones. The Golden Age, however, would not last forever. Technology would eventually outrace tradition. Soon the Golden Age of Sail would be a memory, a memory that could be clouded by mythology and longing.

Certainly these had been grand times but they were not necessarily easy times. Nor were all the captains of heroic proportions. Life on a sailing ship was a hard one; there is no masking the facts. If you grew up in Nova Scotia in the nineteenth century, there were few great job opportunities ashore and many a young man felt he had to get away from home to earn enough money to survive. Boys of twelve or thirteen might sign onto a ship and begin a life's work at sea, sometimes cut short by disease or the other dangers inherent to sailing the seas. Captains would take their families along on the larger vessels and some children literally grew up aboard ship. Perhaps they travelled around the world once or twice before they ever set foot in a school house.

For those who worked on a ship, it was a physical life and a hard one. If you couldn't take it, you went back ashore and would have to live down a reputation as being soft; if you stayed with it from a young age, you might find yourself stepping up a notch or two in your profession—second mate by sixteen, first mate by eighteen and a master sailor even as early as twenty-one. There was no formal institution where you'd learn the ropes. You were educated in the trade while you worked and earned your own keep.

Aboard ship, the captains were all powerful. Some were kind men but many were cruel taskmasters, brutal even. One of the legendary tyrannical captains was reported to have punished six disobedient sailors by having them hang, tied by their big toes and thumbs from the rigging. Of his contemporaries, some were worse, some were better. Whatever the case, the captain's words were law, usually enforced by the first mate. Questioning authority could bring severe ramifications. Nonetheless, mutiny and insubordination occurred and so captains were always on the lookout for signs of rebellion.

Mice and rats have always been common shipmates for sailors and in the nineteenth century, cats were kept on board to control the rodents. Some cats lived their whole lives without ever setting foot on shore.

Many ships' captains could almost boast the same as these cats. There was something truly addictive about the life at sea. It was not uncommon for a captain to make his fortune and attempt to retire—buy a farm and settle in—only to return to sea the following year. This scenario might repeat itself several times before the captain became too old or feeble to guide his vessel to foreign ports. Most of these men had never been schooled in navigation but learned it aboard ship. A good captain would know the construction of his vessel down to every screw and nail. Invariably, things would break, fall apart or disappear on a long voyage and the captain would have to see to replacement or reconstruction with whatever resources were aboard.

Most captains wore no particular uniform, although they might take care to remain well dressed throughout a voyage. If the captain's wife had sturdy sea legs, she often joined her man at sea and was obliged to earn the respect of the crew through both her demeanour and her work. A captain also functioned as a doctor, sometimes delivering his own wife's baby during a voyage. He controlled the finances of the ship and kept a "slopchest" to sell tobacco and clothing to his men. Many were meticulous about cleanliness and maintenance of the ship and there was a strong sense of personal identity with the vessel.

Hard Tack, Potatoes and Putrid Pork

In the chain of command, the captain would give a directive to his first mate who would carry out whatever the task might be—this regularly included physical punishment involving kicking, brass-knuckle beatings or something worse. Stanley Spicer in his book *Masters of Sail*, argues that the physical punishment was often necessary and usually handled in a "fair" manner. Why was it so necessary? Well, sometimes a crew had been mustered in a port where men were conned into signing up while they were drunk or even drugged. Sometimes men signed on to escape punishment for crimes. So if a captain ended up with a rowdy lot of losers, then there was only one thing to keep them in line—or so the logic went. No captain was going to turn his ship around and head back to port to get rid of a deck hand who had changed his mind about the long journey. Sometimes, however, a captain found his own amicable crew from people in his own community. Men might be selected for their "character" rather than out of desperation in a foreign port, and there would be little need at all for discipline.

The second mate was a kind of deputy to the first mate. He might be a young man expected to give orders to sailors twice his age. If he failed to gain their respect, then he'd lose his job. The bo'sun or boatswain was third in rank and assisted the second mate. A ship required a carpenter aboard to fix things when they invariably broke and a cook played the vital role of keeping everybody fed. A bad cook would inevitably lead to an unhappy voyage, so a captain picked his cook with care. Many meals were made up of salted pork and beef, potatoes and onions. There was dried fruit, hash, soup, molasses and fresh food like baked bread for as long as it lasted. Unfortunately, voyages often lasted much longer than expected. You can't always count on the winds doing what you want them to do. Food supplies would dwindle and rationing would be necessary. If the planning had been poor or the winds unkind, men might have to finish a voyage surviving on nothing but hard tack, potatoes, cabbage or whatever was left. Needless to say, morale suffered and everyone was unhappy.

Meals, in general, were quite often dismal events aboard sailing ships. Benjamin Doane was a young seafaring Nova Scotian aboard the brig *Reindeer* in 1843 who was having a truly rotten time on his voyage to Alexandria, Virginia. His writings were collected in a volume called *Following the Sea* in which he detailed this trip. While the captain supped plentifully from a ten-gallon keg of brandy and ate fine food at his table, exotic refreshments and culinary delights were not to be savoured by the crew. When the cook opened a barrel of beef and found it rotten, he boiled it anyway for dinner and most of the men tossed it overboard. "The pork was a little better," Doane reports, "although it was rancid and rusty. The only bread we had was hardtack which had been in the bread locker two voyages, and it was black and hard and full of great fat weevils nearly as big as centipedes." The peas and beans were too hard to eat even after cooking all day and the coffee was too bitter to swallow. The cook admitted that if the crew wasn't satisfied with the fare, they didn't have to eat it. But what was the alternative?

For some reason, cooks were almost always foreign—either Canadian men were thought to be notoriously bad at shipboard cuisine or the job was not considered manly enough for a sailor from a Nova Scotia port town. The cook was usually assisted by a stewardess (sometimes the cook's wife) or a steward.

Seamen were of all ages, origins and colours. Some might have come from the home ports but others were enlisted along the way. For all the glamour and seduction of sea life, it seems odd that drastic means were necessary to put together a crew. The "crimp" was the man who had the job of rounding up sailors in any way necessary. The situation was not unlike the early days when the British Navy "impressed" sailors by beating them unconscious and hauling them aboard. A crimp might scour a port town and kidnap a healthy looking young man or get him drunk and carry him aboard or, like his predecessors, simply pound the poor sod into senselessness and drag him aboard ship. Having a crew pieced together by coercion would sometimes backfire into violence and mutiny or a captain might just end up with a bad bunch of lazy landlubbers who knew nothing of the ways of the sea. Even for the honest, well-intentioned sailor, life aboard ship was often simply too taxing or too dangerous. Many a port town had a hospital for sick or disabled sailors. Sailing was a job that took a heavy toll.

Running a vessel at sea was a twenty-four-hour-a-day business, so the labour was divided into "watches," usually four hours at a stretch. The crew could be divided into two groups who would work four hours on, then four hours off, throughout the day. One of the toughest watches of the day was the eight p.m. to midnight watch. Tradition deemed that the captain would take this shift on the way out from home port and the first mate would handle it on the return voyage. Sailors of the day were fond of putting it thus: "The Captain takes you out like a man, the mate brings her back if he can."

While not on watch a crewman might doze, play music or cards, loaf, carve, dream of home or faraway ports, or scheme trouble for the captain. Or he might worry over what a damn dangerous job he had volunteered for, if indeed he had volunteered at all.

Accidents were plentiful and danger was all around. You could fall from the rigging and be maimed or swept overboard by a wave. One of the luckiest of sailors that the men in the nineteenth century might talk about was Peter Carrol, who on the 1789 voyage of the *County of Pictou* was swept overboard by one wave, pulled twenty-five metres from the ship and then picked up by another wave and deposited back on deck. Not all hands would be so fortunate.

Men sang sea shanties while they worked—songs with stories or songs of protest—to make the hard labour go more easily. Singing saved the sanity of many homesick or overworked men aboard ship.

Despite the necessary wisdom and knowledge that it took to sail a large ship, men of the sea, including captains, tended to be a superstitious lot. For Nova Scotians, it was bad luck to launch a ship on a Friday or to name a ship for a fish. Whistling would conjure up bad fortune as would putting on a hatch cover upside down. Tomorrow's wind could supposedly be determined by the direction of a shooting star. Other portents were also used to predict the weather from day to day.

"Hard Squalls" and Hard Labour

Colin McKay (1876–1939) was one of the great story writers and commentators interested in the Age of Sail and, unlike other authors who might have referred to the harsh life under the rule of a tyrannical captain as merely "the school of hard knocks," McKay was willing to expose the downright abuse and exploitation of the men and boys who went to sea. In an article titled "Windjammers and Bluenose Sailors," first published in the *Dalhousie Review*, McKay masterfully describes life aboard one of the smaller sailing ships that continued to ply their trade from many Nova Scotia ports right on into the time of the new steamships.

The men sailing these ships encountered frostbite and frozen sea spray turning to rock hard ice that threatened to capsize a boat. There were also tropical hurricanes to endure and malaria as they sailed from Nova Scotia to the Caribbean, Brazil, Spain, Portugal and Greece. There was money to be made but a very high price in lost ships and lost men. McKay notes that in one year, Yarmouth lost thirty-one ships and more than a hundred men who sailed from her wharves.

Nonetheless, the windjammers were considered a healthy and vital part of the commerce going and coming from dozens of Nova Scotia ports. Building the ships provided a considerable number of jobs. Fish and wood were sent to foreign markets aboard the vessels. Young people grew up with employment to look forward to and a life of "adventure" at sea. On the way back to Nova Scotia, the ships were filled with coffee, molasses, sugar, rum, coconuts or any combination thereof. Sometimes they didn't return home directly but carried mahogany from Central America or tropical fruit from the islands to U.S. ports. On other trips they might have shipped coal, flour, or oil to Canadian ports.

Whatever the cargo, McKay assures us, it was a life of hard labour. The crews were amazingly small and, of necessity, efficient. Four to six men might be all it took to keep a ship moving from port to port. Obsessive attention was paid to keeping the vessel in perfect working order. On both the outward and homeward leg, men aboard would occupy their time scraping, painting, repairing rigging or, of course, simply wrestling the sails and the sea in an effort to survive. With a small crew, fourteen- to sixteen-hour work days, divided up into watches, were not uncommon. If an emergency occurred in the middle of the night—like a ripped or lost sail—everybody aboard would have to help fashion a new one and get it into place no matter what the state of the sea. When the waves began to pound against the sides of the ships, loosening the oakum in the seams or cracking the boards in the hull, sea water would flush into the ship. Then the men would have to spend hours, days, even weeks taking turns at the dastardly job of pumping, pumping, pumping.

If a mate aboard ship was satisfied to be leaving behind a cold November Nova Scotia gale, he might be less than pleased to find himself in the Gulf Stream with "hard squalls of wind and streaming rain swooping down from a heaven-filling wrack of gloomy, low hung clouds." If a calm occurred, the sails had to be worked meticulously to milk every tiny bit of energy from whatever puff of air was in the neighbourhood. Then there might be more rain and another squall after that. The trade winds further south provided some respite from the snarly Atlantic to the north. These winds tended to be "orderly" and useful, pushing the ships on with considerable speed toward their destination.

Once in a tropical port, however, the scene grew grim again. The thrill of walking about an exotic seaport town might quickly wear off as a sailor tried to sleep in a deathly hot and mosquito-infested cabin. If it wasn't the mosquitoes, it was another flying insect too tiny to be kept out by mosquito netting. To avoid the bugs, men would sometimes sleep aloft in impromptu hammocks among the rigging, only to be drenched periodically by thunderstorms.

If the wrong mosquito took a sample of your blood, it also left something in return: malaria, which brought on fevers, chills, madness and agony. McKay notes, however, that Canadian men, "Mostly abstemious with the bottle enjoyed a surprising immunity from tropical diseases." What he means is that fewer died from sickness than from the multifarious other hazards of life on the high seas. If your voyage ran into problems, for example, and your captain and cook had not fully counted on the thirty or fifty extra days, you might simply starve at sea or, worse yet, die from dehydration.

Chapter Twenty-six

Sea Crimes of the Nineteenth Century

Engraving of the ill-fated Saladin; Illustrated London News, 1844.

To Kill a Captain

If it wasn't the weather and waves, then it just might be an unruly crew that created disaster at sea. While Nova Scotian captains had considerable skill at harnessing the power of natural forces to propel their ships, they were not always able to govern the greed, jealousy and bloodlust of some of the men who sailed on their ships. Some Nova Scotian sea crimes of this century happened close to shore and others far away. One of the most notorious shipboard crimes of the nineteenth century took place on the *Saladin*. The story begins in October of 1842 when Captain George Fielding left Liverpool, Nova Scotia, on the 460-ton *Vitula*, headed for Buenos Aires with a small crew, including his fourteen-year-old son, George Junior. Business didn't look so good for the return journey, so he sailed on to Valparaiso, looking for a profitable cargo and later on to the Peruvian island of Chincha where he hoped to spirit away a full load of guano. That's right, he was hoping to steal a shipload of bird droppings and sell it in some northern port. Odd as it may sound, this bird poop was worth a lot of money and it was owned (and protected!) by the Peruvian government, which would not want to let it go without payment of a hefty tax.

George figured he'd cut through the red tape by sneaking in and stealing the valuable smelly stuff and then hightailing it back to sea. But he got caught and shot in the shoulder in the process. He was held in custody in the town of Pisco and his ship confiscated. George was subsequently caught in a plot to escape and free his ship and that landed him in prison. Cloaked in a poncho, however, he succeeded this time in escaping and he fled to Valparaiso. By now it was July of 1843 and Fielding, though free, considered himself a ruined man.

Fielding and his son were desperate to find passage back home to Nova Scotia. Captain Sandy Mackenzie of the barque *Saladin* agreed to take both of them on and not charge a cent. Mackenzie's vessel had a load of legal guano but it was also carrying twenty tons of copper, thirteen 150-pound bars of silver, a money chest and some "money letters" that included cash. On February 8 of 1844, the *Saladin* left Valparaiso but it would never arrive at its destined port.

Mackenzie and Fielding were both captains but one of them had lost his ship. Fielding was desperately jealous of Mackenzie and craving to work out his frustration, even if it meant taking it out on the benevolent Captain. He began to plot to take over the ship. Fielding convinced shipmates George Jones, William Trevaskiss, John Hazelton and Charles Anderson—all men in their early twenties—to join him in his mutiny. Why did they go along with it? Good old-fashioned greed is the most likely answer.

They planned to kill the captain, his first mate and anyone left who didn't go along with them. They would sail the *Saladin* to some isolated spot in Newfoundland or the Gaspé where they would abandon the ship and carry off the valuables. They wanted the money in the letters, the cash box and the silver. There is no mention in the court records as to anyone wanting possession of the guano.

Using an axe, Hazelton first murdered another sailor aboard named Byerly who had just finished his watch. Next, the carpenter was attacked with a hammer and tossed over the side, the conspirators ignoring his pleas for help as he sank beneath the waves. While his son watched, Fielding himself chopped twice into Captain Mackenzie, the very man who had offered a free ride home during his time of desperation. Then Fielding declared himself captain. Jem Allen, a sailor at the wheel of the ship, was the next to go, struck from behind with an axe and heaved to the depths. Three more men were struck down viciously, leaving only two others on board who were not part of the conspiracy—the cabin boy Galloway and an Englishman named William Carr. When these two learned of the dirty deeds, they agreed to throw in their lot with the blood-spattered pirates.

It was around this time that the men took advantage of the ship's liquor supply but they also prudently agreed to throw most of the weapons overboard to insure against killing each other. As Sunday rolled around, in the spirit of Christian fellowship, they brought out a Bible, swore an oath "to be brotherly together," and then kissed the Good Book. The oath did little good because a sub-conspiracy was already being hatched so that fewer men would be involved in the splitting of the wealth. A fight broke out and a general reign of terror persisted aboard. Fielding, the man the others feared most, was bound and gagged. It was decided that the two men who had not shared in the killings, Galloway and Carr, should be required to share guilt with the rest by killing the evil captain. Galloway refused, so Carr and Jones heaved Fielding into the sea where it took him four minutes to drown. George Junior, despite his own appeals for compassion, soon joined his father to a watery grave.

The *Saladin* was still headed north with Galloway as navigator, although he was poorly equipped for the job. The men heaved some of the copper overboard and nailed boards over the ship's name. The plan was to sink the ship and leave in a boat, along with all the money they could carry. Unfortunately for them, on May 22, the *Saladin* grounded on an island just outside Country Harbour, Nova Scotia. When Captain Cunningham of the schooner *Billow* came to assist, he found everything aboard the *Saladin* just a little too weird for his liking. The men's stories didn't mesh and Cunningham began to suspect piracy. He had the sailors arrested and they were brought to Halifax. The ship itself, left stranded in shallow water, broke up at what is today known as Saladin Point.

It was a big story in Halifax with a special court created to deal with this heinous crime on the high seas. While in prison on the Northwest Arm, Carr and Galloway confessed to their part in the affair. Jones, Hazelton, Anderson and Trevaskiss admitted to their crimes as well. The charges of piracy, which called for death by hanging in chains, was "reduced" to murder—which meant simply death by public hanging. Some critics thought the court too lenient. While four of them would swing for their crimes, Carr and Galloway were acquitted, having convinced the court they had been forced into their actions under threat of death.

The hanging was a grand affair on the South Common that brought out thousands of the city's population. Haligonians were big fans of a good hanging, as were others from around the province. Crime historian Dean Jobb notes that one man from Lunenburg County walked fifty miles to be there. On July 30, four nooses were readied and, when the trap doors opened, the *Saladin* pirates got what was coming to them. Galloway disappeared after that, but Carr settled in Digby County, where it was noted that he rarely walked but instead "trotted" everywhere he went.

Murder on the Zero

In 1865, a ship with the unlucky name *Zero* had loaded with coal in Cow Bay, Cape Breton, and was cruising toward the South Shore of Nova Scotia. The captain was Colin Benson and his cabin boy, aged fifteen, was Frank Stockwell. Also on board were the first mate John Douglas, the cook Henry Dowcey and two German crewmen named Marlbey and Lambruert. Somebody murdered the captain on this voyage and it was most likely the cook or the mate. The story most accepted is the one told by the young Stockwell, who later testified so convincingly that, according to the Halifax *Evening Express*, people were "impressed with the conviction that he was telling the truth."

According to Stockwell, he first became aware of the violence on board when he saw the captain himself wrapped in a sheet and hauled on deck with one side of his head bludgeoned. He believed that Dowcey had attacked the captain with an iron bar as the poor man slept. The captain was about to be dumped over the side, but he was still alive enough to plead with his men to spare him. Stockwell saw his captain tossed into the calm sea where he floundered and struggled and ever so slowly disappeared.

What were the intentions here? Apparently the crew had thoughts of sailing the vessel someplace, the Caribbean perhaps, and selling the cargo, and then selling the ship itself. But if so, they must have changed their plan, realizing that they'd likely get caught. Douglas ordered Stockwell to burn the ship's papers and they divided up the captain's clothes. Dowcey kept the captain's gold watch. This was all they could muster in reward for having murdered an innocent man.

It was then decided they would try to sink the *Zero*. A lifeboat was lowered and the men began to drill holes in the hull with an augur until the tool broke or they lost the augur bit to the sea. Next they tried to chop holes into the ship with an axe only to have the axe head fly off and sink in the deep. The ship was still afloat when they gave up and rowed ashore.

James Baker was a La Have Island fisherman who was out to sea on the morning of September 11 when he spied the brigantine under full sail. But something looked very odd. He boarded the ship and discovered that the only crew left was a dog. The wheel was tied with rope and there were obvious signs that someone had tried to sink the ship.

Salvage laws allowed for anyone who found such a gift at sea to rightfully claim it as his own. Baker knew nothing about a crime but he sure knew that he had lucked onto a good thing. He sailed the *Zero* into La Have Harbour and claimed his salvage rights to the ship and her cargo of coal. Other fishermen went out in search of the missing crew. They located Douglas, Dowcey and Stockwell. The other two crewmen had run away in the night. Douglas did most of the talking, with a concocted story about a captain who had been accidentally knocked into the sea by the boom and a leaking ship that had to be abandoned.

Everything looked too suspicious and the trio ended up in jail. Marlbey and Lambruert were tracked down as well. The mystery prompted yet another murder trial in Halifax that November. The cabin boy's story seemed credible and it was backed up by Marlbey, who claimed that he had heard Douglas and Dowcey *plotting* to kill the captain in order to take the ship. Marlbey claimed to have informed the captain but the captain turned a deaf ear to the news.

Dowcey claimed Douglas had murdered the captain and Douglas claimed Dowcey had performed the deed. The judges in the case had a hard time sorting out the truth. In the end, they allowed Douglas to live but committed him to a life in prison. Dowcey, however, would face the famous Halifax hangman. The *Halifax Colonist* reported it this way: "The hand that committed this cruel murder will soon be cold in death."

Strangely, Haligonians, usually anxious for the great entertainment value of a good hanging, were not convinced that justice was being served. Because of the publicity of the trial, many were convinced that Douglas was the true murderer or that both were equally guilty. Four thousand people signed a petition asking for leniency for Dowcey. The law blundered forth anyhow and in January of 1866, Halifax had its final public hanging. A mere 200 people showed up for the event.

Message in a Bottle

Another ill-fated Nova Scotian ship was the *Lennie*, built in Belliveau Cove and captained by Stanley Hatfield of Yarmouth. On October 31 of 1875 the ship was in the English Channel when Captain Hatfield told the 4 a.m. watch to tack the ship. The men must have done a poor job of it and the captain gave them a chewing out. A Greek sailor couldn't handle the insult and he pulled a knife and stabbed Hatfield in the stomach, while another man stabbed him in the head. The second mate tried to help, but he too was murdered, as was the first mate who was killed by the cook.

This unhappy lot of seafarers may not have pre-planned this mutiny, but now they had to get rid of the evidence and figure out where to sail. The bodies were weighted and pitched into the sea. The steward, Constant Van Hoydonck, refused to take part in the mutiny and he was locked in his cabin until the rest of the men realized he was the only one who could handle the ship. When Van Hoydonck was allowed above, he was ordered to steer the *Lennie* to Greece. He agreed to the request, but instead steered her toward Bristol. The crew caught on to the trick and Van Hoydonck was forced to change course for the coast of France. Periodically the steward was dismissed to his cabin as the men tried to sail the ship on their own, each time giving up and calling the poor man back to the helm. Eventually, they anchored off the French Île de Ré. The steward and the cabin boy sealed messages for help in bottles and tossed them to the tides, hoping for salvation.

Somehow, the steward figured a way to hoist a distress flag as well. That signal was seen from shore. A French gunboat arrived and the mutineers and murderers were rounded up to be put in jail. Tried in London, four of the conspirators received the death penalty. Van Hoydonck received salvage money from the ship's owner, gave up a life at sea and opened up a tavern in London with the cash received for his loyalty.

Chapter Twenty-seven

Confederation: Nova Scotians Become Canadians

Joseph Howe   *Charles Tupper*

The American Threat

U p into the middle of the nineteenth century, most Maritimers felt no great desire to be absorbed into a larger country. In 1838, when the British high commissioner had suggested a new kind of union for all of British North America, he was soundly chastised by most Nova Scotians. The province of Canada may have thought it a prudent move, but Maritimers had become staunchly independent folk and they were feeling good about themselves, thanks to the world links forged by the sailing ships that brought commerce to and from their shores.

In 1861, Nova Scotia had a population of 339,000 made up of a diverse ethnic mix of English, Scots, Acadians, Irish, Germans, Blacks and Mi'kmaq. Most still lived in rural areas. Halifax had a population of only 25,000. The economy was a diverse one based on fishing and the lumber trade, coal mining, farming and all the jobs related to ships and shipping. The trading links were strongest with England, New England and the Caribbean. There was simply no pressing need or desire to forge stronger ties with those people living further west on the continent.

Some have argued that soon after this high point in her history, Nova Scotia quickly faded from glory. Wooden ships driven by the wind no longer dominated world travel and commerce, overtaken by the new technologies of coal-fired steamships and railroads. Nonetheless, economic decline for Nova Scotia may have been due more to politics than technology. The province had more than its fair share of inventors involved in the new technologies and the people here were not so far out of step with advances elsewhere. By 1858 a rail line was completed from Halifax to Truro and plans were on the books for major construction linking Halifax to New Brunswick, Maine and even Quebec. Most Maritimers, however, weren't solidly convinced that rail transport was in any way better than travel by sea.

As in so much of Nova Scotia's previous history, once again, military and political events well outside of her borders would play an important role in shaping events here. Early in the 1860s, the United States was headed for its great Civil War which would tear that country apart. When the war began, Britain declared its neutrality, but many in British North America had strong sympathy with the Yankees. Back in Britain there was, however, a strong undercurrent of support for the South. Then in 1861, the U.S. Navy boarded the British vessel *Trent* in international waters and arrested two Confederate agents who were aboard. Britain viewed this as a form of piracy and tensions began to mount. The American secretary of state, W.H. Seward, had pushed things further by suggesting that an invasion of British North America was a possibility. Great Britain responded by sending 14,000 troops to defend her colonies if necessary. After a while things cooled down, but the political effect of such a threat was pivotal and long-lasting.

The provinces of Nova Scotia, New Brunswick and Canada now saw the need to strengthen their ties and agreed to forge ahead with the long-discussed rail link from east to west. In Quebec City in 1862, the rail deal was signed, with Canada footing the lion's share of the bill. Nonetheless, by 1864, Nova Scotians weren't talking so much about union with Canada but simply a Maritime union. Britain liked the idea but politicians in Canada were hoping to up the ante in any way they could by getting in on the action while the players were at the table. The province of Canada had been a melding of both Upper and Lower Canada, bringing together the French and English populations. It had never been an easy marriage and the early 1860s saw the collapse of a series of administrations leading to a coalition of political forces.

Entering the Dominion

A larger union of provinces might be useful in resolving problems between rivalling factions in the province of Canada, it was argued by a handful of men at the top. (Canada, at that time, included what is now Ontario and Quebec.) Therefore, the government of Canada wanted to be sure to have a foot in the door when Nova Scotia, New Brunswick and PEI discussed their own arrangements. And so it was that in September of 1864, the eight delegates from the *province* of Canada showed up to take part in the Charlottetown talks among Maritime leaders. Accommodation was scarce because the circus was in town and Charlottetown hadn't seen elephants for over twenty years. But the conference went ahead and the Canadians prodded and bullied the discussion around to the topic of a broader union.

Once things were moving, it seemed there was no turning back, whether the citizens of the Maritimes were interested or not. Another meeting was called for Quebec City and a plan made up of seventy-two resolutions was put forward. It would eventually lead to the British North America Act of 1867, creating the Dominion of Canada. (Newfoundland had been given the option to join but, in 1869, the electorate there gave the proposal a thumbs down. Their will would prevail well into the next century on this matter.)

In 1866, with Confederation looming as the hottest of current issues, two powerful Nova Scotian politicians were at loggerheads, representing two completely opposing views on the matter. Charles Tupper was in favour of joining; Joseph Howe was against it. Howe lost but went on to become one of the best leaders the province would ever see. Tupper succeeded in bullying the people of Nova Scotia into Confederation but quickly lost favour with his electorate and was booted from office. Had the system of government been a fairer one, that is to say, had the people had the right to determine their own fate there in the middle of the nineteenth century, Nova Scotia might have evolved into its own small but dignified nation. The same flaws of the political structure that allowed Tupper to act decisively against the will of the majority still exist today. NAFTA and GST legislation of the 1990s, while patently unpopular, became law because of a ruling party holding a clear majority. Having attended law school at Dalhousie in Halifax, Brian Mulroney may have learned his lesson from the man whose name is affixed to the medical school next door—Sir Charles Tupper.

Joe Howe—the Fiery Reformer

Tupper believed himself to be a man of vision, but so did his worthy opponent, Joseph Howe, one of the most popular politicians this province ever knew. The son of a Loyalist printer, Howe was born near Halifax's Northwest Arm in 1804. In his writings he described himself as being filled with "restless, agitating uncertainty." With little formal schooling, he ventured into the newspaper business as a young man, first as part owner of the *Weekly Chronicle* and then as publisher of the *Novascotian*. He read voraciously and travelled all around the province, filled with curiosity about people and places, spending sometimes two months at a time in the saddle on his horse.

As a writer, he penned more and more articles and editorials about the state of politics in Nova Scotia. He was bold and accused magistrates of being nothing better than thieves. Charged with libel in 1835, Howe read a pile of law books and proceeded to defend himself in court. He gave a legendary six-hour-long speech that resulted in his acquittal and many of the corrupt magistrates began to resign their posts.

All of this public attention launched Joseph Howe into political life and the next year he was elected to the Assembly, where he would remain for twelve years, working for the reform of government. He loathed party politics and the party system which demanded loyalty to the party line and his opinions were well heard. More reform-minded candidates found themselves elected.

Howe's popularity outraged many of the old line, none more than the son of Chief Justice Haliburton who challenged Howe to a duel. Fortunately, no one was killed. Haliburton fired and missed and Joe Howe simply fired his shot into the air.

Howe helped stage a major defeat of the Conservatives in 1847 and became provincial secretary under Premier Uniacke. He was fired up over the idea of a railroad from Halifax to Windsor and then beyond to Quebec by way of Maine. In 1860, Howe became premier but his Liberal party's hold was shaky and he was out of there by 1863.

During the 1860s the move toward Confederation was underway and Howe was staunchly opposed to Nova Scotia being consolidated with Canada. Even after Premier Tupper had signed the deal, Howe went to London to try to undo the damage but it was too late. At that point, hoping to improve the deal for Nova Scotia, Howe himself became involved in the new federal government. He died at Government House as lieutenant-governor in 1873. Howe had written, "If I could be content to go along quietly and peaceably like my neighbours and in the end of some fifty or sixty years tumble into my grave and be dust, I should be happy—very happy." But, of course, he was speaking of a life he never lived.

Against the Will of the People

Howe's rival, Charles Tupper, was born near Amherst in 1821, the son of a Baptist minister. He had an extensive education, including medical studies at Edinburgh University. By the age of twenty-two he had returned to Nova Scotia to set up a medical practice. Like Howe, he spent a good deal of time travelling the province on horseback.

Tupper became enamoured with politics and the issues of the day and the Conservatives went after Tupper as the man to take on the people's hero, Joseph Howe. Although Tupper's Conservative party lost in 1855, he had personally outmanoeuvred Howe in their Cumberland County riding. He ascended in the ranks of his party and ultimately became premier in 1864 when the leader resigned.

Tupper was instrumental in passing the Free School Act in 1864 and a taxation act that would support the schools. No doubt he was both loved and hated for this twin blessing and curse. Along with the other premiers, Tupper had been part of Confederation talks. He believed that unification was a wonderful, monumental idea and Nova Scotia should play a key role in the provinces coming together. When he went to the conference in Charlottetown to discuss *Maritime* union with the premiers of PEI and New Brunswick, the delegates from Upper and Lower Canada had already arrived to push for a larger confederation.

The move toward a larger union was partly due to fear of American military strength as apparent in the American Civil War. Tupper continued to meet with the other premiers in Quebec and London and, as representative of Nova Scotia, he endorsed Confederation in 1867.

Very few Nova Scotians actually supported their premier in this and so Tupper put off his re-election as long as he could until later in 1867, after the deal was already signed. The Conservatives were soundly defeated but the deal was already done.

Tupper persuaded Howe to get involved in federal politics at that point and he himself went on to undertake a series of ministerial duties at the federal level. In 1896 Charles Tupper, upon the resignation of Mackenzie Bowell, became prime minister but he had a short tenure. The Conservative party was unpopular by then as Tupper took up the post of Leader of the Opposition until the turn of the century. After that, he retired and spent a goodly amount of time in England. Perhaps there was a little of the philosopher king in Tupper. A well-educated man with a vision, he was willing to overrule the views of the majority in favour of an idea like Confederation, which he personally thought was good for Nova Scotians. Friend or foe of the people, Tupper was a principal figure in Nova Scotian history and painted a sharp contrast to his feisty foe, Joseph Howe, who had so wished for a more truly democratic form of government for Nova Scotians.

Avoiding Annexation

Confederation spelled the end of political autonomy for Nova Scotia. The people had been taken against their will into the arrangement by means that were nothing short of unscrupulous. The changes ahead would be both political and economic. The rail link with the West would begin to shift the political, economic and social focus away from the sea and toward the continent. While Nova Scotia had once been at the very hub of international trade activity, it would soon find itself on the fringe of both trade and industrial growth that was taking off in the interior of the continent.

Would Nova Scotia have survived on its own as an independent nation? Could the Maritimes, and possibly Newfoundland, form its own strong union? Charles Tupper ensured that these questions could never be answered by history. Howe's passion for democracy, free speech and Nova Scotian independence looks very appealing in retrospect but Tupper's vision may have been more clear. Had this province not aligned with Canada, it might have found itself eventually annexed to the United States. Trade and family ties with New England were already very strong. Undoubtedly, annexation would have led to unrelenting economic and political dominance by American interests. For Nova Scotia this would have been a disaster much greater than the loss of autonomy that occurred during Confederation. Charles Tupper, acting more like a philosopher-king than a democratically elected leader, may have spared us this fate. Yet here in the late-twentieth century, the separation of Quebec and the potential disintegration of Canada remain a real possibility. We may once again find ourselves wrestling with questions of political independence or alliance not unlike those faced by Howe and Tupper.

Chapter Twenty-eight

The Plight of Nineteenth-century Nova Scotian Women

Early postcard depicting "the simple life" of a Nova Scotia coastal family.

Limited Rights or No Rights at All

As was the case throughout North America, equal rights for women in Nova Scotia were slow to evolve. Laws gradually emerged in the nineteenth century, initially recognizing some privileges for women in terms of property and family. Nonetheless, an inflexible, patriarchal notion of the institution of marriage remained at the heart of these laws.

Women played a vital role in the economic well-being of a family and it was fairly common for a rural wife to supplement the household income by weaving. In the city, she took in boarders and provided meals for them. Men owned almost all property, housing and the means to generate an income—a fishing boat, for example. Throughout most of the nineteenth century, women had, at best, limited rights under the law to protection and safety from harm, but the law itself could only do a symbolic job of enforcement, particularly in domestic situations.

Wife battering was all too common in Nova Scotian homes. To a great degree, it was tolerated by the male-dominated society and only rarely surfaced in the court system. If a man deserted his wife and family, the woman was left in a very difficult and vulnerable situation because she had no legal ownership of anything belonging to the family. Everything technically belonged to the husband, whether he was there or not. Later in the century a court might allow a woman ownership of her family's house and goods, if her husband could be proven to be a drunk or otherwise "worthless."

When women became essential in the public workplace, some changes in their legal status were unavoidable. In 1838, for example, the Nova Scotia Assembly discovered there was a desperate need for teachers in the province. Not enough men saw the occupation as worthwhile and, besides, the pay being offered was pitifully low. To meet this crisis, the Assembly magnanimously decided that women could now be hired and receive personal wages, rather than having the money paid directly to a husband or father. This legislation also set a standard for double standards regarding wages for men and women in the province. Despite the lower pay for women, forty years later women would occupy two-thirds of the teaching positions in Nova Scotia.

It seems that poorer counties enlisted more women than men for the teaching ranks—to save money presumably. While there continued to be some staunch political opposition to women working at all, Joseph Howe didn't see what the fuss was all about. He argued that these women would be married soon enough anyway, so they posed no threat to any male income earner. Once married, women teachers were expected to give up their jobs and take care of the husband and home. Even if there were not enough qualified male teachers to replace them, there were always plenty more young women to fill the jobs until they too took an early retirement into matrimony.

Legislators, lawyers and judges were painfully slow to consider the needs of women. It was not until 1866 that an enlightened law was passed to protect a wife from debts incurred by her husband and further along, in 1882, women were officially decreed to be individuals with personal rights, including the right to collect children's wages if they were needed to help pay household expenses. Few married women in these days could earn an income outside of the home, so, whenever possible, boys in the family were put to work at menial jobs to bring money into the house. It wasn't until 1897 that the laws fully permitted a woman to have her own possessions during marriage, including a right to personal savings.

"A Nest of Brothels and Dance Houses"

While women endured a decidedly hard life in rural Nova Scotia, their counterparts in Halifax during much of the nineteenth century may have had it even worse. In her book *The Dark Side of Life in Victorian Halifax*, historian Judith Fingard documents the dire straits of the so-called "underclass." Women of low economic means suffered from all manner of mistreatment, often without much hope of ever improving their lot in life. Nowhere was the situation worse than on the notorious Barrack Street at the base of the Citadel which was lined with drinking dens known as grog shops, brothels and pitiful tenement housing. Visitors to Halifax were appalled by begging children, filth, squalor, prostitutes and, of course, drunkenness. While the military presence cannot be blamed entirely for the problems, Fingard points out that the economy of this district was based on providing female companionship and cheap, plentiful booze for the multitude of soldiers and sailors in the city.

R.H. Dana, legendary author of *Two Years Before the Mast*, visited Halifax around this time and described Barrack Street as a "nest of the brothels and dance houses." He saw prostitutes who were "broken down by disease and strong drink," and felt much pity for them.

Halifax was a crime-ridden city and newspapers prospered by publishing lurid stories about notorious criminals, both men and women. In her book, Fingard resurrects the sorry tale of one Margaret Howard and how the legal system failed to help this down-and-out character who the *Morning Chronicle* of the time publicised as the "Wickedest Woman in Halifax." Margaret Howard first went to court in 1863 when she was twenty, charged with drunkenness, and went on to serve more than fifty-two sentences in jail, although sometimes she was able to avoid a stay behind bars by paying a fine as small as one dollar. Unlike many other criminals from the lower class who actually committed crimes to have the luxury of the shelter of a jail cell and regular meals, Howard preferred to be free on the streets and avoided jail whenever she could. She escaped from Rockhead Prison at least once, increasing her notoriety, but little or nothing was ever undertaken by the authorities to improve her lot in life.

What heinous crimes had Ms. Howard committed to earn the title of "wickedest woman in Halifax"? Well, she drank quite a bit on many occasions and raised a ruckus, she got into fights and she tried to commit suicide during one of her jail terms by hanging herself with pieces of cloth from her dress. Newspapers of the day reveal the moral repugnance felt by the middle and upper class toward women like Howard, who was undoubtedly a product of much hardship brought on by Halifax poverty.

Margaret Howard was viewed as an out-and-out criminal, but most city prostitutes were tolerated by authorities as nothing more than a nuisance. Fingard suggests that "In terms of income, prostitution was an attractive alternative to the drudgery of household service. For some women it was an occupation which led to capital accumulation and upward mobility." Most, but not all, of the customers were in the military, who made up nearly twenty-five per cent of the adult male population of Halifax. For the most part, the legal system tried to ignore prostitution altogether. Brothels were located close to the military bases and away from the middle- and upper-class homes, so most Haligonians preferred to ignore the problem, if they saw it as a problem at all.

The army discouraged its men from marrying, preferring to keep them unattached and ready to move out to the next campaign when needed. Only about six per cent of the soldiers in Halifax succeeded in gaining permission from their commanding officers to marry, mostly to women who had been domestic servants. Many Halifax women, however, became unofficial wives, living on and off with army men or sailors. Such an arrangement might provide some companionship and financial support for a while, but it was also quite unstable and an unofficial army wife might find herself at any time left to fend for herself if her husband was ordered to a new posting.

While prostitution may not have been respectable, it was one of the few avenues for a lower-class Halifax woman of these Victorian times to earn a steady income. By the mid 1860s there were somewhere between 600 and 1,000 women earning a living through prostitution, although there may have been many more part-timers.

If the law, for whatever reasons, wanted to apply pressure or control over any woman engaged as a prostitute, she could be charged with vagrancy, lewd or disorderly behaviour, or indecency. Most who ended up before a judge were women of the street rather than regular employees in bawdy houses. If men and women were caught in the act, invariably the women were charged and not the men. Men had many privileges under the law, but women had few.

Not unlike today, prostitution was a perilous trade, fraught with dangers of venereal disease, alcohol problems, pregnancy, unsafe abortions and physical abuse. Women who became prostitutes did so out of desperation. Victorian culture also forced single women into a catch-22 situation. A woman living alone or abandoned on the street was considered to be disreputable; once she was disreputable, she could no longer hope for respectable employment or be considered as a good prospect for a wife. Hence, she had nowhere to turn but to a life as a "dishonourable" woman who could at least earn an income.

Taking Note of "Improper Conduct"

Not everyone turned a blind eye to the abuse of women that was so prevalent in Nova Scotia. The Society for the Prevention of Cruelty was established in 1876, with its initial focus on animals, but it soon recognized the dimension of the human problem as well, particularly the plight of women and children. As a result of the SPC lobbying, husbands could now be dealt with in the courts for negligence or battering. Even then, a woman only went to the law under the most desperate conditions, because if her husband was locked up she would most likely be left without any form of income whatsoever. Sometimes she turned to the courts for help if her man was constantly drunk or if her children's lives were in danger. The SPC would become directly involved in these cases and documented the proceedings. (The society never kept written records of sexual abuse, however, arguing that it was too distasteful to be written down.)

Nonetheless, the SPC continued to bring more and more cases of child and wife abuse before the courts and also attempted to improve laws to relieve the plight of victims. Matthew Richey, a Member of Parliament who was also the president of the Nova Scotia SPC, failed in his attempts in 1881 to pass federal legislation for the protection of children, but the organization forged ahead in Halifax in its efforts to ensure criminal punishment for men proven to be cruel to or neglectful of their families. SPC secretary-agent John Naylor, a driving force in the organization, recorded in 1884 and 1885 cases involving neglect or harm by a drunken husband, husbands eloping with other women or "improperly conducting themselves with wife's sister," as well as cases of outright murders of wives by their husbands. Similar cases involving harm to children were also investigated. It's safe to say, however, that most instances of physical harm by men to wives and children still went unreported despite the best efforts of reformers and social activists.

As women entered the workforce beyond the classroom, they found themselves in low-paying factory or fish-plant jobs. Only the fairly destitute remained working after marriage; these ladies were often abandoned or widowed wives. Even by the turn of the century, a female worker in a cotton textile factory in Halifax could expect little in the way of generosity from her employer. This young, unmarried woman would work through an unpaid training period of five or six weeks. When wages started, they were low, and if she had come in from out of town, up to half of her salary might end up going to pay for her lodging in a rooming-house. At work, fines were imposed for lateness, poor work, breakage or even talking to other workers. The bosses might also alter the way women were paid to save factory costs, according to whether it was a busy or a slow week.

If women and men worked at the same task, men were paid a higher wage. Women endured long hours in noisy, unhealthy environments. It wasn't until 1906 that some limits were set on time: a work week of seventy-two hours was ordained as the limit for women under sixteen and boys under fourteen. If a woman tried to organize even a small protest or suggest some form of union, she was quickly released from her job.

Chapter Twenty-nine

The Savage Seas

The fury of the sea, with Cape Split in the background; 19th-century engraving.

Never Give Up the Ship

The coast of Nova Scotia is a rocky one and there's very little of it that has not seen some sort of shipwreck over the years. There are countless stories along this coast of drownings, rescues and recoveries. Whatever the fate of a foundering vessel, shore-dwellers often harvested the goods—anything that floated ashore. Houses and fisherman's shacks sometimes displayed the most curious and sometimes expensive items that would literally wash up on the doorstep. The old law of the Nova Scotia shore was that if it arrived by sea and you found it, it was yours—whether it be a few good boards, a barrel of rum or a chest of money.

In April of 1873, for example, the White Star liner *Atlantic* smashed up against some unyielding rocks on a stormy night off the coast of Prospect, not far from where the ill-fated *La Tribune* sank in 1797. The steel hull of the ship was pounded into scrap and 560 people on board died that night as they were swept overboard. The story goes that the coast was strewn with the bodies, many of the women still wearing expensive jewels. Not all of the jewellery lay intact when the bodies were carried off to the morgue.

Sea disasters do not always end in tragedy, and many times Nova Scotian seafarers have been pushed to their mental and physical limits to outwit the forces of nature. Such was the case with the *Research*, a vessel built in Yarmouth in 1861, weighing in at 1,459 tons, the largest ship constructed there to that time. Her price tag was a walloping $65,000. Toward the end of November in 1866 she was sailing from Quebec to Scotland with a heavy load of timber. Sailing out of the dangerous Strait of Belle Isle and into the Atlantic, Captain George Washington Churchill ran up against a monster gale and heavy seas that were to test his abilities. The topmast sail was ripped away and, worse yet, the rudder was broken off.

The bad weather persevered while the crew jury-rigged a rudder out of spare parts. In order to fix the rudder in place, Aaron Churchill, first mate and nephew of the captain, was let down over the side in a bowline. Figuring that wet, freezing clothes would impede his progress, the brave young man did the job totally naked. In reporting this story later, a newspaper would report that the younger Churchill, "when taken back on board was insensible but recovered."

Unfortunately for all aboard, this rudder too was wrecked by the continued hammering of the storm. Another one was painstakingly constructed as the ship was driven along by the storm. As the new rudder was being lowered over the side for placement, a wave smacked into it hard enough to send it floating away. The undaunted crew created a huge manual pole-like rudder from the timber aboard but it too proved useless. Mountains of water smashed over the ship and wrecked the deckhouse where the men lived, sweeping away many of the provisions. To add to the calamity, the oakum began to work its way loose between the boards and the ship started to take on water below. Heavy with wood, the ship and its cargo wouldn't exactly go the bottom of the sea but everything was becoming waterlogged and soon the ship would be a helpless pile of floating wreckage at the mercy of the unforgiving winter Atlantic. A third rudder was put into place and the men pumped away to get rid of the constant flush of water. Rudder three was lost, as was rudder four.

Unimaginably, the ship kept up a haggard westerly path on into January of the next year until she was within eighty kilometres of Tory Island, north of Ireland, and only a hundred and sixty kilometres from her destination port, Greenock. Bad weather, described by Archibald MacMechan as "a series of hurricanes and heavy seas," shoved the *Research* off course again. The newspaper in Glasgow would later say, "The officers and men were frequently greatly exhausted and upon several occasions the crew desired the captain and officers to give up the ship." No one would have to wonder why.

Passing vessels *Empress Eugenie* and *Palmyra* came close enough to offer up some desperately needed provisions. Amazingly enough, the captain and crew stayed with the *Research* rather than give up the battle with the North Atlantic. More rudders were lost or broken and more setbacks occurred, some of the cargo was heaved overboard to lighten the load but much of it was still on board when they were finally towed into Greenock on February the fourth. For once, man had won the battle with an adversarial sea.

Saxby's Storm

Storms at sea were the most obvious cause for the wrecks of ships and the monumental loss of life at sea. Sometimes the collateral damage of Atlantic-born storms spills over onto land. One of the most famous of all Nova Scotia storms was the Saxby Gale, predicted almost a year in advance by Lieutenant James Saxby from the British Navy and written up in the London papers at that time. He calculated that on October the fifth of 1869, the moon would be at its closest point to the Earth and located directly in line with the equator, while at the same time, "lines drawn from the Earth's centre would cut the Sun and Moon in the same arc of right ascension." To Saxby's mind, this was an extraordinary celestial circumstance and it meant big trouble for mariners.

Sure enough, the following October an Atlantic storm was moving up the seaboard wreaking havoc on Washington, D.C., and flooding Philadelphia and New England. On October the fourth it arrived at the mouth of the Bay of Fundy and by nightfall a wind of hurricane force hammered the coastline. Roads were flooded, bridges washed away, ships were smashed ashore and wharves beaten to a pulp. Incredible stories were reported, like the one about a barn, complete with livestock, being lifted off its foundation and floated for one hundred metres. Other barns simply drifted away on the super-high tides, as did a great number of haystacks. Telegraph poles were knocked down. Fields in the lowlands remained flooded for weeks.

The town of Windsor saw her streets in full flood and in nearby fields many cattle and sheep drowned. The great dyke at Grand Pré was breached for the first time since it was built by the Acadians, more livestock drowned and the salt that remained wrecked the crops for three years.

Along some parts of the bay, tides rose twenty to fifty feet above normal and some shorelines were permanently altered. An unlucky mail carrier and his passenger were crossing the Tantramar Marsh at the time the waters swept over the dykes, carrying them almost a kilometre and drowning the passenger, poor Miss Huldah Bray. At Minudie, near Amherst, an old gent named Steward who was sleeping in his barn after a hard day of cutting hay, found his barn afloat and breaking apart around him. He jumped onto a passing haystack, so the story from the *Amherst Gazette* reports, and surfed it off into the wild night until it grounded on a dyke where he was rescued the following day.

For weeks afterwards, stories were reported about the devastating and sometimes amazing effects of the storm on people's lives around Fundy. A house was turned completely about on its footing in one case. In another instance, while a low-lying house was flooding up into the second floor, its occupant climbed into a coffin and floated out the second-storey window to eventual safety. Many survived by sitting it out on the top of barns stubborn enough to stay put during the high tides and blasting winds.

Ships, like the *Genii*, whose captain had not been wary enough to take Saxby's early warning or frequent reminders as the date approached, ended up wrecked in the Bay of Fundy. In this instance, eleven men drowned. Meanwhile, the capital city of Halifax was spared nearly all of the mayhem and the *Chronicle Herald* reported the next day in a slightly miffed tone that, "The storm of Monday night was not a success in the city—did not come up to the expectations of the public."

The Mystery of the Mary Celeste

Not all sea disasters involving Nova Scotians occurred along our own coast. In fact, the setting for one of this province's most famous sea tragedies was thousands of miles from home port but it nonetheless constitutes an important legacy of the golden age of Nova Scotian sailing ships. When disasters occur far from port, it is often difficult to piece together the events. Unlike the wreck of the *Atlantic* or the *Cherokee*, there might not even be bodies washing up on the shoreline to confirm the final chapter of the story. The case of the *Mary Celeste* is one such occurrence.

Spencer's Island on the Bay of Fundy was one of those tiny Nova Scotian communities that produced fantastic sailing ships in the third quarter of the nineteenth century. One of the most notable and most talked about was the *Mary Celeste*. First christened the *Amazon* when it was launched in 1861, this brigantine had her name changed in 1868 after an unlucky accident in a gale. She was salvaged by a group of Americans and thus became their possession. On the morning of November 7, 1872, the *Mary Celeste* left New York for Genoa, loaded with 1,700 barrels of alcohol. Master mariner Benjamin Spooner Briggs was in charge and was accompanied by his wife, Sara, and two-year-old daughter, Sophia, along with a small crew of only seven men. What happened on this fateful voyage remains a mystery, but the fragments of that mystery continue to be an intriguing puzzle.

On December fourth of that year, another brigantine, the *Dei Grata*, was on its way to Gibraltar from New York. It had been a stormy crossing for the most part and about halfway between the Azores and Portugal, David Morehouse, captain of the ship, spotted some sails on the horizon. It was the *Mary Celeste*. The seas were high but not dangerous and the wind was blowing out of the north. Three of the *Dei Grata*'s crewmen boarded the *Mary Celeste* and discovered it was deserted. Two of the sails had blown away but three were still set. The mainsail had been hauled down and other sails furled. Some of the rigging was missing or damaged. One of the *Mary Celeste*'s lifeboats was missing but there was no sign that the tackle had been used to put it over the side.

Some water had flooded the hold but not enough to cause serious worry and the pumps were working away as designed. The binnacle, a stand for the compass next to the steering wheel, was knocked over and the compass itself was smashed. There was no sign of an explosion, and in the kitchen the stove had been knocked out of place but everything else looked neat and orderly. Seamen's gear was stowed properly away, including the foul-weather gear, the sailors' pipes and tobacco. Plenty of food and water was aboard, there was no sign of booze or drunken activity and, in the captain's quarters, the child's toys and clothes suggested everything had been quiet and orderly. The captain's sword was under his bed but his sextant, chronometer, navigation books and ships papers were missing. The final entry in the captain's log read, "Monday, November 25. At 8:00 Eastern Point bore S.S.W., 6 miles distant."

And here was the ship sailing along mid-ocean without anyone aboard. The mystery surrounding the *Mary Celeste* drew a good deal of interest and speculation, and while no one really knows what happened, theories abound.

One story at the time suggested that the crew got drunk and murdered the captain, his wife, child and first mate. The murderers dumped the bodies in the sea and then left in the small boat. Some believed that a man named

Winchester, one of the owners of the ship, had planned the event as some kind of insurance scam. One investigator claimed that stains on the captain's sword were blood, but it turned out to be rust.

A story later surfaced that one of the men from the *Dei Grata* had discovered the pillow in the baby's bed still warm and a lukewarm meal upon the table in the galley as he arrived, suggesting that something had just happened.

The mystery never seemed to die away fully from public consciousness. In 1884, a story was published proposing a complicated series of murders revolving around the ship. A 1929 book proposed further that the whole thing was an elaborate hoax to collect insurance. At least four men surfaced and claimed to be survivors of the *Mary Celeste* but none could give a convincing account of the voyage or details of the ship.

Had this been a more recent event, theories about UFO abduction might have fitted neatly into the picture. Nonetheless, an explanation by Dr. Oliver W. Cobb is probably the most convincing. His story runs as follows.

The ship's cargo of alcohol was affected as it moved from the colder climate of New York to the warmer reaches of the Atlantic. The alcohol expanded with the heat and fumes began to leak. On the morning of November 25, the captain decided to ventilate the hold. When the hatch was opened there was an explosive rush of gas—a kind of blast but no fire. Thinking that a fiery disaster was at hand, the captain launched the ship's boat with everyone aboard. They would stay tied to the ship and wait to see if it was safe to return. A storm could have come up quickly and the boat was cast adrift from the ship. The tiny boat was overloaded with the entire crew and eventually went down, drowning all aboard and leaving the *Mary Celeste* to sail on for nearly 965 kilometres with no one at the helm and no one aboard.

They "Held Onto Their Manhood"

Lumber was a common cargo that brought profit to the Nova Scotian ship owners. Trees were plentiful and there was a ready market to the south. All you had to do was deliver the goods. That's what the brigantine *Louisa* was trying to do when she shipped out of Bridgewater late one December, headed to Barbados with her cargo. She soon ran into a North Atlantic blast of a storm that started the ship leaking and forced the crew to cut the lanyards and some of the rigging. As the storm raged, the foremast broke clean off and the maintopmast did as well. The men survived the night on the roof of the forehouse only to face a worse nightmare the following day when the whole stern of the ship was ripped apart by waves. The lumber from below began to drift out into the open sea and the boats that had been in place for emergencies disappeared. The vessel was literally disintegrating beneath them, but as the ship was full of wood, what was left was still afloat.

Nonetheless, it was a pretty sorry state of affairs.

On Christmas Eve, the crew attempted to get the attention of a passing ship by lighting impromptu torches made from jackets soaked in oil, but failed. The weather improved somewhat, however, and they found some bread, carrots, turnips and tinned water on board. The ship was still afloat, thanks to the lumber below, but there was no way to steer it. Miraculously, the galley stove had been above deck in the forehouse, and as the water ran out, the men figured out how to capture the steam of boiled salt water, and painstakingly distilled desperately needed fresh water a few drops at a time. Each of the men was allowed four teaspoonsful of water a day as their ration. Luckily on December 27, the liner *Olympia* arrived, having been blown far off course herself. Soon after the men were safely aboard the *Olympia*, another gale came up and bashed what was left of the *Louisa* to pieces. So the crew was saved by a fluke of fate. Had the *Olympia* remained on course, all aboard the *Louisa* would have certainly perished.

After the loss of a ship, the captain was obliged to make a formal report to the Nova Scotia "Wreck Court" and in it Captain Bain stated that any sailing ship should have withstood the storms he encountered and "no wooden ship of her age should have gone to pieces, if she had not been suffering from some defect of workmanship in her building or some defect of material." He did, however, praise his men for their "stoic demeanour" and said, "they even showed cheery defiance to the cold, the hunger, the thirst, the menace of annihilation."

The captain had high praise for all aboard the ill-fated *Louisa* and he surmised that they survived because each of them "held onto their manhood"—an ambiguous but lyrical phrase that sums up much about life aboard a sailing ship when caught in the grip of some tumultuous exercise in maritime survival. All one could do was to "hold onto one's manhood" and hope for good luck, a passing ship or a painless watery death.

Chapter Thirty

The Decline and Fall
of the Age of Sail

Steamships like this Cunard liner led to the decline of the sailing-ship industry in Nova Scotia.

One Big Ship Instead of Two

The Golden Age of Sail was fuelled not only by wind and a quest for adventure. It was driven by greed, or at the very least, a strong desire for profit. The W.D. Lawrence was one of the largest sailing ships of her time, or any time for that matter. She was built by a William Dawson Lawrence in the small, sea-sheltered village of Maitland on the Fundy Shore. Lawrence had begun his shipbuilding career by cutting his own frames for his first ship and hauling them by hand out of the woods. He had prospered and gone on to build a number of ships but, thinking that one large ship could be operated *more economically* than two smaller ones, he set about constructing a vessel larger than any that existed. He first carved out the traditional miniature model and then proceeded to build the monster-size ship that he would modestly name after himself. The enterprise attracted fame for Lawrence and curiosity-seekers from near and far descended upon the little village. Lawrence disdained the critics who showed up to suggest that such a large vessel made of mere pine and spruce would not weather rough seas. Some thought it would be too unwieldy and hard to steer and they told Lawrence this to his face. Some simply came to laugh at him. Whenever Lawrence tired of his critics or the job of overseeing the massive construction project, he would escape by locking himself away in his study and playing the fiddle.

The W.D. Lawrence was launched in October of 1874 and according to the Halifax *Morning Chronicle*, 4,000 people came out to watch. She weighed in at 2,459 tons, at a price tag of $107,453, a pretty penny in those days and much of it was Lawrence's personal investment. Lawrence himself sailed her to Liverpool, then on to Aden in the Middle East and back to France. In 1882, he sold the big ship to some Norwegians for $140,848, realizing a hefty profit which, of course, was why he had undertaken the massive endeavour in the first place.

"Boundless Fleets of Magnificent Steamers"

If the emergence of the steamship rang the death knell for the Nova Scotian sailing industry, it is somewhat ironic that the entrepreneur who was so successful at embracing the new technology and making a great fortune from it was a Nova Scotian. Samuel Cunard was born in Halifax in 1787, the son of a Philadelphia Loyalist who had moved north during the American Revolution.

Samuel Cunard worked as first clerk in the Royal Engineers' lumber yard and in 1813, along with his father, opened a shipping business by purchasing a sailing ship from the "prize court"—that is, a ship that had been hauled to port by privateers. They succeeded in landing His Majesty's mail business

between Halifax, Newfoundland, Boston and the West Indies and later
nailed contracts to protect fishing rights and perform customs inspections.
Pretty soon, father and son had nearly forty vessels at work and they were
involved in everything from mail service to sealing and whaling.

A razor-sharp businessman with an instinct for making money, Cunard
also had a passion for navigational aids and became the first Commissioner
of Lighthouses. It made good sense: he had a lot of vessels afloat and wanted
to protect his own interests. Cunard had his hand in all sorts of things from
charitable soup-kitchen work to military activity and fire protection for the
city. He became involved with an early insurance company and helped in
establishing the first bank of Halifax. After all, he needed some safe place to
keep his money.

The really big deals were in London and so Cunard made a number of
trips across the Atlantic to compete with the big English shipping firms. He
successfully landed a contract with the East India Company and sailed his
ship the *Countess of Harcourt* into Halifax Harbour amidst considerable fanfare as it carried 6,000 chests of tea from China. By forty, Cunard was a
wealthy man and had negotiated more English contracts, including one with
the General Mining Association.

A fan of new technology, he became enamoured with the steamship and
fostered a dream to create a kind of "ocean railway." He became a central
figure in forming a company to build the *Royal William*, the first ship to cross
the Atlantic entirely by steam. She was launched in Quebec in 1833 and
made port in Halifax, then to Pictou where she took on 300 tons of coal,
and then proved herself by crossing the Atlantic in three weeks.

Cunard tried to ignore the opposition of the naysayers who believed the
big sailing ships run by the Shakespeare, Dramatic and Black Ball Lines were
the epitome of oceanic travel. Even though he had proven that the
steamship could be used for reliable trans-Atlantic travel, he was scoffed at.
Sadly for Nova Scotia, Cunard was right and the die-hard sailing men would
see progress outstrip them, robbing many of them of their dignity and
income.

Wheeler-dealer that he was, Cunard and his ever-growing body of associates took on more mail contracts, including the big one with the English
government to shuttle mail across the Atlantic on a fortnightly basis. The
service proved to be successful and Cunard courted passengers as well, once
offering 2,000 free dinner invitations to the people of Boston. He found
plenty of people willing to take passage across the Atlantic and provided
plenty of high quality food and spirits. At one point, he found his passengers consuming too much of the free-flowing wine so, like the airlines of the
1990s, he reluctantly decided to charge extra for wine.

In 1859 Cunard was knighted by Queen Victoria—for shipping all that
mail, capitalizing on steamships and, presumably, making a fortune. He died

in 1865 at age seventy-eight. A verbose and slightly skewed biographer of a later day, Abraham Payne, would write, "Let the mind's eye survey the boundless fleets of magnificent steamers traversing the seas at this very hour in every quarter of the globe. The first standard bearer of this host of leviathans was— Sir Samuel Cunard, who remodelled the Ocean Navigation of the world."

Steel, Not Wood

To some, Cunard may have been a heroic figure, a forward-thinking pioneer of world shipping. But to those who lost their livelihood on sailing ships, he may have appeared more like an enemy. One might wonder why the seven seas were not immense enough for both sail and steam to prosper. How exactly did steamships diminish the sailing industry so quickly and why couldn't Nova Scotia have prospered and adapted, as Cunard and his company did, to the new technology? It should have been a natural evolution.

Shipbuilding in Nova Scotia was greatly diminished by the fact that the new massive vessels were made of steel, not wood. Most of the ships plying northerly waters were built in England in huge shipyards. This factory production was a stark contrast to the craftsmen of tiny Nova Scotian villages who carved wooden models, cut the trees from their own forests and built handsome schooners with local labour and minimal capital expenditure.

Steamships were faster, alas, less dependent on wind, more reliable, and easier to maintain. They made importing and exporting cheaper. Some sailing ships would navigate on into the twentieth century carrying whatever cargo they could muster, but they could not compete in the new age of coal, steam and iron. Why, then, didn't Nova Scotian shipbuilders, unarguably among the finest in the world, adapt to the times? One of the big problems was the tariff structure of the day. You could buy a ship already built in England and register it in Canada without paying duty. *But* tariffs on shipbuilding materials were costly if you wanted to assemble one in Nova Scotia, and a considerable bulk of the materials involved would have to be imported. It would just cost too much to build a ship in Nova Scotia if it wasn't made of wood and fitted with sails instead of steam engines.

Around the World Alone

The Golden Age of Sail would eventually fade but sailing itself would never go away. It was an integral part of the psyche of anyone growing up in coastal Nova Scotia. The stories of life aboard the sailing ships involved the exhilarating drama of the high seas and the sometimes tumultuous interaction of the high-spirited men aboard vessels. But in the case of Joshua Slocum, it was a story of a loner in the truest sense. Slocum was the first man to sail around the world alone, a circumnavigation of some 74,000 kilometres.

Joshua Slocum was born near the Fundy Shore on the North Mountain above the Annapolis Valley on February 20, 1844, the son of a farmer trying to make a living by cultivating some very rocky soil. After the family moved to the fishing community of Westport, Joshua ran away at fourteen to work as a cook on a fishing schooner and, after his mother died, he went off to toil on the big ships that would travel to foreign ports.

Slocum learned everything about ships quickly and by the time he was twenty-five he was the skipper of a fishing schooner that sailed between Seattle and San Francisco. The American West Coast was far from his home in Nova Scotia, but Slocum found himself drawn to even farther ports. In 1870, he became the captain of the *Washington*, a barque that he sailed across the wide Pacific to Sydney, Australia. Here he met and married Virginia Walker. For a variety of reasons, Slocum moved on from ship to ship. In 1875, his current ship, the *B. Aymar*, was sold out from under him in Manila and he decided to take a year off to build his own sailing ship. He sold that one (presumably at a profit) and used the money to buy another ship to haul freight between Pacific islands, then sold that one and bought the *Amethyst*, which he also later sold as business began to slacken. Next, he signed on as part-owner and captain of an 1,800-ton ship called the *Northern Light*. Working as master of the *Northern Light*, he sailed for the first time around the world and ended up in New York, where again his ship was sold to new buyers.

Always eager to take on new work, Slocum became captain of the *Aquidneck* and, with his wife aboard, shipped out of Baltimore in 1884, headed for Brazil and Argentina. Virginia died from illness along the way and Slocum was devastated. His son, Victor, would later write, "…father was like a ship with a broken rudder." In 1886, Slocum married his first cousin Henrietta. He was forty-two; she was twenty-four and, unlike Virginia, didn't adjust readily to life aboard ship.

In 1888, still working off the coast of South America, the *Aquidneck* went aground and the captain considered her unsalvageable. He sold what was left of the wreck and with little money left in his pocket, Slocum, Henrietta and two sons lived ashore on a strange island with little more than the tool kit, charts, chronometer and compass salvaged from the *Aquidneck*. Ever resourceful, Slocum set about building a ten-metre canoe-style boat which he rigged like a Chinese sampan. He christened her the *Liberdade*, launched the day that slavery was abolished in Brazil—May 13, 1888. The cost of the boat had been less than a hundred dollars and Slocum sailed his family over 8,000 kilometres to South Carolina and then published a book about the experience.

Slocum's wife and children settled into life ashore in East Boston, but Joshua was feeling unsettled and depressed over the loss of his first wife, the wreck of his ship and his faltering finances. In 1892, he got his hands on an old sloop and decided to rebuild it into something that would be uniquely his own. He also got it into his head that he should sail it around the world, with no one but himself on board. Eleven metres long and four metres wide, the *Spray* was designed to be a ship that could pretty well sail itself for long stretches at a time.

So this very confident, somewhat alienated fifty-one-year-old master mariner set sail from Massachusetts in April, five years before the turn of the century. "A thrilling pulse beat high in me," he wrote. He also admitted, "I had taken little advice from anyone for I had a right to my own opinions in matters pertaining to the sea." The obvious advice he was ignoring from everyone was that he would be completely crazy to undertake such a treacherous adventure.

Slocum took his time getting adjusted to his craft and sailed first to Gloucester, where he bought an old dory which he cut in half to use as a dinghy. Next he went home to Westport in Nova Scotia and on to Yarmouth for final provisions, including a tin clock with a smashed glass which he bought for a dollar. It would be his only man-made reference point for time on the trip.

Slocum had no particular interest in the shortest, fastest route around the world. First he sailed from Nova Scotia to Gibraltar. On his way he stopped in the Azores, where he contracted some form of food poisoning. Sick at sea, he had a vision of Christopher Columbus guiding him on. After Europe he sailed back across the Atlantic to South America. He probably figured a couple of trans-Atlantic crossings was a good warm-up for what would come next. He nearly drowned off the coast of Uruguay trying to get his vessel unstuck from a reef. Keep in mind that, like so many Nova Scotian sailors who spent their working lives at sea, Slocum had never learned to swim.

Passing through the Strait of Magellan, he had a rough time tacking through the stormy and difficult passage. He was also boarded by some of the local Native population who failed to sneak up on him asleep because he had mined the deck with carpet tacks dumped all over as protection against intruders. He claimed that the leg from Thursday Island to the Keeling Cocos Islands, a distance of 4,300 kilometres, was accomplished with the need for only one hour manning the helm. His design of a sailing ship that could very nearly sail itself had paid off. As he arrived at ports in the South Pacific he was often treated royally by governors and kings and given presents of food and supplies.

On July 3, 1898, he sailed back into harbour at Fairhaven, Massachusetts, but there was no one there to make a fuss over his return home. When he finally made it ashore, people asked him who he was and where he had come from.

Joshua Slocum must have had a hard time readjusting to landlocked life as he moved into an apartment in New York City and then back to East Boston. He sold his story of sailing alone around the world to the magazines and then book publishers and tried to settle into a small farm on Martha's Vineyard. A few trips sailing south didn't seem to cheer him up enough and he grew cranky and silent. In November of 1909 he set sail from Martha's Vineyard in the *Spray*, an aging, out-of-shape vessel with an aging and unhealthy captain. He was never seen again.

Chapter Thirty-one

Dreamers, Schemers and Telephone Screamers

A meeting between Alexander Graham Bell and Helen Keller.

Yarmouth's Unsung Inventor

Nova Scotia has often been fertile ground for inventions, particularly those related to ships and shipping. In the eighteenth and nineteenth centuries it was common practice for someone to simply dream up some new, innovative device for a practical purpose and then build it for himself or share it with his neighbours. Patents were rarely considered, often because the patent office was too far away or because the formality was too expensive for a fisherman or sailor. Occasionally, a Nova Scotian sailor or shipbuilder would create an ingenious improvement in ship design or fashion a completely unique maritime device. If either worked well, it found its way into sailing technology worldwide without any great rewards for the inventor.

Such was the case for John Patch of Yarmouth, who invented the marine screw propeller, a major advance in ship technology. Patch had also come up with some improvements for steam engines and paddle wheels, but it was the propeller device that would revolutionize the shipping industry. Patch had created a wooden model of his screw propeller as early as 1833. It was powered by a hand crank that turned wooden gears. Patch tried it out at night in Yarmouth Harbour with a handful of witnesses nearby to watch him propel himself across the water by turning a hand crank that in turn rotated a prop at the back of his boat. In 1834, his new-fangled propulsion system was installed in the schooner *Royal George*, and the grateful captain, Silas Kelly, found that he could now move his boat around even when the wind had gone dead on him. Patch went off to New York to apply for a patent but was denied. He was told his invention was worthless and that he would just be wasting his money. He tried again in Washington but was turned down there as well.

It was probable that the patent offices were manned by corrupt employees who took advantage of their positions to seize on a good idea and try to make money by getting a patent for themselves. Patch was an uneducated seafaring Nova Scotian who looked like an easy mark to the shrewd American patent officers.

The patent design finally did get registered in England but not by Patch. It's possible that this English design was invented quite independently of Patch. This doesn't change the fact that the Yarmouth resident had come up with the idea on his own, had tried to register what had previously not been registered and was turned down. By 1858 poor old John was seventy-seven, crippled, broke and living in the Yarmouth poorhouse. The good folks of that port had watched John's invention become a vital tool of marine technology and they were outraged that Patch had not received credit or money. They made a solid case to the Nova Scotia legislature for compensation, but it was turned down and so John Patch went to his grave without ever getting much in the way of credit or cash for his invention or his inventiveness.

The Deep Divers of Pictou

Another more worldly-wise Nova Scotian inventor was John Fraser of Pictou County. While his brother, Dr. J.D.B. Fraser, was the first physician to make use of chloroform in Canada, John was the first man to use a diver's helmet in North America. While this may not sound like a monumental "first" to a landlubber, it was a pretty big deal in the salvage industry. As the stories in this book reveal, a multitude of sailing ships and uncountable tons of valuable cargo ended up on the bottom of the sea and any means available to return such booty above sea level would earn significant rewards.

Fraser had been doing salvage work for Lloyds of London off the European coast and when he came home to Nova Scotia in the summer of 1842, he had the gear necessary to descend to the bottom of the sea while still breathing air. Along with another Pictonian, Alexander Munro, he set off to Cape Bear, PEI, where, in 1839, the *Mallabar* had once floundered, dumping her seventy-four guns and tons of valuable "shot" to the bottom. Munro and Fraser were able to raise thirty-five of the cannons and a few tons of the shot to produce a good profit for themselves. After that they set up operations in Pictou, where they demonstrated their bizarre-looking new equipment to the wide-eyed fishermen and townspeople. The diving device was large and unwieldy, weighed down by ninety kilograms of lead. The hood had three windows and the "suit" was made of India rubber. Air was pumped into the helmet by way of a long tube. To the amazement of the Pictou crowd, Munro stayed under for more than a half hour and then went down a second time to bring up some ornaments—an anchor and a chain—to show off.

Undersea Messages to Europe

In 1849, Nova Scotian Frederick Gisbourne thought that the island of Newfoundland should have a more dependable communication link with his own province and the outside world. His plan involved a land cable and a steamboat connection to Cape Breton. The Newfoundland legislature gave him 500 pounds to perform a survey of the land route which would carry the cable from St. John's to Cape Ray. That venture in itself was dangerous, leading to the death of one man and near-starvation for the rest of the crew.

Not one to be discouraged in pursuit of profit and better communication, Gisbourne went to New York to find investors to back him for yet another project, the first successful North American submarine communications cable. In the summer of 1852, it would link PEI to New Brunswick, giving

Charlottetown instant telegraph communication with the island for the first time.

The troublesome Newfoundland project, however, eventually led to bankruptcy for Gisbourne, but he didn't let that get him down. Instead, he enlisted the support of big money man Cyrus Field, and together they decided to finish the Newfoundland project, complete with an underwater cable to Cape Breton. Next, they grew more ambitious and proposed putting in a submarine cable all the way from St. John's to Europe. Gisbourne liked big projects and this was an enormous one which took thirteen years to finish and five times the money originally expected. Field and Gisbourne had also enlisted other investors and the help of Samuel Morse, inventor of the electric telegraph.

In the summer of 1854, 600 men were at work on the land leg of the Newfoundland route, cutting a swath a mere two and a half metres wide through the rugged terrain. The first try at putting down the undersea cable from Cape Ray to Cape Breton across the Cabot Strait was scrubbed when a storm walloped the sailing ship that was trying to lay the cable. In the process they lost seventy-two kilometres of costly cable. The next year they succeeded with a steamship to get the insulated strand-core copper wire in place and the telegraph link came into service.

More money was raised, including $70,000 from the U.S. government, and the Atlantic Telegraph Company continued on its way to forge the undersea link with Europe. There were still plenty of setbacks, including cable lost or damaged by storms, and accidents, but by 1866 the transatlantic cable was pulled ashore at Heart's Content, Newfoundland, and Gisbourne saw his vision fulfilled.

While Frederick Gisbourne was concerned with improving communication by laying cables, geologist Abraham Gesner would hope to supply something even more fundamental: a better way to provide light in the darkness of one's own home. Gesner was born in Cornwallis Township, Nova Scotia, in 1797. He studied in London to become a doctor, but he also had a lifelong passionate interest in geology. In 1836 he published a book about the rocks of Nova Scotia, then moved to New Brunswick to act as provincial geologist. When he was fired from that job, he opened a museum of natural history. It turned out not to be a very good way to make a living, so he returned to Nova Scotia where, in his disappointment, he started to study coal.

During those days many people provided night-time lighting by burning smoky and smelly oil from plants or animals, including whales. The lighting itself was quite dim and the fuel sometimes expensive. When Gesner met the British commander, the Earl of Dundonald, he found a kindred spirit interested in the possibility of providing light from coal. Burning a chunk of coal for light in itself would be a smelly, unsatisfying business but, with

Dundonald's encouragement, Gesner figured out how to distil oil from coal. He made a big demonstration of it in a church in Charlottetown and the event was a huge success.

The new synthetic fuel, called kerosene, was adopted for use in illuminating lighthouses. Gesner started the Kerosene Gaslight Company to light the streets of Halifax but there were a few snags in getting the business running smoothly. Gesner's new fuel was still somewhat smelly as it burned but was a major improvement over the past. Kerosene would go on to be used for cooking, lighting, heating and even to fuel jets, but in his day Gesner never made a big profit from it and moved on to teach natural history at Dalhousie University.

The Bells of Baddeck

In 1885, the greatest of all inventors associated with this province, Alexander Graham Bell, took a vacation in Cape Breton and became hooked on the place. For the next thirty-three years, Bell lived from the spring into the fall at Beinn Bhreagh, his home near Baddeck. For Bell, Cape Breton would be just the place to ambitiously explore new technological possibilities that would help change the world.

Bell had no real professional training in the area of electricity. Instead, his prime area of interest was sound and vocal physiology. He had been brought up in Scotland and first travelled to Canada in hopes of improving his health. He had an inquisitive mind and was interested in all manner of scientific endeavours, especially something that would improve the telegraph device. In Boston, where he worked at a school for the deaf, he moonlighted in his research and in 1875 patented something called the harmonic telegraph, which involved sending messages at varying harmonic frequencies.

Because of his interest in human speech and hearing, he conceptualized a device that could transmit and receive human speech and, along with his assistant Thomas Watson, invented the telephone, which was patented in 1876. Bell married a woman of great inspiration to him, and Mabel Bell, herself deaf, would join Alexander in Baddeck to perform her own research in horticulture.

During the years after the invention of the telephone, Bell worked non-stop on a disparate range of projects involving photoelectric cells, the iron lung, desalination of sea water, the phonograph and steam-powered aircraft. Much of his research took place in Cape Breton. One of his odder experiments was an attempt to create a kind of super-sheep. These were multi-nippled ewes which would give birth to twins or triplets most of the time.

In the U.S. Bell had dabbled with the possibility of steam-powered aircraft but it was in Baddeck in 1907 that he formed the Aerial Experiment Association with J.A.D. McCurdy, F.W. Baldwin, Glenn Curtiss and others.

They made kites which lifted men into the air and went on to make gasoline-powered "aerodromes." On a cold day in February of 1909, Bell and his buddies succeeded in putting a man aloft in the *Silver Dart*, the first such flight in Canada. Bell also toyed with creating hydrofoil boats that rose up and "flew" across the water. The first one appeared in 1908 and the HD-4, handcrafted in 1917, pushed the world water-speed record to 114 miles an hour.

Bell loved his time at Baddeck and died there on August 2, 1922.

Cape Breton Island also had another claim to fame when it comes to telecommunication firsts. Guglielmo Marconi, who had invented the radio, transmitted the first-ever wireless communication from North America to Europe in 1902 from his radio station at Glace Bay. The curious message read thus: "The patient waiter never loses." It made history. Marconi kept improving his system and, by 1907, he had a communication service running from Port Morien, Cape Breton, to Clifden, Ireland. He had also set up shop in Glace Bay to manufacture his own equipment. In 1919, Marconi's Louisbourg station received the first wireless transatlantic voice message from Ireland.

The Chignecto Ship Railway Dream

Some blame for the death of sailing ships can be attributed to the advent of steamships, but the rapid growth of rail travel also heralded a decline for the schooners. Nova Scotia's first railroad was created in Pictou County in 1838. It was also the first freight railway in Canada and, powered by a British locomotive, it hauled coal from the Albion mines to ships in need of fuel docked in Pictou Harbour. Most of Nova Scotia, however, was slow to catch on to the great railway boom happening across North America. The most efficient means of transport was still by ship.

Nonetheless, by 1854 a rail link was created between the train-happy Pictonians and Halifax. Halifax was also linked to Windsor by rail. These rail lines would later be absorbed into the Intercontinental Railway as part of the deal to bring Nova Scotia into Confederation. Then, as travel and commerce shifted westward, trains were partly responsible for the great decline of the sailing ships.

One of the most intriguing railroad endeavours in the history of Nova Scotia, however, involved the hauling of entire ships across land. For nearly 300 years, ship owners and captains had daydreamed about a possible short-cut from the Bay of Fundy to the Gulf of St. Lawrence, across the narrow Chignecto isthmus that lashes Nova Scotia (a near-island) to the rest of North America. The shortcut that would lead from East Coast North America to the Gulf and the St. Lawrence River could create a potential fortune for anyone with the capital and equipment to bring it about.

Between 1875 and 1886 nearly twenty studies were undertaken for the building of a canal across the leash of land. Cost, however, would be the critical limiting factor; the price tag was estimated to be as much as $8,000,000. And then along came Henry George Clopper Ketchum, who proposed that it would be much cheaper to build a railroad. Ships could be hoisted out of the water at one end, trundled across the marsh and lowered gently back into the water on the other side.

George Ketchum, a civil engineer born in 1839 in Woodstock, New Brunswick, was a true believer that railroads could be adapted to carry nearly anything. His project would be a privately funded railway designed to accommodate all manner of ships, including paddle-wheel steamers. The rail line would be twenty-seven kilometres long with a dock on the Fundy side capable of handling up to six ships of about 1,000 tons each. Ships would be floated over a cradle with 192 wheels on a rail bed that began underwater. The vessel would next be lifted by hydraulics and propelled by steam engine across the isthmus, at a maximum of ten miles an hour, to be slowly deposited back into the water on the other side. The rail owners could charge a hauling fee of a meagre fifty cents per ton and still collect more than $500,000 each year, even if only a fraction of the sea traffic used the service.

Ketchum started out investing his own money but was forced to find other backers, which included the Government of Canada kicking in $150,000 per year. Cumberland County magnanimously gave him the land free of charge and construction began in 1888. Three-quarters of the work was completed by July of 1891, when tighter economic times put a pinch on the project. Tracks had been laid and machinery manufactured, nearly ready to go. Another $1,500,000 would have seen completion of the dream project. Ketchum was sure it would be the first of many such ship railways for North America but he would never see the completion of the job. It all went down the tubes. The Chignecto Ship Railway would fall into ruin and little would be left to show to the world.

Chapter Thirty-two

Toward the Turn of the Century

Transportation on land: the old and the new in the late 19th century.

Off to the "Boston States"

From the outset, many Nova Scotians resented their annexation to Canada. If they had ever had faith in the faltering democracy of Nova Scotia, it was shattered by Tupper's success in dragging the province into Confederation against the will of the people. Had the terms of Confederation been more appealing, perhaps the deal would have caused less resentment. By the end of the 1860s, however, most dissenters realized the impossibility of bringing about a repeal. The most radical of the discontented still spoke of joining Nova Scotia to the United States and shifting alliances south instead of west. But, fortunately, this movement too faded. By 1869, Joe Howe was a minister in the federal cabinet and he too had been persuaded that Confederation was never to be reversed.

While well-educated Halifax lawyers and newspapermen may have still been hammering out the rightness or wrongness of Confederation, it was probably of little concern at all to a great number of Nova Scotian subsistence farmers and families in fishing villages who scraped by in poverty. Their concern was daily survival. The great age of sailing ships that was creating mercantile fortunes had passed these farmers and fisherfolk by. All the new politicking in Halifax and Ottawa would have very little influence on their lives or provide improvement, not in this century anyway.

In the 1870s, industrial growth in Maritime cities was not keeping pace with expansion in Ontario and Quebec. More and more manufactured goods from outside the region, including the U.S., were finding their way to Nova Scotia, depressing the local economy. In the 1880s, there was not even much growth in farming, forestry, fishing or shipping. Coal production was slightly on the increase, but otherwise, the economy in Nova Scotia was in a kind of holding pattern. Wealth once generated by the sailing ships was falling off, while the government subsidized rail transport, which was not yet proving to be a great asset to Nova Scotia.

As a result of the slack economy and the promise of jobs elsewhere, there was a great out-migration of Maritimers during this decade. Nova Scotians moved west or they shipped off to the "Boston States;" many would never return home. So, while populations in Ontario and Massachusetts exploded, the number of people in Nova Scotia grew by only two per cent during the entire decade.

The exodus of Maritimers took young men away from jobs in the forests and away from the hard toil of life in seaport communities. The lure of a factory job in Boston seemed more desirable and credible than a hard but adventurous life at sea on an outdated ship that might not turn enough profit to pay all the crew. Even fishing proved to be an unreliable occupation due to fluctuating prices determined by economic factors far outside the region. And so, for those who would move away, the vital tie to the life of the sea was cut forever.

As workers flowed out of the region, so did money. Economic downturns in the 1870s and 1880s had prompted local banks to invest their clients' savings *outside* of the region, where growth was stronger. This obviously did little to help the Nova Scotian economy and meant a less certain economic base for future development. By the middle of the 1880s, Nova Scotians were in the midst of a depression and had some reasonable grounds for holding the distant federal government to blame for their dire straits. W.S. Fielding got himself elected in 1886 by talking again of seceding from the Dominion of Canada and forming a Maritime Union of provinces, even though the other Maritime premiers were only lukewarm to the idea. Once settled safely in office, however, Fielding backed off from his secessionist ideals when a new federal government was elected in 1887 and the outlook for enhanced provincial rights looked more promising.

Despite economic setbacks, social and cultural progress found its way to Nova Scotia during this decade, much of it in the form of public works. Halifax opened a large indoor public skating rink in the Exhibition Building in 1879, and amateur sports began to flourish as well. The Halifax Infirmary was opened by the Sisters of Charity in 1886 and the Victoria General Hospital opened in 1887. Dalhousie University moved away from downtown and expanded.

"The Mist of Virgin Ramparts"

Halifax in the nineteenth century had received its share of literary travellers, many of whom had strong opinions about the place. Charles Dickens, on his tour of North America back in 1842, arrived in Halifax Harbour, where his ship promptly ran aground on a mud bank. His very first impression of Nova Scotia was that it was, "dark, foggy and damp and there were bleak hills all around us." Halifax itself was a "curiosity of ugly dulness," and his correspondence reveals that he was not overly impressed with his host, Speaker of the House Joe Howe, the best conversationalist Halifax had to offer. Nonetheless, Dickens somehow left with a favourable impression of Halifax and countered his earlier observation by reporting in the British press that Halifax was ultimately "cheerful, thriving and industrious."

In the fall of 1882, Oscar Wilde even lectured here on a tour that took in Halifax, Amherst and Truro. While in Halifax, he wrote, "I am having charming audiences…but it is a great fight in this commercial age to plead the cause of Art." It may well have been the capital "A" in Wilde's discussion of "Art" that was troubling Bluenose audiences.

Rudyard Kipling did better public-relations work for Halifax after his trip here. In his lengthy poem "Song of the Cities," published in 1896, he had this to say of the city:

> Into the mist my guardian prows put forth
> Behind the mist my virgin ramparts lie,
> The Warden of the Honour of the North,
> Sleepless and veiled am I.

Oscar Wilde had not been quite so impressed with the virgin ramparts but Kipling obviously had a strong feeling about Halifax fitting into the grand scheme of empire. It was also around this time that a young woman from PEI, Lucy Maud Montgomery, was attending Dalhousie University and preparing herself to become one of Canada's most beloved writers.

Better Pay For Boring Jobs

For those Haligonians who could afford it, city water, sewage and electricity made life more comfortable. In sharp contrast to the new comforts for the middle and upper class, the urban and rural poor still suffered the ravages of malnutrition and a host of diseases. Childhood illnesses like smallpox, diphtheria and whooping cough took a staggering toll on lives.

Poorhouses for the downtrodden did little to alleviate the problems of poverty. From 1882 to 1886, the homeless, including many elderly, sick or mentally ill, were cloistered away in an old Halifax penitentiary where they at least had the small luxury of meals, beds and what medical care was available. Blacks were kept segregated from whites and for all, space was cramped and uncomfortable. As many as four hundred people were crammed into a living space originally intended for eighty prisoners. Physically fit boys or girls might be sent out to work as farm hands in the Annapolis Valley or elsewhere but this could not exactly be considered charitable adoption. Instead, the boys and girls acted as a pool of cheap labour, and to further augment this workforce, children were imported from the ghettos of English cities.

While the ravages of poverty continued on into the 1890s, this was also a time characterized by urban growth, industrial development and immigration into Nova Scotia. The province was also fragmented, however, with divergent (and sometimes opposing) local interests rather than unified regional or even national concerns. Once, even the smallest harbour communities felt linked to the four corners of the world; they now felt isolated and abandoned. Nothing had come along to replace the vital link that sailing ships had provided for commerce and travel.

For those mobile individuals who had moved from rural villages into towns and cities, there was a marked difference in lifestyle dictated by the job. In the outback, fishing, lumbering and farming might all have fit together as part of a Nova Scotian's occupation. He had lived in a world of self-reliance where he was directly responsible for providing his family's food and the basics of living. Now the factory demanded a worker who could stand for long hours at a machine, repeating a single dull task over and over for the reward of pay. Some young men and women would be discouraged by the sheer boredom of the work and return home. Others moved on farther yet in pursuit of better money or more challenging occupations.

Industrialism would create a new order of working-class people whose livelihood would be controlled by the tides of economy rather than the tides of the sea. Whether the new urban lifestyle was an improvement or not is arguable but it led to a clear-cut shift of population. At the time of Confederation, only one in ten Nova Scotians lived in a town with a population more than one thousand. By the turn of the century, one in four lived in such a town or in a larger city.

Those who remained working on farms, at fishing or in the woods maintained some semblance of the independence and self-reliance that had characterized the most successful Nova Scotians from the early days on. The 1890s, however, saw a true decline of the skilled craftsmen. Men with highly refined abilities at shipbuilding, furniture-making or other artisan crafts had no real place on the assembly line, where all that was required was the ability to follow instructions and repeat a mind-numbing manoeuvre over and over. The creativity, ingenuity and individualism required of a shipbuilder had no place in the new factory that demanded conformity and complacency.

By 1896, Halifax boasted electric street cars that picked up workers near their homes and deposited them at the doorstep of the factories. In Halifax and Dartmouth, this new breed of factory labourer produced sugar, cotton textiles, clothing, rope, books, magazines, boots and shoes. The companies that employed these Nova Scotians, however, continued to be buffeted by market forces outside the region and jobs came and went accordingly. Rather than providing for more job security, integration into the new North American economy would continue to erode what self-reliance was left in Nova Scotia.

Coal had brought plenty of jobs to Cape Breton, jobs certainly not as dull as factory work, but far more difficult and dangerous, jobs that lured farmers from their fields and fishermen from the sea. The mining attracted workers from abroad as well. Along with the new immigrants arriving, Premier Fielding was anxious to see outside money from investors also coming into the province. He was particularly fond of American money that would go toward developing the coal fields. Unfortunately, what he had not bargained on was the outside control that would go with it. As a result, coal production and attendant jobs would be at the mercy of distant corporate decision-makers and external economic factors that would play havoc with job security and with the lives of generations of Cape Breton men and women to come.

Social Reformers and Working-class Warriors

In 1899, when the Boer War broke out in far-off South Africa, it brought a revitalized sense of duty and allegiance to the British Empire in the still-heavily militarized city of Halifax. In 1900 a contingent of twelve hundred men, along with military horses, shipped off across the Atlantic to fight for territorial rights and expansion, although there was a patriotic and idealistic fervour attached to the event that made it seem more like a religious crusade. Halifax was perennially energized by military campaigns involving the British, and war never failed to bring profits and vitality to the old garrison town. The burst of military activity in Halifax for the Boer War was a mere foreshadowing of the commitment that would put the city in such a vital and pivotal role during the looming world war to come.

The new century also brought continued efforts to industrialize Nova Scotia. Manufacturing activity jumped nearly one hundred per cent in the frenzied first ten years. Coal mining in Westville, Springhill, Inverness and Glace Bay flourished, but often at the expense of the lives of coal miners. The Dominion Iron and Steel Company, with the capricious acronym DISCO, used coal to fire the furnaces and forge steel at its mills, and those of the Nova Scotia Steel and Coal Company, in Trenton and Sydney Mines. By 1910, the DISCO and Scotia mills were producing nearly one-half of all the steel in Canada. In terms of industrial development, it seemed that Nova Scotia had finally come of age.

Cape Breton Island was changed forever by this industrial boom, which would lead all too soon to a boom-and-bust cycle that at times was more crippling to the people of the island than was rural poverty. The *Sydney Post* declared the ghettos of industrial Cape Breton to be "a positive disgrace to the most filthy parts of Constantinople."

In 1901 33,000 men and 9,500 women worked at industrial jobs throughout the Maritime region. Trade unions came into existence and grew in influence and authority to enhance the rights and wages of these workers. Conflicts, including bloody strikes that looked like open warfare—class warfare—erupted as the interests of workers and the company owners proved to be in direct opposition.

The population in rural areas continued to decline as Nova Scotians moved into towns and cities, except in a few areas like the Annapolis Valley where apples were grown and then successfully marketed to far-flung parts of the British Empire. New progressive ideas found their way into many areas of agriculture, leading to the expansion of the Agricultural College in Truro and modernization of dairy and vegetable farms. But these efforts were not enough to keep young men and women from moving toward the brighter lights of the city, lured by the promise of progress, progress, progress.

Social and health reformers of the first part of the century concerned themselves with trying to eliminate alcoholism, smallpox, tuberculosis and venereal diseases. Tuberculosis alone was killing off at least two thousand people per year in the region. A provincial TB sanatorium was set up in Kentville in 1903, the first of its kind in the country.

The momentum of industrial change and social reform had finally caught up to Nova Scotia during this first decade but would not bloom into the full promise of everyone's expectations of health and wealth. Much of the ownership of the new industries was now outside of the region. Battle lines were being drawn between workers and their capitalist bosses and nowhere would the fighting be bloodier than in the coal-mining towns of Cape Breton.

Social reformers of the new century would continue with efforts to rescue the poor, curb drunkenness and end cruelty to women and children. They also called for better education, juvenile courts and improved city planning. They boldly hoped to improve the morals of Nova Scotian communities, too, by ending prostitution, pornography and even public swearing. Women were vitally active in these reform movements and it led to empowerment in other areas of education and employment as well. One ebullient Halifax feminist, Edith Archibald, stood before a cheering crowd in December of 1912 and announced, "Women of Nova Scotia! You stand today in the growing light of an early dawn of the most wondrous epoch that shall ever be."

As women were celebrating their new-found rights, boosters in the business community kept touting the advantages of industrialization with little regard for the fact that they were turning over the keys to the Maritime kingdom to outsiders who might not have their best interests at heart.

Gearing Up for War

Near the end of July, 1914, a new enthusiasm swept through the region as Canada was being drawn into the war in Europe. The patriotic fervour recently induced by the African Boer War was stirred up again. Soldiers were shuttled from Halifax to Sydney and on to Glace Bay to protect the Marconi wireless station there. This one small incident prompted the Halifax *Herald* to predict that Nova Scotia was about to be sucked into a war of such proportions that it would affect the lives of everyone in the province, even people living in Cape Breton, and far from the centre of military activity in Halifax.

In May of the following year, Halifax Harbour was already mined and soldiers of the Twenty-sixth Nova Scotia Battalion were aboard a converted Cunard steamship heading for battle in France. Many of the high-spirited men aboard felt that they were heading off on the greatest adventure of their lives, but many would return to this same harbour disillusioned and shattered physically or mentally from gruesome battles they were totally unprepared for.

Nova Scotians were unified in the war preparations as never before. Unemployment in many parts of the province disappeared almost overnight as industry geared up for war production and businesses prepared to provide services and supplies for soldiers. More than one Halifax entrepreneur would guiltily admit that the catastrophe in Europe inspired his sorrow but that this would not stop him from making a serious profit.

One man who reaped considerable financial rewards from the war was Thomas Cantley of the Nova Scotia Steel and Coal Company. In 1914, he geared up his shaky steel plant in Pictou County for making top-notch military ammunition. By 1916, he was manufacturing 300,000 shells a month at a fair profit. The war effort had far-reaching economic spin-offs for fishermen and farmers, the lumber industry and even builders of wooden ships. Economic optimism and patriotism melded together. Strikes declined dramatically and productivity increased.

As always, war would be good for Halifax, the city founded on military need. Unfortunately, there was a heavy price to be paid for the economic upswing. Death and destruction would not be limited to the battlefields of France. Halifax would feel the full impact of the war right here at home.

Chapter Thirty-three

"A Sound Past All Hearing"

SS Calonne, *damaged and forced into a wharf by the Halifax Explosion.*

Subs, Spies and Seventeen Million Tons of Cargo

Military activity in Halifax had been on the decline since the British pulled out their naval forces in 1906. As historian Joan Payzant puts it, "The Citadel, the Dockyard, the forts, and the batteries on the outskirts fell asleep, except for a few soldiers who were little more than caretakers." The city and much of the rest of Nova Scotia would soon come back to full alert when war was declared in August of 1914.

As the Canadian government centred its attentions on the war, money, men and machines poured into Halifax, the focal point for defence and embarkation of men and supplies to Europe. Submarine nets were stretched across the harbour. The water between Point Pleasant and McNab's Island was seeded with mines, while all manner of small boats, including fishing craft, were coaxed into use for mine-sweeping.

Canadian troop ships loaded up men at Pier 2 and they were sent off to a war they could little comprehend. Haligonians waved goodbye to Canada's young men, still healthy and in one piece and then, months later, returned to the harbourside to greet the survivors and also the casualties—the victims of this new technologically advanced warfare. Camp Hill Military Hospital opened in 1917 to help deal with the overflow of war casualties.

The same returning ships also brought along prisoners of war, who were relegated to the cold stone cellblocks of the Citadel or the prison on Melville Island, where now stands the genteel Armdale Yacht Club. One of the more famous guests of the Citadel prison during these years was Russian revolutionary Leon Trotsky, who predictably had little positive to say afterwards about his prison days in Halifax or Amherst.

There were persistent rumours of German spies walking the streets of Halifax and news of German subs within a stone's throw of the coast. Nova Scotian German families who had lived here for generations were often snubbed or viewed with suspicion. In my own coastal community of Lawrencetown, if a local resident with a German last name was seen standing on the headland gazing off to sea, he might openly be accused of spying or signalling those elusive German U-boats.

Submarines were a constant threat to shipping, and in 1917 a monumental effort was made to reduce the losses by sending ships across the Atlantic from Canada in protected convoys. Halifax was the perfect staging area for corralling a large number of ships in Bedford Basin. The ships then proceeded under escort across the open Atlantic. Between August and November of that year, over fifty convoys with more than five hundred ships steamed out of Halifax for Europe. From a commodity point of view, it was a spectacular feat, with something like seventeen million tons of cargo moving in and out of Halifax.

The Hourglass Harbour

When the U.S. declared war on Germany in 1917, the U.S. Navy became a frequent visitor to the harbour. An American sea-plane base was also established in Eastern Passage.

The Halifax–Dartmouth ferry service, the lifeline between the people on each side of the harbour, was working well over capacity, jam-packed with civilians, soldiers and military vehicles. Ships often blocked the ferry lanes and there were at least two collisions between ferries and large ships. Well before the big boom of the Halifax Explosion, boats and ships were bumping into each other in the impossibly heavy traffic.

There is a long list of bumps and scrapes, near misses, close calls and downright smash-ups in the harbour during World War I, but nothing rivals the collision that set off the Halifax Explosion of December 6, 1917.

The harbour has been described as an hourglass in shape. The main part of the harbour on the ocean side is ten kilometres long and two kilometres wide. The Narrows is about one kilometre in length and a mere 450 metres across. This opens up into Bedford Basin, six kilometres long and four kilometres wide. The Basin is where the convoys could safely assemble, well-protected from anything beyond the harbour mouth. Any incoming vessels would have to stop for clearance between Lighthouse Bank and McNab's Island. If everything went by the book, ships would pass in or out of the Narrows in a safe and orderly fashion. But as it turned out, the Narrows was not nearly wide enough to allow for human error.

A Grave Miscalculation

The *Mont Blanc* was a ship destined for Bordeaux, France, loaded to the gunwales with explosive cargo that included guncotton, 200 tons of TNT, 2,300 tons of wet and dry picric acid, and 35 tons of benzol in thin steel barrels loaded at the last minute lest any cargo space go unused. The *Mont Blanc* was not a new ship but it was considered serviceable in wartime when everything afloat was being put into the war effort. Owned by a French transport company, she was captained by Aimé Le Medec, with a crew of less than forty. Loaded with her tonnage of deadly cargo in New York, she was too slow to join the convoy going to Europe from there, so she headed north to Halifax, arriving on December 5.

A local pilot with twenty-four years' experience, Francis Mackey, came on board to usher her into the harbour. He didn't understand much French but had a good record of never having been involved in an accident. After being checked out by the naval authorities, the *Mont Blanc* was given permission to move through the Narrows to the Basin.

Leaving the Basin that morning and headed for New York was the *Imo*.

The *Imo* was a Belgian relief ship of Norwegian registry and had once been a passenger ship for the White Star Line. Now she was referred to as a "tramp steamer," but she was in good enough condition to be called into service for the war. Her captain was Haakon Fron and the local pilot was William Hayes. She should have left the previous day but there had been delays with the loading of coal.

The chain of events leading to the disaster began when an American tramp steamer entered the Narrows on the wrong side. Behind this ship was the *Stella Maris*, a 36.5-metre-long tug towing two barges. The *Imo* was on its way out to sea. The *Stella Maris* turned to avoid the oncoming *Imo* and found herself heading for the Dartmouth shore and directly into the path of the incoming *Mont Blanc*. There are conflicting reports as to who did what when both ships realized that a collision was imminent, but whatever the case, the *Imo* ended up ramming into the bow of the *Mont Blanc*. Archibald MacMechan, who had the honour of writing up the official reports on the ensuing city-wide disaster, suggests that the pilot of the *Imo* gave a critical order to change direction—in English—but it wasn't understood by the French crewmen. MacMechan reports that "the *Imo* came with great violence against the starboard bow of the *Mont Blanc* and crushed the plating to a depth of ten feet." Sparks from the collision set off a fire almost immediately. "Dense clouds of smoke rose into the still morning air, shot through with flashes of fierce red flame…"

The crew of the *Mont Blanc* might have been the only ones to realize just how dangerous the situation was. They abandoned ship and rowed their lifeboats like madmen toward Dartmouth as their vessel began to drift toward Halifax's blue-collar Richmond neighbourhood on the other shore. People along the waterfront in Halifax and Dartmouth could see the fire and knew there was trouble. Crowds gathered to watch.

Firefighters were ready to respond and sprung into action, while the noble captain of the *Stella Maris* left her barges and put a line onto the *Mont Blanc* to tow her away. HMS *Highflyer*, anchored nearby, sent a whaler and seven men to help. Also handy was HMCS *Niobe*, a sort of floating dormitory described by MacMechan as resembling "Noah's Ark." Men were dispatched in a tender to help in any way they could.

At this point, good intentions were not enough to avoid the inevitable— a gargantuan blast just seconds before 9:05 a.m. that would go down in the books as the single largest man-made explosion in the history of the earth until the dropping of the Hiroshima atom bomb. Novelist Hugh MacLennan was living in Halifax at the time and documented the horrific event in his novel *Barometer Rising*. He writes of the earthquake, "air-concussion" and tidal wave produced by the blast he describes as producing a "sound beyond hearing." The water opened up and the rock beneath the harbour transferred the shock onto the city, where the ground "rocked and reverberated, pavements split and houses swayed as the earth trembled." Up above ground, "the forced wall of air struck against Fort Needham and Richmond Bluff and shaved them clean."

According to Archibald MacMechan, the walloping blast vaporized the *Mont Blanc* in a "spray of metallic fragments." Metal shards rained down around the harbour and in the city along with a black oily precipitation. The ship's cannon was launched through the air and crashed down more or less intact three kilometres away on the Dartmouth side near Lake Albro, while her anchor went the other direction, landing even further away on the far side of the Halifax Peninsula beyond the Northwest Arm. The *Stella Maris* and her poor crew were catapulted into the air and crashed down near Pier 6. All who had been aboard were killed.

The *Highflyer* and *Niobe* suffered serious damage but immediately sent crews ashore to help fight fires and treat victims of the debacle. At the sugar refinery wharf, longshoremen were unloading a ship named the *Picton* when the shock wave slammed into them, killing most, shredding their clothing and blackening their bodies with the oil-laden rain. Ships all around the harbour sustained damage. The *Imo* was shoved aground near Tuft's Cove in Dartmouth. Amazingly, there were survivors aboard, including the helmsmen and ship's dog who refused to leave and howled long after the disaster.

In the Path of the Shock Wave

A hundred kilometres away in Truro people heard the blast. Plates were rattled in Charlottetown, PEI, and houses shook in Sydney, three hundred and twenty kilometres away. A mushroom cloud, not dissimilar to a nuclear blast, vaulted two miles up into the sky. Some say the blast momentarily swept clean to the bottom of the harbour, making the harbour floor visible. Rocks were ripped from the bottom and shot up into the sky only to fall back to earth in what seemed like a deadly meteor shower. The explosion set in motion a tidal wave measuring at least four and a half metres high. It crashed up onto the shores of Halifax and swept up the hill of the North End of the city. On its way, it tore up piers and pilings, smashing tugs and small boats, depositing them on the lower streets. As the water drained back toward the harbour, it carried hundreds of unwary victims to a watery grave.

Citadel Hill acted as a barrier to buffer the effect of the explosion and somewhat protected the well-to-do families living in the South End of Halifax. But the working-class North End, the Richmond area in particular, had no such protection. Very few houses were left standing. Entire families were killed, some trapped in collapsing houses, others caught in the raging fires that ensued as stoves burning coal or oil tumbled over. All around the city, people were blinded or otherwise injured by flying glass as windows shattered.

The North End railway yards were in the direct path of the shock wave. Railroad engines were picked up like toys and tossed. Rails were ripped up and the steel bent into odd and fantastic shapes. The railway station had a glass roof which collapsed onto passengers waiting below.

The collateral damage of the event would take weeks, months and in some cases, years to repair. Electric and phone lines were down. Gas was cut off from the North End to prevent further fires and explosions. A huge volume of natural gas was lost when the enormous holding tank near the South End of town had massive metal plates sheared off. Miraculously, the vapour did not ignite, but rose upward into the atmosphere, sparing most of the South End from a fate similar to that of the North. The sugar refinery near the Narrows, however, was decimated, collapsing on its employees or trapping them in the fire, as "syrup-soaked timbers" were torched.

"Dartmouth in Ruins"

Miracles of survival abound in the midst of this horror. Two ferries were making the crossing at the time of the blast and, while some passengers were injured by flying glass, no one was killed. Dorothy Chisholm was on the ferry, making her way from Dartmouth to work at the Royal Bank in Halifax that morning. She remembers first seeing the fire on the *Mont Blanc* and then feeling the blast, but the ferry apparently kept right on its way to Halifax. She reported for work but was told to go home, and on the way back, observed fires throughout the North End. Joan Payzant, in *Like a Weaver's Shuttle*, logs an account of great understatement by one ferry worker, Charles Pearce, who entered the following into his diary:

> Dec. 6: Weather Fine
> Mr. W. Pearce, Machinist on *Chebucto* until the Great Explosion, then went home to fasten up windows and doors.
> Frank Green—Extra help on *Chebucto* until 9 a.m. went home badly hurt by the explosion.
> Ferry steamers kept running all night.
> Ferry Boats and property badly damaged.
> City of Dartmouth in ruins. Everybody boarding up windows and doors.

Loyal to their jobs, many ferry workers saw the importance of their task to keep people moving that day and stayed on rather than going home to check on their own families.

At the Royal Naval College in the Dockyard, a class overlooking the harbour had been watching the burning *Mont Blanc* when the window shattered and sprayed glass into the faces of the unwary students. While the

junior class on the far side of the building escaped serious injury, the building shook hard as wood and plaster smashed down around them. Cadet
Orde, Petty Officer King and Captain MacKenzie received serious damage
to the eyes from the flying glass.

It was a bloody, ravaged crew of cadets who marched themselves first to
the Naval Hospital, then the Military Hospital on Cogswell and finally to
the Camp Hill Hospital seeking medical help. At every stop the scene was
one of overcrowding. Hospital staff tried desperately to move out anyone
who was not seriously injured—this mainly included those not dying of
bleeding or in need of removal of a severely injured eye. Petty Officer King
had succumbed to shock and appeared to be dead to the examining medical
staff. He was sent to an emergency morgue at Chebucto School, where he
awoke and grabbed a passing soldier who was thoroughly shocked.

Families near the hospital took in strangers in need of a place to stay close
to medical services. MacMechan reported the typical case of a widow, herself badly wounded by glass, who lived near the hospital with her two daughters. Her home had sustained major damage and most of the windows were
shattered, but she readily volunteered to take care of a wounded stranger
with serious eye injuries who required hourly medical attention. She and her
daughters gave up their bedrooms to this man and his parents who arrived to
care for him while they "slept where they could."

A Train Ride into Hell

The night express train from Saint John was a fortunate ten minutes late
coming into the Halifax North End station, missing the full impact of the
blast that devastated the station that was so close to the harbour. Even at its
location in Rockingham, the train nearly derailed. Windows broke but there
were few injuries. As they drew nearer the city, the train slowed and injured
people came seeking assistance. More than two hundred explosion survivors
were loaded on board where passengers tore up table cloths and bed sheets
to make bandages for all the bloody wounded.

Other passengers left the train to search for survivors in the burning
houses, sometimes rooting through rubble with their bare hands or using
train axes, saws or boards to pry up fallen walls. One of the passengers was
Colonel E.C. Phinney who organized rescue crews that saved between forty
and sixty Haligonians. They went from house to house as the fires raged.
Phinney himself saw a boy with a rivet though his right eye and two shrap-
nel-like pieces of metal from the *Mont Blanc* imbedded in his chest and
thigh. Although the young man's death was imminent, he told Phinney
quite clearly that he was in no pain.

The conductor, J.C. Gillespie, took on coal and water and then headed
the train for Truro with one doctor, Major DeWitt from Wolfville, on board.

DeWitt began to perform operations as they trundled along, removing irreparable eyes with forceps and scissors. In Truro most of the doctors had been dispatched to Halifax and DeWitt had to rely on himself and the few other doctors arriving from rural areas. He worked for five days, nearly nonstop, day and night, before returning home to Wolfville with a hand infection and total exhaustion, only to find he was needed in nearby Camp Aldershot for more surgery.

A City on Fire

The Wellington Barracks, up the slope from the Dockyard, was hit hard by the blast. It contained an ammunition magazine, and many feared it too would set off a second explosion. Lt. C.A. McLennan pulled together sixteen men to put out the fire that had begun there. He discovered that a three-hundred-kilogram chunk of the *Mont Blanc* had slammed into the iron fence around the magazine. But he also noticed damage to the magazine itself. The furnace room adjacent to the ammo had a smashed door and roof. The damage had allowed the spread of the fire that had been burning in the furnace and indeed a second major blast could have sent another shudder of great intensity through this part of the city. MacLennan, assisted by Private W. Eisnor, put out the fire with extinguishers and staved off another potential calamity.

At the North Ordinance, another depository of ammunition, nearby fires on land and shipboard prompted the military leaders to order their men to start dumping ammunition into the harbour. They did this for a while, until some felt it was too great a waste of good materials, so they piled it by the water's edge just in case they had to dump it in the drink.

Fires burned everywhere and no city fire department could have been equipped to control the flames. The fireboat *Patricia* had gone to aid the *Mont Blanc* only to be decimated when the blast hit, killing all but one of the men aboard, William Wells, who was thrown ashore, slammed into a post and was nearly drowned by the ensuing wave that rushed up the slopes of Halifax.

There was not much wind but fires spread nonetheless from the ruins of many houses and buildings in flames. While Halifax firefighters did what they could to save the lives of anyone left in buildings, they were soon aided by firemen who raced to Halifax from as far away as Amherst, Springhill, Truro and New Glasgow.

False Rumours and a Trail of Blood

By ten a.m. that same morning, rumours spread that a second explosion from one of the ammunition magazines was inevitable and this ignited a panic in civilian and military circles. Everyone was instructed to evacuate both Halifax and Dartmouth. As MacMechan stated, "There was nothing vague about the rumour. The definite statement was conveyed by soldiers through the streets." They went door to door and turned back the curious onlookers and would-be rescuers headed to the most damaged parts of the city. Houses were to be abandoned in favour of open spaces, where one would at least not be killed by falling buildings. Having just witnessed the most horrific event of their lives, most Haligonians followed orders.

The sites for assembly were the Commons, Point Pleasant Park, the sides of Citadel Hill, Halifax Golf Club, the sporting field at Dalhousie University and the locale of today's Armdale Rotary. The Armoury building at the corner of Cunard and North Park was a focal point for both rescue parties and for channelling human traffic to the supposedly safe areas.

Was the evacuation order a mistake? In the sense that many victims trapped in buildings would not be saved, yes. But even though the second explosion did not occur, the cautionary move may have made perfectly good sense at the time. In his report, MacMechan tried to get at the root of the evacuation orders and found it unclear as to which officer had issued the statements. "A heavy responsibility rests on the officer who gave them," he says. Perhaps the details were covered up, once the order was discovered to be a mistake. Nonetheless, soldiers travelled about town insisting that people leave their homes and most obeyed.

MacMechan goes so far as to call the second alarm a "second disaster." Bedridden old people, as well as the sick and injured, were forced to go out into the open, where many were laid down on the ground. Certainly some of the explosion victims died as a result of being moved out into the cold. As one observer stated about the path of travel to any of the open-air gathering points, "The route could be traced by the trail of blood."

Chapter Thirty-four

Aftermath of the
Halifax Explosion

***Devastation at the corner of Kaye and Gottingen streets caused by the
explosion.***

The Walking Wounded

By eight o'clock at night on the day of the explosion, a city of tents was set up on the Commons as temporary housing, but most of the explosion refugees were reluctant to stay there. Many preferred to return to their own damaged houses or stay in public buildings. It was December, after all, and despite the military warnings and the intended goodwill, to many Haligonians, it still seemed to make good sense to get inside.

There was a general feeling of terror that a second blast might equal or exceed the first. No one in Halifax or Nova Scotia—or the world for that matter—had ever experienced a blast of such proportion. This fear hung around for a day or more, sending people out wandering the streets or even walking miles into the countryside to get away from the danger zone. The streets themselves were scenes of horror, with anguished wails of pain coming from the blinded or maimed victims stumbling around. Men, women and children with burns and gashes were a common sight on the streets. Everywhere, people were trying to help the victims. The shock of the blast had not stunned most Haligonians enough to suppress their feelings of compassion.

Survivors Seeking Help

While much has been reported about the death toll and destruction in Halifax, it should be remembered that Dartmouth too took heavy damage.

The stories of the survivors are well documented, thanks to MacMechan's records and the research undertaken by numerous writers, including Janet Kitz, author of *Shattered City*. The event left powerful haunting memories for the children living near the harbour. Pearl Hartlen was nine at the time of the explosion. Her house collapsed and her unconscious mother was buried under the debris. According to MacMechan, she dragged her mother to safety and, when her mother's dress caught on something, Pearl had to rip the cloth with her teeth to free her. Agnes Foran, twelve, lived on Merkel Street in Halifax. She was looking through the front windows with her mother when the glass shattered, knocking them both to the floor. Agnes led her now-blinded mother downstairs and then returned for her baby brother. She could find no one in the neighbourhood to help and waited until her father arrived at 1:30 in the afternoon to take them to the hospital. It wasn't until later that afternoon that a huge glass fragment in Agnes's stomach, which required removal and twenty-nine stitches, was discovered .

Kids who were in school fared better than those at home on those days, but the Bloomfield School, situated close to the harbour, was pretty hard hit. At St. Joseph's School near the Wellington Barracks, the attic roof toppled on a grade-eight class below and then crashed onto the floor below that. Sister Maria Cecilia McGrath was entombed with most of her class in the wreckage and yet most of them emerged relatively unscathed. She somehow managed to locate her students by groping along what was left of the floor joists. She then led them out the window and helped them climb down one and a half storeys. Other students were rescued by soldiers. By the time Sister Maria left the school and went to check on her own home, she saw her mother engulfed in the flames of her house.

As a result of the Halifax Explosion, 25,000 people were without shelter and more than 6,000 had their homes completely destroyed. The damage was estimated at $35 million in 1917 dollars. Official claims suggest there were 1,963 killed and 9,000 injured although these figures are considered low and not necessarily accurate. Many of those on ships in the harbour had simply disappeared without a trace. Some estimate the death toll closer to 3,000, but a final and absolute statistic will probably never be known.

As was so often the case in Nova Scotia history, weather was to further complicate an already catastrophic circumstance brought on by man. December 6, a Thursday, was sunny and calm, but it snowed that night and by the next morning the weather had turned to a frigid blizzard with forty centimetres of snow. It snowed all day Friday and Saturday and on Sunday gale winds splattered the city with freezing rain, turning the streets to sheets of ice. On Monday, December 10, more snow returned with high winds. All of this hindered the efforts of rescue workers and aid volunteers trying to make their way to Halifax and out into the streets to help the multitude of victims.

People from across Canada and beyond were ready and willing to lend what assistance they could, despite the weather. The Red Cross in Saint John was the first to assemble major outside assistance, gathering medical supplies and volunteers and putting them on a train for Halifax. The Ottawa Red Cross shipped down eight train cars full of clothing.

Relief trains from Truro, the South Shore and the Annapolis Valley brought medical help and supplies. Moncton and Charlottetown sent supplies and personnel and more assistance was on its way from Massachusetts, Maine and Rhode Island. Financial aid even found its way here from Australia and New Zealand. Two ships from Boston soon headed north with glass, building materials and twenty-five glaziers aboard to try and repair some of the damage to homes.

"That Arch Fiend, the Emperor of the Germans"

Before anyone fully understood why the explosion had occurred, there was a wave of rising anti-German sentiment. Many still thought that the devastation was a German act of sabotage or some kind of planned attack. It seemed that the compassion, kindness and generosity shown toward the victims of the explosion was soon replaced in Halifax by prejudice in the extreme toward anyone with a German-sounding last name.

One headline a few days after the explosion stated flat out, "Practically All the Germans in Halifax Are To Be Arrested."

Michael Bird, in his book *The Town That Died,* reports that "Men, women and children, with names like Richter or Schultz, were stoned in the streets or chased by angry crowds that were largely made up of people who, only a week earlier, had been friendly neighbours." There were even rumours that some families of German descent had underground gun emplacements to aid in some mythical German invasion or that some of these families had prepared themselves for the blast, having been informed ahead of time.

The newspapers helped increase the animosity with stories playing on the fears and hatred that arose. On December 12, the *Herald* ran an editorial concerning the explosion that said, "We now know, too, that the prime responsibility for this, as for every other catastrophe which has afflicted the peoples of the earth as a by-product of the war, rests with that close co-partner, that arch fiend, the Emperor of the Germans…"

The editorial went on to discuss "certain people of German extraction and birth…who have repaid us within the past few days by laughing openly at our distress and mocking our sorrow."

All of this hate-mongering probably didn't do much to alleviate any of the suffering or get at the root of understanding what went wrong and who was to blame. It did, however, help to bolster support for the war against Germany, even though this blast was undoubtedly only indirectly a result of warfare in Europe.

The explosion fostered a more vivid sense of the calamity of actual warfare: no other city in North America in the twentieth century would know firsthand the ravages of modern war as did Halifax.

Rebuilding a City

By December 13, an official inquiry was underway in Halifax and Justice Arthur Drysdale heard testimony that the *Imo* had not been given permission to leave port. It was also revealed that the ship pilots in the harbour didn't always follow instructions. However, when it came to pinning the blame on someone, charges were laid against Aimé Le Medec, captain of the *Mont Blanc,* and his local pilot, Francis Mackey, as well as naval Commander Whyatt, who was considered negligent. Amazingly all three had survived the blast. They were now arrested on charges of manslaughter but immediately released on bail and charges were dropped three weeks later. Mackey was allowed to continue on as a pilot and Le Medec went back to work for his French shipping company. Whyatt was posted elsewhere for military duties.

A royal commission made the tardy and obvious recommendation for changes to the Halifax Pilotage Authority. The owners of the *Imo* were sued by the owners of the *Mont Blanc* and then issued a counter-suit. This rattled around in the Canadian courts for a while until the Supreme Court of Canada ruled that they were both to blame.

The Halifax Relief Commission was in charge of rebuilding the city. It was a powerful governmental force that was not dissolved until as recently as 1976. It appropriated land in the North End and oversaw thirty million dollars in relief aid. Decisions were often made with little or no public input.

The first job was to clear the rubble of the North End neighbourhoods—a job that took 450 men and three months. It would look like a lifeless, strip-mined piece of earth. Many former residents refused to return, some believing it was a cursed or haunted area. Although the Halifax Relief Commission created short-lived wooden apartment buildings—tenements really—the construction of more permanent housing didn't begin until 1918 when Thomas Adams, an English town planner, drew up plans for street alignment, parks and the distinctive "Hydrostone" housing that still exists in that part of Halifax today. The Hydrostone was a dense concrete block manufactured by an American company in Dartmouth. The cost of one of these abodes was from $1,800 to $2,500 and the housing was completed by 1921. As a result of the damage and the reconstruction, much of the physical city of Halifax was changed forever. The scars left in the bodies and memories of her residents, however, remained to haunt the survivors right up to the end of the century.

Chapter Thirty-five

Rum and Rum-runners

"The Soldiers' Smoking Room" in *Halifax*; Canadian Illustrated News, 1872.

A Province Afloat on Rum

Prohibition created wonderful opportunities for adventure and prosperity for hundreds of Nova Scotians. Commonly known as rum-running, the business was at once illegal, glamorous and respectable in many ports on the South Shore and along the Bay of Fundy. Rum-running was motivated by more than mere opportunism, I might argue, for booze—rum, in particular—has played a meaningful role in shaping Nova Scotia. In fact, rum had been popular in this province for well over three hundred years. Rum had been on hand with the earliest naval expeditions and had remained an integral part of the daily life of the English and Canadian navy men anchored in Halifax Harbour or having their fun ashore.

The beverage that was once viewed on these shores as a kind of medicinal and social luxury evolved into a necessity and over the years created economic prosperity, cultural identity and social havoc. When the legendary *Bluenose* would finally meet her fate in 1946, appropriately enough, a good portion of her cargo would be rum.

Nova Scotian rum historian James Moreira, in *Tempered by Rum*, goes so far as to suggest of rum that "It has made and lost fortunes; it has won and lost elections; it has fuelled riots and provided comfort in the wake of disaster; it has been a factor in rebellion and, by not completely patriotic means, it has even been a source of loyalty." Moreira and other Nova Scotian history professors have even gathered in large forums to discuss the impact of rum on Nova Scotia and have concluded that it is profound.

Rum was never manufactured here until recent times. Instead, it probably originated in the sixteenth century on West Indian plantations when discarded molasses and cane juice from the sugar mills fermented in ponds into a kind of funky beer that was drunk by the slaves, who were looking for whatever form of escape was possible from their cruel owners. Soon, white entrepreneurs were distilling the fermented goo and shipping it to New England, Nova Scotia and Newfoundland. Rum rations began on British naval ships in 1655 after the capture of Jamaica. There was mention of rum at Port Royal in 1710 and Colonel Samuel Vetch was annoyed by the high cost of the beverage for his men in 1711 but he said it was a necessity in place of "beer, which the severity of the winter freezes."

Issuing rum to sailors became a standard practice and it was pretty strong stuff doled out at a half-pint per man, not to be watered down to "grog" in a three to one mix until 1740, when it was becoming obvious that drunkenness was reducing the effectiveness of the military. Rum was part of the trade going to Louisbourg and it found its way to the Acadians in various parts of the province. Halifax, however, became the city that floated on rum. New Englanders who were in the liquor importing business found it a very receptive and thirsty port. To lure settlers, the English were offering an allowance of nearly four gallons per person per year. As if that wasn't enough, the sale of rum became big business in the growing city. A man named George Hick gave up blacksmithing to sell it by the quart. He boasted, "I sell rum by the quart and smaller quantities. I buy it at 3s. a gallon, and lays [sic] out two guineas a week in it, by which I get fast money." Mr. Hick would be followed by a legion of booze vendors, legal and otherwise, who would profit from rum in Nova Scotia.

It was Joshua Mauger, the "Agent Victualler" for the navy, who made the biggest killing, founding his own Halifax distillery in 1751. Some believe he became so wealthy and powerful that the first legislative council here was made up of men he hand-picked. Despite his government contract, he brewed with smuggled molasses, trading with French and Dutch islands alike.

Since Halifax became a kind of warehouse for supplies during the American Revolution, rum again allowed some entrepreneurs from this tipsy city to profit heartily from the trade. During the years of immigration that followed, rum was a part of everyday commerce and seen as a reward for hard work. Licensed merchants and tavern keepers sold it in pints or quarts in black glass bottles or in the economy-size three-gallon stone jug. Five- or ten-gallon kegs could be had at a favourable discount. In a nineteenth-century Halifax tavern you could still buy a cheap "gill" (quarter pint!) from the keg on the bar or have your rum in a punch, a flip (a hot drink) or "folded" into a spruce beer. Gin and brandy were available but much more expensive. Beer just wasn't as popular as the rum and there was still that problem of it freezing on inhospitable Victorian winter nights.

A working day for many labourers involved a rum break at eleven a.m. and one at four p.m. It was sometimes a factor in labour negotiations. Joseph Salter, for example, was willing to give his men a shorter work day if they promised to stay sober on the job of building his wharf. For others, it was considered to be of great value to the maintenance of one's health.

Despite the so-called therapeutic effects, drinking rum produced plenty of family abuse, brawls and even street riots brought on by drunkenness or arguments over the quality of rum. The backlash to all this Nova Scotian booze gave birth to the temperance movement, with societies popping up all over the region by the middle of the nineteenth century. "The demon rum" was now given a very bad reputation by well-meaning religious men and a growing force of women who wanted an all-out prohibition. Battle lines were drawn between the "wet" and the "dry." Tales were told of the destruction— including spontaneous self-combustion—of those who drank too much. For those who converted, oaths like the following could be heard in the jail cells:

If ever I gain my liberty
    that enemy will I shun

Street walking and bad company,
and likewise drinking rum.

Booze Wars and Big Money

Temperance societies proved to be a valuable springboard for all manner of
social reform and helped women to gain some political power. Prohibition-
type legislation came and went, including a province-wide act after the First
World War that could not successfully curtail the great tradition, but stayed
on the books all the way until 1929.

During those dark (or enlightened, if you wish) days of prohibition, liquor
was supposedly available "for medical purposes" only. People bearing booze
were occasionally arrested, but the law did little to interfere with the most
profitable of the bootleggers and the smugglers.

The big profits, however, were to be had from engaging in the smuggling
of booze into the U.S. In 1920, the Americans saw the passage of the
Volstead Act calling for total prohibition. As another rum historian, D.A.
Walker, asserts, "An era of unprecedented organized crime began and millions of usually law-abiding citizens became criminals." New supply avenues
would open up to accommodate the illegal cargo and one of the main
sources would be the French island of St. Pierre. Nova Scotians would be
among the primary players in this smuggling racket, initially hauling booze
in fishing schooners from England and Europe to the U.S. and later opening
up the supply route from St. Pierre to various East Coast destinations.

Along the South Shore, fish prices had been dropping. The same quintal
of cod that brought $13.62 in 1918 was fetching only $6.25 by 1927. The
number of vessels actively fishing dropped in ports like Lunenburg as it
became less profitable to fish and harder to even make a meagre living. The
rum-running business came at a good time for South Shore fishermen who
were being squeezed out of a livelihood by the slump in the fish market.

The schooners which started up the rum-running trade proved too slow
eventually for the U.S. Coast Guard as it geared up for an all-out war using
former naval destroyers to track and nab Bluenose smugglers. The new
American ships proved to be a challenge for Nova Scotian rum-runners, but
the local boat builders were ready to meet the test. The first U.S. destroyer
to get involved in the war on booze, the *Henley*, went into service in 1924
and a fleet of twenty-four more would be commissioned, including former
sub-chasers. The first of the new boats designed as rum-runners capable of
evading these naval monsters saw action in 1926.

Nova Scotian boat builders were probably never in a happier disposition.
Twenty-five craft were made exclusively for this new purpose in Meteghan,
Shelburne, Mahone Bay, Lunenburg, Liverpool, Dayspring and elsewhere. A
true rum-runner was long and low (when loaded) and probably painted

grey—for obvious reasons. It was a wooden boat with a low deckhouse and slightly more formidable wheelhouse. An average runner might be 31.5 metres in length, 6.5 metres wide at the centre. It was built to haul maximum cargo but with a profile as low to the water as possible. Although these boats often had substantial Fairbanks-Morse engines, they were not particularly fast. Cruising speeds would only run at about ten knots. They were also slim, making them somewhat shaky in rough seas. Close to American shores, they met up with the faster forty-knot boats that would scoot the goods ashore before the Coast Guard could show up.

Lacking speed, the Nova Scotian runners used whatever means they could to avoid getting caught if detected, including the environmentally unfriendly method of spewing out a smoke screen from a smoke generator or stuffing oily rags into the engine exhaust.

"Once a Scrapper..."

The story of the Bluenose rum-runners is one of fact, fancy and legend. Lives were lost, great fortunes were made and there was a general sense of high-spirited daring and adventure. For the most part, it was an amoral business entered into by fishermen who saw their traditional livelihood dwindling because of economic factors at work outside the boundaries of Nova Scotia. It may have been a way of fighting back, of making a fortune or asserting the defiant and independent spirit that has always been kin to these men of the sea. Perhaps no one embodies this spirit more than rum-runner *par excellence* Jack Randell.

In his lively book *Bluenose Justice*, Dean Jobb captures the story of Jack Randell of Lunenburg, whose motto was "once a scrapper, always a scrapper." Randell didn't have one of the fancy new specially designed rum-running vessels. Instead, his boss, Big Jamie Clark, had purchased the 38-metre schooner *I'm Alone* for $18,000. It was rigged with a pair of no-nonsense hundred-horsepower diesel engines, just in case the winds weren't favourable or if she needed to run for her life from the U.S. Coast Guard. Randell was a seasoned skipper and couldn't turn down the $500 per month that Clark would pay him to haul rum far away to the warmer parts of the States.

Randell was happy to get the work rather than sit idle all winter and so, in November of 1928, he sailed the *I'm Alone* to St. Pierre, loaded up 1,500 cases of good booze and turned her south. Of course, his job was not to actually run the goods ashore but to meet up with his contacts twenty kilometres off the Louisiana coast. Once in the warm Gulf waters, he unloaded his first shipment and then set about finding new suppliers of freight (alcoholic, of course) from British Honduras, rather than lugging the goods all the way from northerly St. Pierre.

The Coast Guard, however, was catching on to his activities and he had to use his best nautical skills to outsmart them on several occasions. Then on March 20 of 1929, Randell brought his ship to a stop at a rendezvous point which he reckoned to be about twenty-four kilometres off the American coast. On board was more than sixty thousand dollars' worth of assorted refreshments for the parched American shore dwellers. Much to his chagrin, he saw the Coast Guard vessel *Wolcott* approach, prompting Randell to weigh anchor and prepare to outrun his adversary. The *Wolcott* closed in and hailed Captain Randell. Randell did not respond and so the *Wolcott* fired over her bow and issued an order to stop. Randell would have none of it and yelled back over a megaphone that he was in international waters and could not legally be stopped.

Three hours of further pursuit and Randell finally agreed to let the skipper of the *Wolcott*, Frank Paul, board to discuss the matter. Unarmed and in his slippers, Paul boarded the *I'm Alone* and told Randell he had been within the twelve-mile limit of the United States. The Coast Guard, he argued, had a legal right of pursuit to chase and seize the vessel. Randell couldn't be persuaded by the cool logic of the Coast Guard captain and he allowed Paul to return to his ship. Both boats kept heading south until Paul grew frustrated and signalled that he was going to fire if Randell didn't stop. True to his word, the *Wolcott* began firing shells at the schooner and the Coast Guard sailors opened fire with rifles as well.

Jack Randell was struck in the leg by a wax bullet and his ship's sails and rigging had already sustained some damage, but he couldn't quite be convinced that he should admit defeat to this pestering American. The *Wolcott*'s big deck gun had jammed by then and she gave up the pursuit on the twenty-second of March and turned the chase over to Captain Powell of the *Dexter*. The *Dexter* unloaded shells, machine-gun bullets and rifle ammunition into the Lunenburg schooner until it had nowhere to go but down. One of Randell's men drowned as they abandoned ship, but the rest were picked up by the Coast Guard.

Despite the fact that Randell had obviously been carrying liquor destined to come ashore in Louisiana, he swore innocence and even demanded retribution for what he declared as this "cowardly attack." Charged with conspiracy, Randell fumed in his New Orleans cell. Word eventually reached Canada about what had happened and the good skipper became a kind of celebrity. One paper called him "an international hero for upholding British naval tradition on the high seas." Well, that might have been stretching it a bit, but Ottawa politicians jumped on the cause, calling the sinking "piracy" and even "an act of war." After all, the *I'm Alone* was a humble sailing vessel from Lunenburg, Nova Scotia. Was Ottawa really ready to go to war with the U.S. to protect a smuggler's rights?

Not quite. But protest shouts from Canada were heard as far away as Washington for this grave infringement of the international law of the sea.

The case of conspiracy was dropped, and in 1935 the American government apologized with words and money—$25,000 worth—for sinking the *I'm Alone*. Randell had returned to Canada but continued to work as a skipper, this time of a steamship on the Great Lakes.

Chapter Thirty-six

The Bluenose

Crew of the Bluenose (and a few visitors) at dockside in Halifax.

"A Triumph of Americanism"

The official lifespan of the sailing ship *Bluenose* ran from March 6, 1921, to January 28, 1946. It was built to race in a high-profile sailing competition for the North Atlantic Fishermen's International Trophy, which was a pretty big deal for all who lived along this coast, Americans and Canadians alike. But she was never just an élite racing schooner; the *Bluenose* was also built to be a true fishing vessel and she worked the Grand Banks, bringing tons of fish back to her home port, Lunenburg.

Sailing in races had generally been the game of big men with big money. Fishermen sailing daily for a living might have envied the sailors on the flashy racing vessels but secretly many harboured the thought that "real sailors" were a tougher breed, undoubtedly more seaworthy, more sea-knowledgeable and more resilient than anybody else scudding the North Atlantic waves. Around 1920 news arrived north about a race off Sandy Hook, New Jersey, that had been postponed because of so-called strong winds, a mere twenty-three-knot gale. Sailors on fishing vessels in New England, Newfoundland and Nova Scotia thought this show of cowardice absurd and ached for a chance to compete.

William Dennis, owner of the Halifax *Herald* and *Evening Mail*, convinced some of his friends to put up some money to create a competition for fishing schooners that would far outshine the élitist America's Cup. The first two races were held off Halifax and the third near Gloucester, Massachusetts. The rules stated that ships must be genuine working vessels.

In the first elimination race in Canada, Thomas Himmelman in the *Delawana* beat out Angus Walters in his *Gilbert B. Walters*, when Walters lost a mast. In October of that year, the *Delawana* took on the American *Esperanto*, captained by Marty Welch, a "whitewashed Yankee" originally from Digby. The races in a best-of-three series were set off Halifax. The *Esperanto* won. In the second race, Welch took a chance by taking to the shoals off Devil's Island to win the race. The *Esperanto* had been constructed for short hauls and quick trips to sea, nothing like the high-capacity Lunenburg schooners designed for longer trips and bigger catches. The *Esperanto* returned to Gloucester to a hero's welcome and a hail from vice-president Calvin Coolidge who boasted that "the victory was a triumph of Americanism."

Nova Scotians, particularly the fishermen who worked the Banks and the landlubbers who had wagered on the races, were angry and wanted an honest revenge. It was a matter of both money and pride. Revenge, however, came from the Atlantic itself and there would never be a chance to beat the *Esperanto* in a race. She sank with 140,000 pounds of salt cod, while fishing off Sable Island in 1921. The ship struck the wreck of the SS *Virginia* and the crew abandoned her and were picked up by another fishing vessel, the

Elsie. Three attempts were made to bring the *Esperanto* back up out of the ten fathoms of sea water, but it turned out that it would be the *Elsie* herself that would be the American vessel to defend the title when October of that year rolled around.

A Conflict of Interests

Meanwhile, Nova Scotians were preparing a new faster ship to meet the challenge of whatever American vessel would take up the challenge for the next race. At a cost of $35,000, the *Bluenose* was built by Captain Angus Walters and four Halifax investors. Walters turned down the offer to actually captain the vessel, since he was making good money as a working captain of his *Gilbert B. Walters*, which had paid for itself twice over in its first season at sea. The man knew how to make money at fishing like no one else and he was reluctant to give up until he had garnered for himself a controlling share of the *Bluenose*. Then a deal was struck. He would have final say about nearly everything concerning the building and running of the schooner.

A naval architect named Bill Roue (who also ran a family ginger-ale business in Halifax) was commissioned to design the schooner that would be built at the Smith and Rhuland Shipyards in Lunenburg. Roue's innovative ideas concerning the design met some flak from the shipbuilders but they eventually settled on an agreeable shape and, in December of 1920, the keel-laying ceremony was underway. The Duke of Devonshire had come to Lunenburg to take part by driving a gold spike with a silver mallet. The Duke had perhaps over-socialized a bit the night before and missed the gold spike a few times, leaving someone else to finish the job. After that, the shipbuilding moved full speed ahead. By March of 1921, the *Bluenose* was complete and ready to launch on the twenty-sixth.

Marty Welch was back in the 1921 race, this time with the *Elsie*. The event was of passionate interest to people near and far. Perhaps the most intense audience, however, was the one gathered on Sackville Street in Halifax where wires were stretched between two buildings and models of the *Bluenose* and the *Elsie* were run along to show the respective positions at sea in the actual races. The jam-packed crowd cheered as they watched this bizarre little display that was updated by wireless reports coming in from the coast.

The *Bluenose* won and took home the cup and the $5,000. Her owners moved on to another battle, this one with the taxman over whether the winnings were taxable. When it came to money, it seemed the *Bluenose* owners were quite anxious to hang onto what they won and miserly in doling it out. Even Bill Roue had to put up a fight to get paid for designing the wondrous ship. (Later in his career, however, he would make really big money designing the less glamorous sectional barge, which was widely used in World War II.)

In 1922, the *Henry Ford* was up against the *Bluenose*. Named for the famous car manufacturer, it hadn't completed the full fishing season by race time but was allowed to race anyway. The first race was thrown out, the *Ford* won the second, but the *Bluenose* went on to win the third and necessary fourth race. More bitter squabbling attended this series of races, though, as a great deal of money was riding in bets. Angus Walters's nephew Bert (Boodle) Demone made the mistake of going ashore to celebrate and he was later found dead, drowned in the harbour. The *Bluenose* sailed home with her flag at half mast.

The 1923 series was also marred by bad feelings. The American entry, the *Columbia*, had been struck by a trawler and later hit a rock ledge before she even made it to the race. She, too, was not a regular working sailing ship but was allowed to race. In the first race, the *Columbia* forced the *Bluenose* into the dangerous Sambro ledges and the *Bluenose's* main boom jammed into the *Columbia's* rigging. Nonetheless, the *Bluenose* won the first and second race and held her title, only to have it challenged by the Americans who protested over which side of the marker buoys the *Bluenose* had passed on. The International Race Committee then gave the title to the *Columbia*, causing Angus Walters to lose his cool and tell them all to go to hell as he walked away. The befuddled committee told the *Columbia* captain to simply sail the course one more time and be declared the winner. Instead, the *Columbia's* Captain Pine set sail for home. The $5,000 prize money ended up being split between the two ships as a compromise.

Back to the Grand Banks

The Halifax interests were angry at Angus Walters for leaving the race and asked Bill Roue to build a new ship that could beat the *Bluenose*. Roue constructed the *Haligonian* in Shelburne, but in 1926 it was defeated twice by the *Bluenose*.

The *Bluenose* continued to work the Grand Banks through the rest of the decade. While owners and fish dealers were making reasonable profits, the lowly fishermen averaged something less than a thousand dollars a year. Big storms in '26 and '27 hammered the fishing fleets, and in 1930 the *Bluenose* herself ran aground due to pilot error in Placentia Bay and languished for a few days on a gravel beach near Argentia. Later that same year, after repairs, she was back in the race at Gloucester, sailing against the *Gertrude L. Thebaud*, owned by a French-Canadian who lived part of the year in Gloucester. The races were plagued by light winds, then rain. The "American" ship was declared the winner but Angus Walters claimed he wasn't beaten. The next year when the race was held off Halifax, Walters whipped the *Gertrude L. Thebaud*, taking the prize. The two ships wouldn't compete together again until 1938.

In the intervening years of the Depression, the fishing industry went bad as markets for salt fish shrank and nearly everything went bust. Angus Walters had kept on in the fishing business, however, and, later in that decade as president of the fishermen's union, lobbied in Halifax for a small one-quarter-cent-per-pound increase in fish prices.

The *Bluenose* sailed to the Great Lakes to represent Canada in the 1933 World's Fair in Chicago. Arriving with great fanfare, the ship soon became ensnared in a series of legal wrangles. She was sued, she was charged with customs infractions, and her crew found a bullet-ridden body alongside. An article in *Cosmopolitan* would later even suggest that Angus Walters lost his composure when a female sightseer touched the wheel of the schooner and he swore at her for having "violated" his ship.

Despite a few controversies, the *Bluenose* earned respect in many ports for her racing achievements and in 1935 she participated in the Silver Jubilee Sailpast before King George and Queen Elizabeth at Spithead, England. Walters did his diplomatic deed, met the king and proceeded to sail home, only to get slammed by a severe storm that keeled the *Bluenose* over, nearly sinking the great ship.

The Sinking of a Legend

She was already appearing on a Canadian fifty-cent stamp when her image was adopted for the new 1937 ten-cent coin, a little piece of Nova Scotia sailing history jingling around in the pockets of every Canadian. Her last international event was a five-race series off Gloucester, this time with fewer restrictions on sails and crew. The *Bluenose* was in rough shape and showed it. The *Thebaud* took the first race, and the *Bluenose* the second. In the end, the *Bluenose* won the event and, as in the past, there was a furor over how the races were run. Angus Walters said he'd never race in the U.S. after that.

By 1939, the *Bluenose* was an obsolete vessel and considered too vulnerable to submarine attacks. Her owners saw no future or profit left in the ship and Walters bought what was left of the once-grand schooner for $7,200. He tried to raise money to preserve this national treasure but no government office or organization thought it of much concern. Instead, war was on everyone's mind. The East India Trading Company bought the ship in 1942 and Walters reluctantly sent her off to ply the waters of the Caribbean as a coastal trading ship. On January 28, 1946, she hit a reef off Haiti. The crew got off and the ship held together long enough for her engines to be salvaged but after that, she was left to her fate.

In 1963, Walters drove the ceremonial spike for the keel of the *Bluenose II* with a bit more accuracy than the Duke of Devonshire had for the original, but he had stated more than once that "The wood is not grown yet, that will build a boat which will beat the Bluenose." Walters died in 1968.

In his book *Once Upon a Schooner*, Silver Donald Cameron notes that "fully half the Gloucester fleet was manned by Nova Scotians...the Gloucester crews were just about as 'American' as a CFL football team is 'Canadian.'" He points out that these races were competitions between men who were mostly Nova Scotian and that all the bickering was the result of politicians, financial backers and publicity hacks.

Despite the fact that no one seemed to care very much when the *Bluenose* was sent to an ignominious job in the south, her image lives on in the psyche of this province. To many Nova Scotians, the *Bluenose* represents the grandeur of the great days of sailing ships and the spirit of a province integrally tied to the sea.

Chapter Thirty-seven

A Province in Economic Ruin

Annapolis Valley apple farmers of the 1920s with technology both new and old.

Maritime Rights and Marginalized People

The 1920s were a time of economic ruin and rebellion for Nova Scotia. Saint Mary's University historian John G. Reid suggests that the Great Depression which swept the country in the 1930s began much earlier in the Maritimes, as early as 1920, and lasted right through the thirties. Nova Scotians were familiar with hard times, but for that new breed of worker totally dependent on mining and industrial jobs there would be a whole new dimension to the hardships inflicted on them by an economic slump.

Nova Scotians, however, didn't take the punishment lying down. They worked hard to survive and, when necessary, fought back to protect their meagre earnings and their rights. It was a watershed period which shaped attitudes and government policy for many years to follow.

With the end of World War I, the country was readjusting to peace time. For Halifax, this meant continued recovery from the great explosion of 1917, which, despite its devastation, had set in motion relief programs that were the basis for significant social reform. There was a brief postwar boom that quickly fizzled and, because of the new economic changes in Nova Scotia, it looked as though the people here would not have much control over their own destiny.

Between 1922 and 1925, the Maritime Rights movement flourished, fuelled by grievances shared by the three provinces. The Maritimes were suffering as a result of changes in railroad rates and other stumbling blocks impeding the economy of the East. Dartmouth writer H.S. Congdon, a leading exponent of the Maritime Rights movement, put Upper Canada fully at fault for trying to "have these provinces destroyed." Prime Minister Mackenzie King was slow to recognize the inherent truth in what was being put forward by the Maritime Rights activists and, for a while, turned a deaf ear. As a result of mutual problems, the 1920s was very much a time of solidarity for New Brunswick, PEI and Nova Scotia as a strong regional identity emerged.

Not everyone was to share in this feeling of unity, however, especially the marginalized Blacks, Mi'kmaq and, to a lesser degree, Nova Scotian Acadians. Mi'kmaqs were still left isolated on reserves and Blacks continued to go to segregated schools in accordance with the less-than-enlightened 1918 Nova Scotian Education Act.

Although women had received the vote in 1918, significant barriers to equality still stood in their way. Lower-class women worked for very low wages and employers hoped to keep it that way. Like their male counterparts, these workers would not always quietly acquiesce to the boss's demands. In 1925, for example, Halifax telephone operators went on strike for better wages. Inequality in the workplace existed almost everywhere, including Dalhousie University where highly qualified women were relegated to lower-paying jobs than their male counterparts.

"In Terror of Revolution"

Historian T.W. Acheson points out that, as early as 1914, the Maritimes had become a branch-plant economy. It was not unlike the early days of British occupation when major economic decisions were made far away in London. Now, important economic decisions about Nova Scotia would be corporate ones made in boardrooms well outside the province. When companies begin to cut back, they tend to protect their operations close to home and shut down branches farther away. Nova Scotia was very much on the periphery of North American industrial development and jobs here were considered expendable.

More hard times were in store for Nova Scotia. There were problems with the province's coal and troubles in the steel industry. Railroads were not expanding as expected and so there was a smaller market for Nova Scotia rails. Nova Scotia had lost considerable political power as well. By 1921, the entire Maritime region accounted for less than twelve per cent of the country's population, whereas, at the time of Confederation, it had been nearly twenty per cent. Nova Scotians simply had a weaker voice in Parliament and diminished means to insure that the federal government made decisions favourable to them.

A change in the National Policy, for example, reduced a tariff on imported coal that had once protected jobs and kept mines in production on Cape Breton. Freight subsidies that allowed all manner of goods from this region to move cheaply toward Central Canada were also chopped.

Government policy and outside control of industry led to a crisis in employment: almost half of the manufacturing jobs in the region disappeared during the first six years of the decade. The export of fish remained steady for a while, but that too was to decline.

Between the two great wars, another sort of war erupted in Nova Scotia, particularly in Cape Breton. It was a battle between workers and employers and it had its greatest impact on the lives of miners. When the Canadian government reduced the import tariffs on coal, the owners of the mines began to lower the wages for workers. Dominion Coal and Nova Scotia Steel and Coal companies, major employers in Cape Breton, had been merged into BESCO, the British Empire Steel Corporation, headquartered in Montreal but run by directors in Montreal, London, Toronto and New York. The company pretty well had a monopoly on coal and steel in Nova Scotia. They were calling the shots.

BESCO had probably not completely considered the depth of the frustration and the convictions of the highly organized Cape Breton coal miners as they began slashing wages. Under the banner of the United Mine Workers of America, militant leaders like J.B. McLachlan were prepared to cause the mine owners some serious grief, if they were ready to short-change these men for the hard work that was at the centre of their lives.

Activism on the part of industrial unions had grown dramatically in the region since 1900. Strikes were often turbulent and they were lengthy. One at the Springhill mine had lasted for over twenty-two months. Imagine how the miners in Cape Breton felt in 1922 when BESCO announced they were ready to chop wages by nearly forty per cent. BESCO was also closing some of its steel plants (including one in Sydney Mines) and wanted to trim the number of workers and wages in its mines. In June of 1922, Cape Breton UMW members saw a cataclysmic disaster ahead. They were good and riled and went so far as to call for the "complete overthrow of the capitalist system and capitalist state." By August, "Red" Dan Livingstone and J.B. McLachlan had their men looking as if they were ready for just that as they went on strike.

One Member of Parliament reported to Prime Minister Mackenzie King that people were "in terror of revolution." Five hundred troops had already pulled in from Halifax and Quebec to subdue the so-called radicals. Five hundred more, as well as a thousand police, were on hand, and some influential advisers to government were suggesting that British warships should be brought into Sydney Harbour just in case things became really ugly.

This time around, however, there was very little violence. Red Dan signed a deal, "under muzzle of rifles, machine guns and gleaming bayonets," calling for a wage cut of twenty per cent instead of what BESCO had proposed.

Another strike broke out in 1923 as the steel workers fought to regain lost wages. The miners voted to support the strike after they had seen the troops arrive again and the provincial police lead a charge on horseback against the citizens of the Whitney Pier area. Livingstone and McLachlan were arrested for "seditious libel."

There was yet another strike in 1924 when BESCO called for a further twenty per cent loss of wages and a strike again in 1925. These were turbulent, heady times for Cape Bretoners who were tired of being beaten down. In the intense strike of 1925, fighting broke out again and again between miners and company cops and nearly two thousand troops were brought in to keep a lid on things. Grievances between miners and the government, the police, the military and the company would be deep-seated as the result of the tension during these times.

While the miners proved themselves to be dedicated and vigilant when it came to protecting their rights and their wages, there were no clear winners. The life of a miner and his family would continue to be a struggle. BESCO itself was in a deep financial mire before 1926 and the company was out of business by 1930. Dawn Fraser, a Cape Breton poet of the time, had this to say about the death of BESCO: "may Satan's imps attend your hearse—adieu, adieu Cape Breton's curse."

In 1926, Mackenzie King finally decided that the Maritimes really did have some special problems and the serious disadvantages should be addressed. He appointed Andrew Rae Duncan to head a royal commission and look into the mess. As a result of his commission Duncan suggested reform—a twenty per cent reduction in freight tariffs, federal subsides to coal, steel and to the provinces themselves, along with financial assistance in developing the ports. John G. Reid notes that it was a fine-sounding proposal but that King and his cabinet had created it as pretty window-dressing and nothing significant came of it.

The Prophet of Co-operation

The twenties were a rough time for Nova Scotia. In many ways, the quality of life diminished as control over the economy moved out of the province. The union movement brought new militancy out of self-defence, but it also helped to draw a hard line between economic classes. On the other hand, the sense of regional unity had been sparked by the political and economic hammering that the province was taking and it would be a basis for a revitalized identity reminiscent of pre-Confederation times.

One labour-related crusade that was to have a lasting impact on the region was the Antigonish Movement, led by a Catholic priest, Moses Coady. Coady saw that farmers and fishermen were being taken advantage of in their business dealings and wanted to help educate rural Nova Scotians to have more control over their own economic and social well-being. In 1928, Coady began to spread the word of co-operation through self-help groups. Co-ops were set up around the province for housing, consumer goods and medical concerns. Coady was a fiery, dedicated leader who argued that "Co-operation is the only means in our day through which the masses of people can again have a say in the economic processes."

Fishermen and farmers organized to create their own marketing organizations so that they had more say over the price they would receive for their harvest. Some saw Coady as radical and dangerous—after all, this was a kind of "communism." But his approach was down-to-earth and practical and he won over many converts to his co-op way of thinking. Community education was at the heart of the movement and Coady was bolstered in his efforts by the even more "radical" priest Jimmy Tompkins who created Canada's first co-operative housing project outside Reserve Mines, Cape Breton, in 1935. He also helped establish credit unions and libraries to advance the cause.

The co-ops grew and became well established and helped many Nova

Scotians through the critical rough times of the thirties and on into the 1940s. Coady went on to establish the Nova Scotia Teachers' Union and, in 1930, the United Maritime Fishermen's Co-operative. Soon after his death in 1959, workers from the Coady Institute at St. Francis Xavier University were travelling to poorer countries around the world, spreading the methods that had proved so successful in a poverty-stricken Nova Scotia.

Living on a Dollar a Month

The 1930s was the decade of the Great Depression across North America, one that Nova Scotians had already experienced in a head start. Trying to protect their jobs, the Americans closed down the border to Nova Scotian immigrants looking for work, so now there would be no new money sent back home from the Boston States to help support families in the villages and outports. Within the province, the politicians who fared best were those who argued that they could do the most with the least. This was more the skill of the illusionist, not the realist.

Nearly every sector of industry was headed for the basement, and jobs vaporised. Between 1929 and 1933 the forestry business plummeted down seventy-five per cent, fishing production was cut in half and the value of farming goods produced decreased by nearly forty per cent. The need for coal was cut nearly in half and the steel industry fell by a whopping sixty-two per cent.

Nova Scotia was reduced to a bare-bones economy and the system wasn't ready to cope with the needs of the unemployed and their destitute families. Relief responsibility for all the victims of the economic crash fell not to the province or the federal government but to local levels of government. As a result, there were insane discrepancies in the relief money available from one town to the next. A relatively prosperous town such as Amherst doled out a hefty $5.70 per month (close to the Canadian average) to its two thousand impoverished residents in 1933. If you lived in a poorer neighbourhood, like Guysborough, for example, you'd be lucky to receive $1.00 per month, although during many months there was nothing at all to offer to the poorest of the poor.

Those who still had an income to pay taxes were fearful that there was something intrinsically wrong with somebody getting something for nothing, even if it was a scant amount that barely allowed for survival. As a result, work programs were instituted for those on relief, forcing them to cut wood as fuel for their tax-paying neighbours. In the cities they might labour on new streets or public building projects.

One of the more innovative and practical efforts to help out the destitute was a back-to-the-land movement. In 1932, Nova Scotia commandeered about six hundred unused farms and allowed poor families to take them over as a means of supporting themselves. Two-thirds of these families had stayed with their farms by 1938, but in the end only twenty-four families were allowed to gain title to the land, having fulfilled their obligations to the province.

Everybody was hurting for money and work was scarce. The Nova Scotian Mi'kmaq people, who had been robbed of their lands and deprived of traditional hunting and fishing grounds, lived through desperate times as the poorest of the poor. Nova Scotian Blacks found themselves victimized anew as poor whites went looking for scapegoats to blame for their sorry situation. In 1937, a mob of four hundred white Nova Scotians in Trenton demolished a Black family's home that they claimed was in a "white neighbourhood." This despicable act of violent racism resulted in only one arrest: the Black man who owned the destroyed house was accused of assaulting a white woman as he defended his home.

War to the Rescue

Once again, war was good news of sorts for Nova Scotians when it was declared in September of 1939. Halifax would be open for business in a big way and spin-offs would be felt in small towns around the province. The thirties was a time of great despair for a large chunk of the North American population, but Nova Scotians were painfully aware that, for them, things had been even worse. Confederation and the loss of traditional sea links and self-reliant avenues of living had left all of Nova Scotia in a highly vulnerable position. None of the efforts of the federal government had been able to heal the wounds of the loss. As the province climbed up out of the economic abyss, a dispassionate observer might well predict that the boom cycle of war could only be temporary. After that, would anything be different? Was there any way back to a future that re-established the prosperity that had come with sailing ships and global sea trade?

Chapter Thirty-eight

Nova Scotia in the
Second World War

World War II warship Île de France in Halifax Harbour.

A City Stretched to Its Limits

In 1941, Admiral S.S. Bonham-Carter called Halifax "probably the most important port in the world." Perhaps that would be stretching the truth a little, but Halifax had certainly come a long way from its early days of obscurity and insignificance. War had always brought the city back to life and back to work. It also brought with it new demands and new problems to go along with the profits to be reaped by the legitimate and illegitimate profiteers. The Second World War proved no exception.

More than any city in Canada, Halifax had a direct connection to the war in Europe. In the British press, Halifax might simply be referred to as "An Eastern Canadian Port" or in Canada, "An East Coast Port," as if to mask the exact location of military action involving shipping across the Atlantic. Nonetheless, Germany was well aware of what was going on in Halifax, and for some Haligonians the vulnerability of the city to actual enemy attack was a daily concern, if not a reality.

Halifax was in need of a good war, if things were going to improve. The after-effects of the explosion of 1917 and economic depression of recent years had taken their toll on the city. Halifax was on a downhill slide from the glory days in the past. Historian Graham Metson points out that Halifax "was no longer the wild free city of the nineteenth century." It was both "poor and puritan," perhaps the most unhappy of combinations. There was a lack of everything, including entertainment and lodging. To such a sad city would arrive thousands of soldiers and seamen, all getting ready to go off to war. The government in Ottawa didn't seem to have a handle on the situation at all, as they were more interested in moving the men in and moving them out. It would have been logical to treat Halifax as if it was actually in the war zone, a unique situation unlike any other place in Canada. But that was not the case. If things were less than perfect for servicemen and citizens in Halifax, they would just have to chalk it up to the inconveniences of wartime. Everything would be strained beyond limits, including puritanical notions.

Overcrowded and Out of Sorts

Civilians, among them families of the servicemen, flooded into the city. Almost overnight, the population had doubled to a hundred thousand. There were traffic problems in the harbour, in the air and on the pot-holed Halifax streets. There were line-ups for everything from food to entertainment. One concert at the Forum drew a line-up described as "a mile long and four people deep."

One of the hotels in town had converted the ground-floor ladies' lounge into a dormitory with nearly fifty beds, where you could rent a cot for $2.25

a night. Halifax Mayor Donovan blamed much of the problem on the wives and families of military men. He wished they had the good sense to let their men go off to war and not try to tag along as far as they could to the furthest port—Halifax.

F.B. Watt, in writing about the Merchant Navy, described Halifax as "an overcrowded hellhole." Beyond shoving everyone into every nook and corner, makeshift shacks were thrown together in parks and on the edge of the city. Halifax was a sad, depressing place and for those who saw her only briefly during these years it left an indelible impression as a place you would never want to return to.

Watt says, "Many of the newcomers were sick of combing the slums looking for a place to live, tired of eating bad food in bad restaurants, fed up with being exploited by landlords." As in the early days of the city, profiteers were everywhere, trying to sell just about everything at inflated prices to the servicemen and other newcomers. There was good money to be made by taking advantage of a bad situation. Aside from the hucksters and con artists, it seems that almost everybody was snarly about the pressure-cooker life in Halifax. Haligonians saw the loss of whatever dignity the city had held onto through the Depression. New arrivals blamed Halifax folks for being so uncaring. There was anger and tension in the air.

Despite the unifying factor of the war, divisive attitudes prevailed in Halifax. Upper-Canadian snobbery clashed with down-home self-defence and fights broke out. Canadians from away, called "foreigners" by some people in town, didn't like being ripped off by locals making a buck off the war, but these locals who had been living quietly but poorly through the twenties and thirties now felt invaded and, even worse, unappreciated for their sacrifices in the war effort.

Three Close Calls

Despite the fact that much of Halifax had already been levelled by a major explosion in the First World War, all things considered, Halifax was pretty lucky in avoiding such a disaster this time around. Three "near misses" prove that point.

On April 9, 1942, the British ship *Trongate* caught fire in the harbour. In her hold were TNT, shells, casings and ammunition. The harbour was bumper to bumper with two hundred ships, including ten U.S. Navy vessels and four carriers of U.S. troops. The minesweeper *Chedabucto* was ordered to fire four-inch shells filled with sand at the water-line of the *Trongate* to sink her.

Another ship fire broke out in Bedford Basin in November of 1943 aboard the U.S. freighter *Volunteer*. She was loaded with dynamite, depth charges, magnesium, ammunition and bales of tobacco. While the captain and officers drank and played cards, a fire broke out and burned for two hours before word was received at the Port Defence Office. Most of the crew abandoned ship and those who were left with the drunk captain protested when their ship was boarded by firemen. Commander Owen Robertson and his fire party realized that the decks were getting red-hot from the fire below and expected the ship to blow them all to kingdom come. They valiantly attempted to use the tobacco bales to shield the volatile magnesium barrels from igniting and then they cut holes into the decks to release the explosive gases which had to be ignited with a rifle shot. (Does this all sound like a crazy scheme to anyone?)

The release of volatile fumes was a success of sorts, sending flames shooting forty feet into the air rather than blowing up the entire ship. Robertson and his men had been hiding behind those tobacco bales at the time and got off easy. They were only knocked senseless for a mere ten minutes.

When he returned to consciousness, Robertson beached the still-burning ship on McNab's Island, while fireboats continued to pump water on them. There Robertson's men managed to open the seacocks and sink the ill-fated *Volunteer* and thus avert disaster.

The third of the major accidents took place on land, at the Bedford Magazine on July 18, 1945, in the Burnside area north of Dartmouth. The five-kilometre-long arsenal compound was a storehouse and transfer point for all manner of explosive cargo and ammunition. When a barge exploded at 6:30 p.m., it set off a series of other blasts along the shoreline. One after another, the blasts could be heard into the night and there was fear that the entire facility might soon go up in one horrendous burst.

Dartmouth was evacuated, as was the North End of Halifax, where people fled once again to the relative security of Citadel Hill and the Wanderer's Grounds where baseball games continued despite warnings of impending doom. Ships in the harbour were moved out of harm's way as far as possible. The force of several of the explosions did structural damage to buildings on both sides of the harbour, but fortunately there was no single cataclysmic blast as in 1917.

An Emotional Powder Keg

During the war, ships travelled in convoys out of Halifax with supplies for the war in Europe. Along with the troop ships and warships went merchant marine vessels with food, oil and munitions. The first convoy left Halifax before war was actually declared. Eighteen ships, escorted by British cruisers and Canadian destroyers, headed out in the late summer of 1939. Convoys of the older and slower vessels would also head off from Sydney in Cape Breton.

Merchant seamen often felt they were never given the credit they deserved in the war effort. They were sometimes called "zombies," as if to say they were able-bodied men who were avoiding war duty, sometimes even receiving a white feather—a symbol of cowardice—as a gift from a snooty Haligonian. After the war, merchant seamen who risked their lives in crossing the Atlantic were never afforded the benefits that went to military men. Only recently have these men been honoured for their part in helping to win World War II.

Along with all the dangers in Europe, at sea, or even at rest in a floating time bomb in the harbour, there was plenty of trouble ashore. Squabbles broke out frequently between servicemen and townspeople. There were conflicts between merchant and naval seamen as well, and between regular navy and naval reserves. To complement the fever of war, Halifax was an emotional powder keg waiting for the appropriate match.

Chapter Thirty-nine

The Spoils of War

Aftermath of the VE Day rioting in Halifax.

The Kronprinzen Affair

The war had a trickle-down effect on much of the province, sometimes leading to profit, sometimes pain and sometimes to an exercise in sheer absurdity as illustrated by the following. Attack by U-boats off the coast was an ever-present danger for any manner of ship sailing off the coast of Nova Scotia. In July of 1942, a brand spanking new Norwegian ship, the *Kronprinzen*, was part of a convoy headed from New York to Halifax on its way to Britain. Not much more than a hundred and sixty kilometres off the coast of Yarmouth, it was hit by two German torpedoes, with one hole reported as being "large enough for a trawl dory to row through." On board was a cargo of flour, four thousand tons of steel and cotton bales. Convoy veteran Captain Jorgens was a tough nut to crack and refused to abandon ship and lose the cargo. He called for four tugs, two from Halifax and two from Boston, to come to his rescue as his men worked the pumps and struggled to keep the ship afloat as she lumbered a hundred and sixty kilometres to a beach at Lower East Pubnico.

Jorgens was shocked to discover that the locals there wanted a fee of sixty cents an hour to help unload the goods. The captain thought this was an outrage and would report that "They all want to get rich off this one job." Even in those days, sixty cents an hour would not have led to wealth but obviously there was some bad blood between the staunch captain and those people of Pubnico living pretty close to the poverty line. Jorgens decided they couldn't salvage the flour but refused to give it or even sell it to the locals, so he had his men dump it into the sea—which, of course, seems somewhat illogical, given the trouble they were going to in order to save the cargo. It turned out that Jorgens was just following the orders of the war machine that had decreed such goods could never be used for civilian purposes under any circumstances. The RCMP was brought in to use water hoses to keep everyone away so they could properly dispose of the flour by sinking it. The poverty-stricken but feisty Pubnicans, however, would not relent in this battle for food. They rowed out in their dories, scooped up the bales as they floated by and spirited them away, despite the presence of the Mounties and their water cannons. One wonders what a German U-boat captain would have made of this scene had he been close enough to view it through his periscope. Years later, South Shore writer Evelyn Richardson wrote the tale of this event and noted how such bags of flour would often turn up for sale or circulate for free along the coast that year.

The *Kronprinzen* episode was only one of many that illustrate a low government regard for the people of rural Nova Scotia in and out of war. The ship itself was towed off to Halifax, then New York and sailed again.

Just Thirsty

Despite its role as a city "in the war zone," Halifax never sustained all-out catastrophe or invasion during World War II—that is, not until the war in Europe ended in May of 1945. On the seventh and eighth of that month, Halifax was ripped apart by the Canadian military. It would be known as the VE Day riot, part celebration, part outrageous attack upon the city that had been a not-so-hospitable home for men going to and from war.

Five million dollars in damage was the price tag. Three people died in the battle and 211 were arrested. More than five hundred businesses were looted. Cop cars and street cars were burned or smashed. Liquor store windows were shattered and the shelves were cleaned out. Up against the rioting soldiers and sailors (and whoever else cared to take advantage of the situation) were 540 Halifax policemen, 169 army police, 74 air force personnel, 168 navy shore patrolmen and 43 RCMP.

Earlier that year, Admiral Leonard Murray had spoken of a plan for celebrations should the war be over in Europe and, by April, the Halifax North Civic Association asked the city to gear up for the possibility of a big blowout if the war ended. Mayor Allan Butler asked the eleven theatres to stay open, but they all wanted to be closed tight when the day arrived. Of the fifty-five restaurants in town, only sixteen were open on May 7 and all but a handful were closed by the next day. There was no place in town for most men to eat. Edna Hobin remembers her mother answering the door to three polite sailors offering to pay for a meal. She fed them corned beef and cabbage but refused their money. Other servicemen were not so lucky or not so polite. Many must have been outraged that "they" had just won a war and the city of Halifax wasn't even willing to give them a place to buy a meal.

Rumours had been circulating that once the war was over, the men would have revenge on Halifax for all its shortcomings. Poor old Halifax would take a beating for all of Ottawa's lack of concern and the bureaucratic bungling that went hand in hand with it. As novelist Hugh Garner puts it, "Though everyone in authority knew it was coming, little was done to prevent the crisis brewing."

Edna Hobin remembers watching "hundreds" of navy and civilian men carrying cases of booze, although she remembers them as being "non-threatening," just thirsty.

Things started to get weird on the night of May 7 when the bar at Stadacona closed at 9 p.m. Men poured out of there, boarded street cars and went downtown—destination: the liquor stores on Hollis and Sackville streets. Nobody was buying. A couple of dozen men just went in and came back, handing out cases to the crowds. Confrontations were few and there was little in the newspaper the next morning except the good news of the end to war in Europe. VE Day was announced.

Official celebrations were scheduled to take place in churches and there would be a parade to the Garrison Grounds. In fact, much polite and political ceremony would go on as scheduled, with participants unaware that Barrington Street was being ransacked.

Admiral Murray believed it would have been unfair to allow civilians to celebrate and not servicemen. He had a good point. But meanwhile, back at the bar at Stadacona, refreshment had run out by one o'clock on the afternoon of the eighth. A little rowdiness followed and before long, two thousand men were pouring out onto North Barrington Street and headed downtown. Street cars were again commandeered.

"The mob filled the street from one side to the other, breaking the windows of seventy houses as they passed," Hugh Garner remembers. At least four thousand men, thirsty for a little brew, directed their attentions to Keith's Brewery on Hollis Street. Victor Oland remembers his father (who owned the brewery) helping to hand out cases of beer as soon as he realized what was underway. Once all the bottles were given away, he says, "They departed without causing any damage."

"Just High Spirits" or "Just Like Animals"?

Conflicting views about the animosity still abound. Edna Hobin remembers it as a good-natured crowd. Bruce Jefferson thought it all "just high spirits." Charles Sweeny, on the other hand, saw an uncontrollable mob, "just like animals." There were amusing anecdotes but also stories of theft, massive destruction and rape.

What Garner calls "wild scenes of debauchery between drunken servicemen and local girls" might also have been viewed by another observer as serious sexual assaults. If it was the navy who started the riot, other servicemen and civilians were not far behind in joining in the fun (or devastation, depending on what you had to lose).

While all this was going on, most of the guys in charge—the mayor, the politicians, and the heads of the army, navy and air force—were taking part in the memorial service on the Garrison Grounds. Once Admiral Murray got wind of the liquor store break-ins, he mustered up the idea of a military parade for all three branches to calm things down. Admiral Murray and Mayor Butler were out driving around using loudspeakers to talk to the crowds and gather the servicemen for the parade. This must have had some strange soothing effect on a large number of men, many of whom would have been too drunk to march in a straight line but, nonetheless, the great staggering mob was divided into army, navy and air force and marched (more or less) back to barracks.

Navy men were reported to have been the instigators and the major cause of damage. An 8 p.m. curfew was imposed and, by midnight, the war-torn city of Halifax would begin to pick up the pieces and reflect on how calm things had seemed during the war and how devastating the devices of peace.

The very next day, as clean-up efforts began, accusations were flying. Whose fault was it? Who made the biggest screw-up here and why hadn't they all seen this coming?

Admiral Murray, a career navy man from Pictou, was fired as commander-in-chief and resigned his commission by March of 1946, retiring to England. Murray was made a scapegoat for the whole fiasco, and his supporters point out that the armed forces lost an important man at a crucial time of winding down the war. Murray appears to us now as a sort of tragic figure in all this, having done an exceedingly good job in helping to win the fierce Battle of the Atlantic. He accepted the blame for a whole whack of things that went wrong and an emotionally supercharged history of poor relations between Halifax and military men. The royal commission chaired by Justice Kellock, in fact, blamed the whole mess on the navy, although we know now it was much more complex than that.

Chapter Forty

The Fifties and Sixties: "A Friendly Remoteness"

Idyllic-looking Ballantyne's Cove in Antigonish County.

Of Kilts and Cold War

In 1955 the Canso Causeway was completed, linking Cape Breton to the mainland. It was the sort of megaproject that inspired enthusiasm for a number of other grand schemes, many of which turned out to be bitter disappointments. Nonetheless, the Causeway was sure to improve the transportation between this colourful island, mainland Nova Scotia and the rest of Canada. The following year, when Robert Stanfield came to office as premier, his government shelled out $110 million over four years to improve highway transportation, as if to say it was time for Nova Scotians to forget about ships, forget about trains and simply drive, drive, drive.

Urban Nova Scotians were being fully integrated into mainstream North American culture as a result of the automobile, the radio and the TV. In many rural areas of the province, however, the lifestyle and livelihood still revolved around fishing, farming or making a living from the woods. Paved roads and TV signals had not reached every fishing community or farm and, in fact, many Nova Scotians still lived without electricity and had little desire to change that fact.

Meanwhile, Nova Scotia was trying to establish itself as a tourist destination and could still capitalize on the picturesque old-fashioned charm of the province. An article in *Holiday* magazine in 1953 waxed absurdly eloquent about the province, saying, "In the scenic land of Longfellow's *Evangeline*, the haven of the Grand Banks fishermen, the home of heroes, you'll find a friendly remoteness from the confusions of the world." One tourist photo, circa 1957, shows a kilted Nova Scotian of Scottish descent performing on his bagpipes by the highway on the Tantramar Marsh before a very fashionable suburban mother and her two daughters.

Nova Scotia was certainly not at the cutting edge of industry or modern expansionism but the province's "friendly remoteness" helped to put it front and centre in the global peace movement. In 1957, as the Cold War kept getting colder, as Canadians and Americans alike began to prepare for a nuclear holocaust with backyard fallout shelters, Cyrus Eaton brought together twenty-two scientists from ten nations to his estate in Pugwash for the first of the "Pugwash Conferences." The purpose of these gatherings was to promote world peace and solve global problems. Albert Einstein and Bertrand Russell were two major supporters of the conference and helped fortify the foundation for a worldwide disarmament movement, and the work begun by the Pugwash founders continues on to this day, a distinguished and persistent worldwide effort to tackle the most daunting of planetary problems. (It wasn't until 1995, however, that the founders of the movement belatedly received the Nobel Prize for their efforts.)

Another goodwill initiative, Moses Coady's co-op movement which began in the 1930s, had grown by leaps and bounds under the auspices of St. Francis Xavier University. Coady's ideas were being put into action in developing nations around the world where impoverished farmers and fishermen banded together to improve their welfare by establishing better economic control over their livelihood. Co-operative land ownership and housing, as well as fishing and farming co-ops, were part of the new economic salvation being preached by such emissaries of good as Father Harvey Steele of Glace Bay. In Latin America, these efforts proved to be monumentally successful but also drew the ire of dictators and corporations alike who saw Nova Scotia's co-op movement to be a menace.

The "Economic Conquest" of Nova Scotia

As the decade progressed in Nova Scotia, fewer and fewer men were working in fishing or farming. Manufacturing jobs, however, were *not* on the rise and as many as 82,000 workers left the Atlantic region in the 1950s, seeking their fortunes elsewhere. On the other hand, government jobs, including work for the military, were on the increase. The Cold War, like every other war that had involved Nova Scotia, was good for the Halifax economy. By 1961 almost twenty-five per cent of the jobs in that city were related in some way to the naval establishment.

With job shortages in other sectors, women were once again denied equal access to employment, but in 1955 a federal law which barred married women from work in the civil service was repealed. The next year Nova Scotia legislators passed a law calling for equal pay for equal work, but it would take a long while for this legislation to have an effect throughout the working world. Inequality was everywhere, and other less-enlightened legislation actually sustained the problem. For example, women, even working women, were still banned by law from entering taverns. For Nova Scotian Blacks, though, some headway toward equality was being made as segregated schooling disappeared and a 1955 bill was passed making it illegal to discriminate on the basis of race, religion, ethnic origin or even union membership.

For many Nova Scotians life was still a struggle. Ernest Buckler documented just how rough life could be on a North Mountain farm in his beautifully executed novel *The Mountain and the Valley*, first published in 1952. Hugh MacLennan explored the despair and tragedies of life in a Cape Breton coal mining town in *Each Man's Son*. Thomas Raddall of Liverpool was mining a rich literary vein in his novels rooted in Nova Scotia history, perhaps the most daring being *The Nymph and the Lamp*, which concerns inequality of women and the life of a telegraph operator on remote Sable Island in the early part of the century.

In the 1950s most Nova Scotians were aware that they were living in a have-not province. Around the end of the war per capita income was nearly twenty-five per cent below the national norm. By 1955 a Nova Scotian's income was closer to *thirty-three* per cent below average. The promise of prosperity that was supposed to come with Confederation was never to be fulfilled, even after a hundred years. To make matters worse, the opening of the St. Lawrence Seaway led shipping traffic directly into the heartland of Canada. Ports on the East Coast could be entirely ignored. Once again Nova Scotians felt victimized rather than befriended by government. Atlantic Canadian historian W.S. McNutt referred to the sinking of the Nova Scotian economy in military terms as a brand of "economic conquest."

In politics, issues of Maritime Union were discussed in hushed tones and the substance of the previous Maritimes Rights movement was resuscitated. Some still hoped for something grand and ambitious to come from all of the Maritimers' bottled-up frustration. In 1957, McNutt saw some hope that the Atlantic premiers would light the fires necessary for sweeping changes but he worried that "unless the people of the Atlantic Provinces are united behind them the Atlantic Revolution would be one of the great mute inglorious revolutions of history." Such a revolution was really calling for nothing more than simple regional equality for the Atlantic Provinces with the other regions of Canada.

The 1960s and 1970s brought better economic times and heavy government involvement in social welfare and economic development. Stanfield's Industrial Estates Limited, a Crown corporation, enticed industry to come to Nova Scotia. While a handful of companies prospered and became mainstays of the economy (Volvo and Michelin are notable in this regard), other big business boosts were abysmal failures. Clairtone's electronics factory proved to be a bust and a heavy-water industry for Cape Breton proved to be a monumental fiasco. Involving Cape Breton in the nuclear industry seemed to suggest that if workers there were willing to undertake such dangerous underground employment as coal mining, then they would be more than willing to step into an even more dangerous field like the nuclear industry. Long after the heavy-water plant was closed down, Cape Breton entrepreneurs wrestled with what to do with the white elephant. One suggestion was to turn it into a distillery but by then government support for such ventures had pretty well dried up.

The Environmental Price Tag of Progress

Along with economic development came a hefty price tag in terms of environmental degradation. One of the sadder tales in my opinion concerns the building of a pulp mill by Scott Paper at Abercrombie Point in Pictou County. At the time of construction, expedient measures were put into place to deal with the tainted water used in the manufacturing process.

Effluent from pulp mills tends to lower oxygen levels in the natural water it is spilled into. Residues and a variety of harmful chemicals also find their way into the ecosystem, radically changing the natural habitat. Fish die off and other species are adversely affected.

When the Pictou County mill was under construction in the early 1960s, it was decided that the effluent from the mill would be pumped under Pictou Harbour to Boat Harbour, a natural body of water that was used by a local Mi'kmaq community. Boat Harbour would cease to be anything more than a "settling pond" for the pulp-mill effluent before the water continued on its course out into the Northumberland Strait. While the atrocities against the Mi'kmaq people stretch back to the first arrival of the English settlers, it is unnerving to see how even in recent times Native people are bullied in the name of economic expansion. Dan Paul in *We Were Not the Savages* described how the Mi'kmaq families of Pictou Landing were shown pictures of supposedly similar pulp plants where the skies and waters around had remained clean and pure. The Federal Department of Indian Affairs and the province supported the claims of Scott, and the Pictou Landing residents reluctantly accepted $60,000 to allow their land to be used for the mill and ultimately the settling pond.

In the name of economic growth and jobs, the plant was constructed and, as planned, the once-immaculate Boat Harbour was literally killed. This traditional fishing and recreation area of the Pictou Landing Mi'kmaq was destroyed. The province also bought up much of the land around the new black lagoon, realizing that it would no longer be liveable.

Dan Paul notes that Mi'kmaq suicides in the area increased after the deal was signed. Many other Mi'kmaq simply moved away. The community also happens to be downwind of the Pictou plant and many feel that high levels of respiratory illness among the Mi'kmaq children today can be attributed to the gases emitted from pulp-mill stacks.

Recently, a "solution" to the problem has been discussed involving a seventeen-million-dollar extended pipeline that will distribute the toxic effluent further out into the Northumberland Strait. Arguments are being put forward on exactly how this might affect the fragile fish stocks in this region and to what degree the effluent washing back ashore might affect beaches along this scenic coastline of Nova Scotia.

A Drain on the Public Purse

With 20/20 hindsight it seems that both federal and provincial governments, overzealous with plans to improve the economy, all too often failed to recognize the true assets of Nova Scotia: environment and culture. In the race to drag Nova Scotia kicking and screaming into the industrial economy of North America, decision-makers ignored the importance of rural traditions of self-reliance; they failed to protect our richest resources in the sea and in the forests. Efforts at tourism failed to promote the wonder of the wilderness environment that remained and the province was slow to exploit the pool of talent in music that existed in Celtic, Black and Acadian cultures. It wouldn't be until the 1990s that Cape Breton fiddlers, Acadian singers and Black musicians would finally reach a truly international audience.

Instead, the Federal Department of Regional Economic Expansion (DREE), created in 1969, fostered big business and big development. DREE backed a host of big-time money losers, while avoiding serious attention to small-scale, decentralized growth which may have proven to be sustainable. Much of this so-called expansion led to more people moving from rural areas into the cities. By 1971, nearly one-fourth of the entire population of the province was living in the Halifax-Dartmouth metropolitan area.

Following in the wake of so much government optimism concerning growth was a wave of bitter human disappointment. It seemed that more internationally owned industries meant less local control over jobs. Not all Nova Scotia workers were ready to roll over and play dead when foreign-owned companies started to renege on their promises of keeping jobs in Nova Scotia. It would be up to that same overly optimistic government to help put workers back to work. For example, when Hawker Siddeley, a London-based corporation, closed down its Sydney Steel Plant in 1967, 17,000 angry citizens protested in the streets and called for government intervention. The province ultimately did take over the plant and it proved to be a massive drain on the public purse all the way into the 1990s, when a deal was struck with the Chinese to take over operations of the mill.

Chapter Forty-one

The Tragedy of Africville

Africville, before the community was relocated.

The Roots of Racism

What would it be like to wake up one day and be told by your city government that you had to move out of your home, that you had no choice in the matter? And what would it feel like to watch as your worldly possessions were loaded into a city garbage truck to be hauled off to some new designated place to live? If you lingered behind, you would have seen the house where you grew up smashed and levelled by a bulldozer, along with those of your neighbours. And what would go through your head if you returned later to look at a wasteland of rubble which was once the community where you grew up? What thoughts must go through the head of someone who has seen his little home town systematically erased from the face of the earth?

If you were a resident of Africville, Nova Scotia, in the 1960s you would be able to answer these questions. But for these Black Nova Scotians who were driven from their homes, a whole host of other questions remain unanswered and unresolved.

The story of Africville is rooted in the deeper history of Black people in Nova Scotia, one that begins with Mathieu da Costa, a Black man who came from France around 1605 to work in the fur trade at Port Royal. He was a free man, not a slave, and proved to be an excellent interpreter of the Mi'kmaq language, but alas his tenure here was brief, for he died within a year of his arrival.

There are records of a freed slave living around Cape Sable in 1686, but the next evidence of Black immigrants isn't until the founding of Halifax. Some of the wealthy settlers at that time had Black slaves and occasionally advertisements would appear for the sale of slaves on the auction block. Notable among the free Blacks was Barbara Cuffy, who owned land and a homestead in the fledgling town of Liverpool in 1760.

A wave of Black Loyalists came to Nova Scotia by British invitation from 1782 to 1784, arriving at Port Roseway, Annapolis Royal and Halifax. The government had a hand in organizing settlements and there was a clearly unequal distribution of good land and fair justice between the Black and white Loyalists. Impoverished segregated communities emerged near Shelburne (Port Roseway), Digby, Guysborough and Dartmouth. David George was an immigrant of this period, a preacher who wrote an account of his life here and helped to organize churches and education. Another immigrant named Thomas Peters, from North Carolina, proved himself to be a staunch activist, working to gain equality and rights for Nova Scotia Blacks. He travelled the region and lobbied in London to improve the situation for his people here but all too often his arguments fell on deaf ears. Thirty-five hundred Black

Loyalists had made their way to Nova Scotia during this time but of that number 1,196 left in 1792 in hopes of a establishing a better life in Sierra Leone.

The Maroons (whose story is told elsewhere in this book) enlarged the Nova Scotian Black population and arrived here by way of some convoluted political manipulation on the part of the rulers of the British Colonies. They too found Nova Scotia an inhospitable place and in 1800 more than five hundred of them also moved on to Sierra Leone.

More American Blacks were lured to Nova Scotia around the time of the War of 1812. Two thousand fugitive slaves made their way here from the South but most found there were no land grants as promised. They too discovered themselves segregated from the mainstream of society. In 1815, Governor Sherbrooke was more worried about his own public image than the plight of the new arrivals as he admitted Nova Scotia was "totally unprepared" for the influx of Blacks. He was afraid that his lack of preparedness might make him look bad. Of the 727 Black immigrants "housed" in the prison on Melville Island, many died from harsh treatment or disease.

Racist arguments broke out in the House of Assembly over what to do about the arrival of these people of colour. Some argued that Blacks were unsuited to the climate and should not settle here. Ultimately, prejudice and fear led to a decision to stop the influx of any more Black immigrants. Land grants were finally issued to many of those who arrived, directing them to live in Preston, a settlement mostly abandoned by the Black Loyalists and Maroons who had moved on to Sierra Leone. Sherbrooke suggested that a number of the Blacks should be shipped on to Trinidad (where the climate was more to their liking, he argued) and the next governor, Lord Dalhousie, suggested more Nova Scotian Blacks be shipped to Sierra Leone to join their predecessors who had founded a colony there.

The idea of emigration (or exile) was kept alive by Governor Kempt and Bishop Inglis, but by this time, most Black immigrants had settled into a life in Nova Scotia and could not be coerced to move on. These efforts at forced "resettlement" by government decree, however, set a dangerous trend that would plague Nova Scotian Blacks right up into the twentieth century. Government officials were most curious about the fact that Black *women* seemed to be the most vocal in their objection to leaving. One befuddled observer of the day noted, "They seem to have some attachment to the soil they have cultivated, poor and barren as it is." This would not be the last time that Black Nova Scotian women campaigned aggressively for the rights of their people.

By 1850 there were nearly five thousand Blacks living throughout Nova Scotia in well-established communities. The church became a central and driving force in the lives of families in the Black community, with preachers like Boston King and Richard Preston having a powerful impact on the development of a Black Nova Scotian identity.

"A Picture of Neglect"

While the church became a force for social change as well as religious inspiration for men, it also helped foster the push for education and rights for
women, one turning-point being the formation of a provincial African
Baptist Women's Auxiliary in 1917. More Black women were at last receiving some form of education, but it was not until 1945 that William and
Pearleen Oliver helped to finally remove impediments that prevented Black
women from becoming teachers. In that same year, Carrie Best created *The
Clarion*, the first newspaper for Black Nova Scotians. And it was another
feisty Black woman, Viola Desmond, who decided she had had enough of
discrimination when, in 1946, she sat in the all-white section of a theatre in
New Glasgow. She was arrested, held in jail and fined for her act and this
earned her a place in the hearts of the civil rights activists who would follow
her. The forties also saw the success of a Black Nova Scotia singer, Portia
White of Africville, who travelled the world receiving wide acclaim for her
musical abilities.

Racism, overt or obscured in cloaks of bureaucracy, would continue to
haunt the Black citizenry of Nova Scotia for a long time to come. Nowhere
was this more apparent than in the story of Portia White's home community
of Africville, an almost all-Black settlement situated at the north end of the
Halifax Peninsula. Settled in the mid-nineteenth century, it had its first ele-
mentary school in 1883, an all-Black school that didn't close until integration was invoked in 1953.

Through the forties and fifties, Africville men worked as stone masons,
barrel makers, stevedores and garbage men. Women worked stitching bags
in a bone-meal plant. They also cleaned and cooked in the homes of more
affluent Haligonians. As in other Black communities around the province,
the church was very much at the centre of social activity.

Provincial and city governments used land near Africville to locate
sewage disposal pits and hospitals for infectious diseases. A stone-crushing
plant, a bone-meal factory and an abattoir were also located on the edges of
the community. In the 1950s, the city made the ultimate insult to Africville
by locating the civic dump a stone's throw from the homes there. The city
viewed Africville as a place of little consequence and provided lesser or
nonexistent services. Petitions from the community were dismissed with reg-
ularity. City Hall had little regard for those who lived in this end of town.

Fires swept through Africville in the forties and fifties and the absence of
city water hydrants made it a dangerous place to live. Drinking water was
often polluted and likely to generate disease.

A survey in 1959 revealed that half the workers in Africville earned less
than a thousand dollars per year, the lowest wages in Halifax. Sixty per cent
of the kids lagged behind in education and only one student had gone

beyond grade seven. In 1964 William Oliver noted, "the community presents a picture of neglect, poor roads, primitive and unsanitary wells and outside privies." It was a place of poor education, rough housing and few amenities. Who was to blame?

City officials tried to blame the residents themselves, ignoring the legacy of government decisions that had led to the alienation and denigration of life in Africville. Nonetheless, within Africville there was a strong community spirit that was deeply rooted in the place. Some residents at the time were able to claim sixth-generation status. There was a heart and soul to the life of Africville, despite the despair heaped upon the people who lived there. When the urban renewal trends of North America caught up with Halifax, this so-called "slum" could have been revitalized, utilizing available urban renewal resources coupled with the positive spirit that had remained alive here. Instead, the city decided on another option. The community would be "relocated." Houses would be demolished, people would be forced to live elsewhere, some with compensation, some without. Africville would cease to be anyone's problem. It would no longer exist.

Moved Away in Garbage Trucks

The city argued that everybody would benefit from relocation. Residents would move to new homes with clean water and city services. The city would get rid of an eyesore.

Not all attempts at urban renewal were based solely on good intentions; sometimes there were darker underpinnings. Unfortunately for Africville residents, as with other victims of urban renewal, the decisions were often made by politicians, city planners and developers without serious input from those being affected. The city wanted the land at Africville for harbour and industrial development. Some land had already been expropriated in 1957 and, in 1961, a city council housing committee had recommended getting rid of all housing in the area. A common phrase bandied around at political levels was that they were looking for a solution to "the Africville problem."

In 1962, the people of Africville were offered alternative subsidized housing outside of the community. If someone had legal title to the land, they'd be offered something close to "fair market value," but as was often the case, residents who lived in houses on untitled land were offered only $500. The city had budgeted a miserly maximum of $70,000 for the purchase of all property involved.

Africville residents remained under-represented in the whole process, even though human-rights professionals and volunteers were staging dozens of public meetings. These socially concerned activists seemed to be generally in favour of promoting relocated integrated housing as opposed to preserving the mostly segregated Black community of Africville. This altruistic notion was not necessarily in the best interest of those who loved Africville and didn't want to move but rather hoped to see the community improved. A meeting of community residents in 1962 led to an outright rejection of the proposed city plan of relocation.

The city decided to buy out as many residents as were willing to sell and then immediately tear down their houses to impress upon everyone else that redevelopment was already underway and that complete relocation was inevitable. It would be the older people, with deep emotional and historical roots in the community, who were the most reluctant to give up their life-long homes.

The first move took place in 1964 with a woman who received her $500 cash settlement, free moving, public housing and payment of an outstanding hospital bill of $1,500. Before the buy-out was complete, the city had spent considerably more than expected in relocating residents. The city spent a total of $550,000 for the land and houses plus another $250,000 in resettlement and program costs. Some residents of Africville were moved "free of charge" in city garbage trucks, an insult that would reverberate for generations to come.

One of the last hold-outs was Aaron "Pa" Carvery, who was called to City Hall and then presented with a suitcase full of money in hopes he would give in. He refused the money and walked away. Eventually the city acted without his consent and bulldozed his home anyway.

Of the Africville citizens relocated, seventy per cent interviewed in 1969 attested to some kind of personal calamity in their lives as a result of having to move. Africville became a powerful symbol for the entire Black community of Nova Scotia through the seventies and still is today. At the heart of the Africville crisis was the issue of ownership of land and a government's right to revoke ownership of one's own home. There was a clear sense that Africville residents had been pushed around by government because they were Black and because they were poor. The message was clear: it should never be allowed to happen again. In retrospect, the treatment of Africville residents fit into the classic pattern of how Blacks in Nova Scotia had been treated from the very beginning—as second-class citizens.

A newspaper account during the time of relocation uttered the indignity that "Soon Africville will be but a name." But that hasn't been the case. The trauma of Africville has remained alive in the consciousness of Nova Scotia and comes back again and again in the music of Four The Moment, in the writings of George Elliott Clarke, Maxine Tynes, David Woods and Walter Borden. Reunions are held annually at the site of the former community. In the summer of 1995, while world leaders gathered in Halifax at the G7 Summit, two brothers in the Carvery family, who had grown up in Africville, encamped on the land that was once their home to stage a protest covered by the international media and brought to the attention of people around the world.

Chapter Forty-two

Unhealthy Habits,
Unclean Harbours

Lobster traps at the edge of Halifax Harbour in the 1960s; best not to eat anything caught in the harbour today.

Of Oil and Herbicides

In 1971, per capita income in Nova Scotia was a modest $2,661, compared to $4,019 in Ontario. Young men and women raised here were still leaving for greener pastures in Ontario, Alberta and beyond. Don Shebib's 1970 movie, *Goin' Down the Road*, told the story of the dreams and the losses of Nova Scotians who had to move west in search of employment.

There was hope anew, however, as Mobil Oil announced in 1971 discovery of oil and gas fields off Sable Island. The economic bonus for Nova Scotians was never to be as big as expected and the promise of reward is yet to be fulfilled in the 1990s. Oil rigs and oil transport at sea, however, have raised even bigger questions concerning the safety of the environment. What would be the price of destruction, for example, if there were a major accident involving the unchecked flow of oil to the surface around the sensitive and unique aquatic and coastal environment of Sable Island?

Although this event was not associated with the Sable Island oil fields, Nova Scotia had a taste of oil disaster on February 3, 1970, when the Liberian-registered tanker *Arrow* grounded in Chedabucto Bay, ravaging the coastline with a thick coat of oil that spread for sixty-five kilometres, killing uncounted numbers of birds, seals and other aquatic life.

In the forests of Cape Breton, another ecological disaster loomed as a result of the chemical spraying of insecticides to kill the spruce budworm and herbicides to "control" hardwood growth in forests.

The first aerial spraying of pesticides took place in Canada in 1927, and by the late fifties and early sixties, the most popular and potent form of poison was DDT. No one fully knows the damage inflicted on the Nova Scotia ecosystem by DDT, but mass-media attention to the problem brought on by books like Rachel Carson's *Silent Spring* alerted all of North America to the crisis. At the very least, the spray intended to kill off pests was killing useful insects, birds and fish. Bald eagles, higher up the food chain and most likely to consume concentrated amounts of DDT, were headed for extinction.

Local foresters were most worried about the ravages of the spruce budworm. Fortunately, a biological insecticide, b.t., was developed to replace DDT and other more toxic chemicals and has been in use for nearly twenty years.

Unfortunately, the forestry industry, in an effort to make Nova Scotian forests "more efficient," has continued aerial spraying of herbicides to kill off hardwoods in favour of the more commercially useful softwood trees. The long-term effect of such spraying is still very much a controversial matter, but residents who live near affected areas fear the consequence to themselves and their children and argue for safer means of forest regeneration— labour-intensive selective cutting and more holistic avenues of harvesting the forest. In some parts of Cape Breton, environmental activists, in an effort to protect not only wildlife but the health of children living close to the affected areas, have led successful campaigns to reduce or eliminate the most toxic of the chemicals used.

Poison from the Rain

The curse of acid rain became most apparent in Nova Scotia in the 1970s and 1980s. The result of sulphur dioxide and nitrogen oxide from burning fossil fuels, the acids in the sky are carried by the prevailing winds, and driven toward Nova Scotia from as far away as industrial Indiana and Ontario. Although some of the acid is generated right here in the province from automobile exhaust and coal-burning power plants, more than eighty per cent of it comes from away. Nova Scotia has become an indiscriminate dumping ground for Upper-Canadian and American air-borne pollutants.

As a result of the acid rain, more than half of the lakes in Nova Scotia are considered to be highly at risk. As the waters become more and more acidic, plant life dies off and so do fish. The end result is the outright extinction of some water creatures. The higher elevations in the area stretching from the Annapolis Basin to Chedabucto Bay have been the hardest hit. Salmon cannot reproduce in waters with high acidity and many streams and rivers have seen the disappearance of salmon and other fish. If these species cannot migrate to other less acidic rivers, they too will eventually die off for good in Atlantic Canada.

Acid rain also has the problematic side effect of leaching metals like aluminum out of the soil and into the water. Aluminum and other toxic elements from the soil can harm the fish but also the human population that drinks water from these natural sources.

Almost anything that finds its way into the air eventually finds its way into the water as well. This is most worrisome not only because of the acidity of the rain but also because of a whole range of chemicals that are carried aloft from combustion. PCBs and lead are but two of the deadly chemicals that eventually fall back into the rivers and the sea, some produced locally, some drifting from a thousand kilometres away.

Nova Scotian communities continue to dump tons of raw sewage into the waters. Pulp and steel mills disgorge solids, and other chemicals as well. In the early 1980s a section of Sydney Harbour was closed to lobster fishermen because of high levels of some very exotic chemicals—cadmium and "polynuclear aromotic hydrocarbons." The problem has continued to spread, with shellfish being perhaps the most affected. In 1940 about 30 shellfish closings were posted in the entire region, but by 1987 310 areas were closed because of contaminated shellfish. But the shellfish problem might be only the tip of the iceberg.

The worst of the pollution exists in what is known as the Sydney tar ponds, an environmentalist's worst nightmare. The tar ponds contain something like 700,000 tons of sludge, laced with PCBs and heavy metals, that has drained here from the Sydney Steel mill for nearly a hundred years. Run-off from the tar ponds eventually finds its way into the harbour and into the sea. In the 1980s, the province and the federal government realized something had to be done, so they invested more than fifty-two million dollars in constructing a pipeline and two incinerators to burn the deadly goo. Unfortunately, the incinerators never worked effectively. In early 1996, Sydney still had a monumental environmental problem and one of the highest cancer rates in the country. In a time of declining government dollars for health and environment, the best the current government can suggest is a proposal to encase the ponds in cement and leave the problem to be solved in the future.

Twenty-five Million Gallons of Gunk

The early French and English explorers had a clear mandate to come to Nova Scotia to exploit for profit the resources that were here. Sometimes a resource, such as cod, would be harvested for a few hundred years until these fish were simply all gone. Sometimes there are bi-products of industry or populations that wreak havoc on this beautiful and fragile environment. And we simply chalk it up as the price of progress.

I have a deep personal love for Nova Scotia and realize that all of these many generations of immigrants, myself included, have probably done a lot more harm to this place than good. Economic factors have more often than not dictated how we treat this maritime environment that has sustained us. As a result, we have delivered back to our host the least desirable of gifts, for our skills in cleaning up after ourselves are poor.

Along with our international guests who fish these waters, we collect and consume the marketable life of the sea until it disappears. And in line with global market forces, we clear-cut the forests, dig up the land and ship off the trees and the minerals without significant regard for the damage that is left behind. Economics dictate that it is often "inefficient" to clean up after ourselves, so we leave problems to following generations who we hope will magically be better equipped than we are.

Despite the mistakes, Nova Scotia has been spared some of the massive environmental damage that ravaged much of New England and the Atlantic states as well as the Great Lakes region of Canada. With a relatively low population density and a minimum of heavy industry, we're not as badly off as, say, New Jersey, where I was born. The forests and fields of my youth are long since buried by concrete, houses, shopping malls, highways and industrial parks. But change will come to Nova Scotia and the mythical good economic times that always seem just around the corner may prove to be worse for this northerly haven than anyone has reckoned.

In recounting a history, there is the hope that it is more than just a good yarn or a tale of power struggles, heroes, corruption and battles won or lost. There's always the prospect that something is to be learned from history and that such knowledge will bring about change for the better. In one sense, however, the tradition of crimes perpetrated by the early English élite and military men who battered this rural wilderness into so-called civilization are continuing as we do damage to the very land and sea that make this such an attractive and nourishing place to live.

Perhaps the most glaring of all the environmental damage is taking place at the heart of Nova Scotia's population centre in Halifax and Dartmouth where raw sewage continues to be pumped directly into the harbour.

There are only three major cities in Canada that dump raw sewage without any sort of treatment, straight into the waterways. Halifax is one of them, spilling more than twenty-five million gallons of the gunk each day into the sea by way of the very harbour so often boasted about as being one of the finest in the world. For a long time now, citizens and politicians have grudgingly agreed that something should be done. In fact, more than fifteen years ago, a surcharge was put on every Haligonian's water bill, money that would go toward cleaning up the harbour.

Unfortunately, much of the money raised—about seventeen million dollars—ended up being used for various "public works projects," including new and better pipes and pumping stations to move more raw sewage from homes and new industrial parks off into the harbour. As of 1996, property owners in Halifax continue to pay the tax and untreated sewage is still being force-fed into the harbour where it is conveniently flushed into the open ocean.

Ironically, in the late 1980s, the feds and the province drew up an agreement to end the abomination. Halifax Harbour Cleanup Inc. was created to assess the problem and put together a solution. Their price tag was a hefty $400 million.

The HHCI plan was way over budget and there was a lot of protest over the plan to put the treatment plant on McNab's Island. (Remember, the British Navy used to hang disobedient sailors along the shores there for all to view.) Some argued that the chlorine that was to be used in the process could also do some damage of its own and that the whole business was going to take place within a couple of kilometres of where people would be swimming. Local environmentalists obviously didn't like the plan at all and offered an alternative that would cost a mere hundred million. Political appointees on HHCI weren't pleased with the alternate proposal and, like too much crud in a septic line, the whole process became gummed up long enough for 1995 to roll around, at which time the federal-provincial agreement ran out. Obsession with the deficit quashed any hopes of any further federal money coming in to clean up the harbour.

Environmentalists were fuming and are still considering taking somebody to court. The Fisheries Act states outright that it's illegal to spew untreated sewage into the ocean. It could, after all, do nasty things to the fish—well, those less marketable ones that are still swimming. The Department of National Defence—the military—continues to dump sewage and possibly more damaging chemicals from several strategic locations around the harbour. And, of course, the harbour cities continue to spew with unchecked abandon. With all of this blatant law-breaking one might wonder how federal or city authorities can ignore the problem. But ignore it they do.

In 1994, the Metro Coalition for Harbour Cleanup reminded the public that Halifax and Dartmouth were choking the harbour with 35.3 billion litres of raw sewage each year and that it was a "foul mix of water, human excrement, grease, motor oil, paint thinner, antifreeze and many kinds of industrial waste." They went so far as to say it was equal to "two Exxon Valdez oil spills each and every day of the year." Clams and mussels can no longer be harvested from the harbour, but some people are still eating the fish, and a swim at Halifax's once-pristine Black Rock Beach can be an encounter with just about anything your neighbours flushed down the toilet yesterday.

Fragile Environment, Vulnerable Economy

As Nova Scotians have become more and more aware of how fragile their environment is, they have also found themselves rudely reawakened to how fragile and vulnerable their economy remains. The sixties and seventies had brought in a tide of federal concern and involvement in the region, but the eighties saw the tide ebb away again as the Mulroney government sought to cut federal spending and devolve its interest in helping the Atlantic region. Having become ever more dependent on the Canadian government in the hundred plus years since Confederation, Nova Scotia now felt the sting of the loss of federal financial support.

Nova Scotians were resoundingly opposed to the Free Trade pact the Mulroney government negotiated with the United States, but by now the province had little political clout in Ottawa. Free Trade legislation went into effect and, as a result, many jobs in fish plants and manufacturing slipped out of Nova Scotia forever.

Ironically, Nova Scotia's near-unanimous opposition to Free Trade was a signal of the province's fully mature attitude toward national unity. Nova Scotians were shouting out that they preferred a strong and independent Canada. For good reasons, they feared the economic domination of American corporations and the unhealthy influence of American politics and culture on the Canadian way of life. They had already, for decades, lived through the economic erosion that resulted from absentee ownership of industry. Unfortunately, there will be no easy road back to the self-sufficiency permitted by a highly decentralized economy and a rural lifestyle.

Chapter Forty-three

Coal Mining in Nova Scotia: A Chronicle of Despair

THE EMERY COLLIERY, CAPE BRETON.

Emery Colliery on Cape Breton Island, 1873; engraving by Eugene Haberer.

Westray: The Inevitable Disaster

At 5:18 on the morning of May 9, 1992, an explosion ripped through the Westray Mine at Plymouth in Pictou County, Nova Scotia. Twenty-six men were trapped inside and all died underground. It was a tragic mining accident that was only one in a long legacy of catastrophes in which Nova Scotian miners paid with their lives for digging out the coal in this province. Despite significant improvements in mine safety, Westray drove home the realization that coal mining had begun as a dangerous enterprise here and, with modern safety precautions, the death toll in the coalfields might diminish but would not disappear. Once again the question would be raised: is coal worth the price of the men who would die underground?

Westray had only been in business for five months. A build-up of methane gas caused the explosion. Underground workers had been complaining for months that the mine was unsafe. The coal dust had been thick inside the shaft, abandoned machinery had been left lying around inside and, even worse, combustion engines that could produce sparks to ignite unvented gases were in use despite the fact they were illegal in these conditions. Rock falls and work stoppages had been too frequent and the owners had not allowed for time-consuming measures to cover the dangerous coal dust with more stable rock dust, a common safety measure to lower the risk of explosions.

The mine had failed safety inspections yet continued to operate. The imposed deadline for improving the situation was mid-May, too late to avert the disaster. Government regulators moved far too slowly and failed to save the men who perished there and whose fate could have been so easily avoided.

Families and surviving miners went to the media to show how lax the government had been concerning Westray and how the mine's owner, Curragh Resources Ltd., had failed to look out for the welfare of its workers. Bureaucratic bungling, desire for quick profits and a generally cavalier attitude toward safety had led to the accident that took the lives of those twenty-six men.

As TV viewers across North America watched and heard the stories about the events leading up to the tragedy, many wondered aloud why anyone would ever want to work in a mine. A miner's job was, from the start, a dirty, physically debilitating one, an insecure career often subject to erratic economic forces in the energy sector. Yet income from coal mining had been the financial lifeline supporting many families in Pictou County and on Cape Breton Island for generations. Coal is very much a part of Nova Scotia history and it is a tale punctuated all too frequently with anger, heartache and tragedy.

A Dirty, Difficult Job

The origins of coal in Nova Scotia go back to those hot and humid days of three hundred million years ago when a lush, thick covering of vegetation grew over the land. Eventually, everything fell to the ground, rotted, got buried and compressed by the weight of other organic matter and sediment settling on top of it. The stuff below would evolve first into peat and then, after several million years, it would fossilize into coal. The Sydney coalfield is said to be one of the richest in the world and it stretches beyond the island far out under the water, so that by the twentieth century Cape Bretoners would find themselves in man-made tunnels beneath the ocean, mining the dark and dangerous black rock, while above them in the waters of the Cabot Strait their neighbours fished for cod and haddock. These submarine coal seams and the mining that tapped them are unlike any other in North America.

In 1720, French soldiers first began to chip away at the exposed coal at Cow Bay, Cape Breton, and it was sent off as fuel for the homes of Louisbourg. When the English took charge of Cape Breton, they made a good profit on the resource by selling it in Boston or other American cities and for use by the military in Halifax. By 1870, more than twenty collieries were in full swing on the island and the value of this energy-rich mineral was recognized by some as Cape Breton's greatest asset.

Coal mining would always be a dirty, difficult and heartbreaking job for the miners, but for owners, the main concern was profit. By the latter part of the nineteenth century, Cape Breton was dotted with one-company towns where almost all of the decision-making for those who lived there was in the hands of the men who ran the companies. The company would decide who could work, how much they would be paid, where a miner's family could live and what supplies would be available to them. The infamous "company store" would be the only local source of food, household goods and clothing. Everything was bought on credit and then the costs were docked from the workers' wages. The stores would even be happy to supply any frivolous or luxury items a miner's wife might be lured into buying, so they remained well stocked with all sorts of frilly dresses and expensive meats and candy.

The further indebted a family was to the company, the more control the owners had in keeping miners in line with long work hours and low wages. If a miner ever put up a significant fuss, he could be out of a job and out of a house, with no chance of returning to work ever. Any other mining family who acted charitably toward the victims might find itself kicked out of the fold. Needless to say, this left Cape Bretoners in a very vulnerable position. This plight of the miners and their families continued well into the twentieth century and was brought vividly to life in the 1995 movie *Margaret's Museum*, starring Helena Bonham-Carter.

While the companies had created nearly a slave economy for their men, they did little to offset the dangers awaiting their workers below. Gas explosions, not unlike the one at Westray, occurred regularly. A huge ball of flame might produce a blast that killed anyone in its path. It might spew through several sections at once, curling steel rail lines into fantastic shapes and dismembering the men and horses below ground. Those who weren't torn apart by the explosion often died as the oxygen was burned from their lungs. If for any reason you still survived, you stood a good chance of being asphyxiated by remaining methane and carbon monoxide. Small explosions, which killed only a few men at a time, were common and considered a run-of-the-mill hazard, virtually unavoidable. Bigger disasters drew more attention.

Lessons Not Learned

Nova Scotia has a long legacy of pirates, privateers and profiteers, all motivated by the same thing: greed. The story of coal mining in this province illustrates just how extreme human exploitation can get in order to improve the bottom line. The real history of coal mining in Nova Scotia is a chronicle of tragedies that underscore the negligence of bosses and governments set in sharp contrast to the fierce courage and humanity of the men who worked below.

The Westray hearings of the late-twentieth century reminded Nova Scotians that the Pictou coal seams on the mainland had always been dangerous. The coal is imbedded in unstable shale. One early disaster occurred here in May 13 of 1873, when a coal fire swept through the mine. Before the miners could get to the surface, the gases exploded, killing fifty-five men, and the mine was sealed off because it was deemed too dangerous. Only two years later, however, the mine was put into operation again, despite the international notoriety of the 1873 explosion that was considered to be one of the most violent blasts in the history of coal mining.

"In the Town of Springhill"

For anyone living in North America in the 1950s, the name of Springhill, Nova Scotia, is well known as the focal point of not one but two major mining disasters. Nineteen fifty-eight was the year of the worst disaster, but in the forty previous years, at least five hundred "bumps" or rock bursts were charted in the Number 2 mine. Here too was another mine that company and government alike knew to be a killer but profits were good and the mine lived on. The deeper the shaft went, the more frequent became the bumps and they increased in magnitude as well. By 1953, a team of experts began to investigate the recurrence of these disturbances, but they were still looking into the problem as late as October of 1958 when the underground explosion rocked the earth so hard that it was recorded on seismographs as far away as Ottawa.

While reports piled up and studies stretched out over decades, the mines around Springhill continued to operate. On Thursday, November the first in 1956, an ore car jostled free of its underground track and cut through a high-voltage electric line. The spark set off an explosion and fire at the 600-metre level, trapping 118 men below at 900 metres. The fire sucked up the available oxygen and, in its aftermath, was more methane gas and carbon monoxide. Compressed air was pumped to the men below and two miners crawled and climbed to the surface under their own power, reporting on the situation of the men further below. Rescuers and doctors scrambled bravely below and hauled out collapsed miners along the way who were trying to escape. They had to descend past the gas pockets and a fire that still burned, until they reached 1,600 metres below ground where they found fifty of the trapped men. Some could walk but others had to be carried out on stretchers. Back on the surface, rescue workers realized that there were still at least eight men below. Again, volunteers went down and found the remaining miners, but only two of the eight were alive. The return to the surface nearly took the lives of the rescuers as they inched forward in impossible conditions. While so many men were saved by the valiant efforts, thirty-nine perished in the accident.

Less than two years later, Springhill again made the headlines. On October 23, 1958, another bump occurred as the ceiling of a mine collapsed onto the floor. Eighty-one men made it to safety and eighteen bodies were recovered, but seventy-five were still missing. Rescue workers kept at it day and night and six days later, far below the earth, they heard the sound of men singing. Ten men were alive, sealed in a tomb fifteen metres by five metres wide, but it would be nearly impossible to tunnel through the fallen rubble of rock. In order to send them some nourishment, a doctor poured tomato soup into an orchard sprayer and fed it to the trapped men one by one through a copper tube shoved through the air line. After fourteen hours of feverish digging, these victims, still alive, were hauled to safety, but forty-nine miners were still missing.

Seven more were found on November second at the nine-hundred-metre level and were brought up to tell the horrors of their days in darkness below. That would be the end of underground mining in Springhill. Some blamed the recklessness of the mining technique which involved carving out entire coal faces instead of "step mining" which would have allowed for better ceiling support.

A Future for Coal?

Mining declined in Nova Scotia not so much because of its dangers but because it was no longer the lucrative business it once was. By the 1950s, mining costs were increasing as the mines went deeper to follow the seam of available coal. Cheaper natural gas and oil were replacing coal as well. It was a dying industry but not a dead one. Small family mines continued to operate in Inverness and Cumberland counties right up into the 1980s. Mining today in Nova Scotia remains perilous to both the body and the pocketbook. As recently as the summer of 1995, bankruptcy loomed in the air for the Cape Breton Development Corporation which runs the mines on the island. The privatized Nova Scotia Power Inc. was ready and willing to sacrifice jobs locally to buy even cheaper coal on the world market. Cape Bretoners and Pictou County men may be spared the hardship and tragedy of life as miners, but it won't be as a result of the concerns for safety by the federal or provincial government as the Westray disaster so sadly illustrates. Instead, it may simply be bad economic forecasts for the industry that will close the mines for good. If coal once again finds itself in serious demand, however, Nova Scotian miners will again be lining up for jobs, aware of the dangers, but ever anxious to earn a respectable living, no matter how treacherous the job.

Chapter Forty-four

The Death of the Fish

Fishing was rarely an easy livelihood.

Pushed to the Point of Extinction

As I look out the window of my home, out across the vast expanse of the blue November Atlantic, it's easy to imagine that I'm looking at sea where very little has changed in thousands of years. Beyond the sand dunes is the same salt water, the same wind-spirited waves, and above, the same cumulus clouds driven by the restless winds. Everything seems to be as it should be.

What I can't see is how much has changed beneath the surface of the waves. It would be an exaggeration to say that the fish are all gone. Some species still thrive, while others, such as the cod, have been brought to near extinction, primarily by man. The Grand Banks that once teemed with sea life are bereft of much of the life it once knew. John Cabot had written of the sea that could be harvested of cod by merely dipping baskets from the side of a ship. Now, on that same patch of ocean, it might be nearly impossible to find a fully grown cod. We have allowed for a kind of salt-water holocaust and now the social and economic after-blast has come to haunt us here in our very lives ashore.

The phrase, the "death of the fishery," may sound like melodramatic politician's rhetoric to landlubbers beyond the Atlantic Provinces, but here it has profound, ominous implications. Something has gone out of this world, our maritime world, and we may never be the same. We will be the worse for it; many of us will be forced to leave the shorelines and our homes.

Those scientists best equipped to tell us about what went wrong suggest they are not a hundred per cent certain. We fished too much, that's for sure. We fished carelessly and stupidly. And nature figured into this as well. Something changed—most likely the water temperature. A scant degree or two was enough to throw off the cycle of reproduction. Will the cod and other decimated stocks of fish come back? Perhaps, the experts suggest...with a little luck. On the other hand, there is no compelling hard evidence to say that the cod population can bounce back. Like so many other species, we may have pushed this one to the point of extinction.

Uncontrolled and Overfished

Early in the eighteenth century, fishermen in the French fleet off Newfoundland and Nova Scotia began to notice some decline in the fish population. And then things got worse. Canadian historian Christopher Moore came across the writings of a 1739 "expert" on the fishery who reported, "There has not been the slightest appearance of fish stock this fall. This has greatly astonished our fishermen—who will all be wiped out." This news may offer some small comfort and hope to those of us here at the tail end of the twentieth century. Perhaps the fish population is cyclical. It has disappeared before and returned. With a little luck, we're just in a bad patch for the cod themselves and for the fishermen who scoop them from the sea.

The other possibility is this. As the cod population dwindled this century, rather than backing off and allowing for a natural cycle of decline and recovery, we fished on, harvesting those few survivors who could have been breeders leading toward a recovery. In other words, when the cod numbers were low, we swooped in for the kill. If that's the case, cod fish may be gone for good.

As technology advanced in this century, we were painfully slow to realize its deadly side effects and legislate some kind of control. The situation off Nova Scotia and Newfoundland was obviously complicated by the fact that it wasn't just Canadian fishermen involved, but ships, some of them massive factory ships from around the world, harvesting fish.

The story of government controls of fishing in the second half of this century begins in 1949 with the formation of an international commission (ICNAF) whose job it was to do research and "bring order" to fishing in this part of the Atlantic. ICNAF was later renamed NAFO (Northwest Atlantic Fisheries Organization) and, despite some symbolic attempts at control, the Northwest Atlantic was a bit of a free-for-all until 1970 when the Gulf of St. Lawrence, at least, was declared an exclusive Canadian fishing zone. The following year, actual fishing quotas were set for all NAFO members, but not all countries were in the club and not everyone, including some members, would play by the rules.

By 1974, number crunchers in the fishing industry realized that something big-time was going wrong. There was a major drop in the size of the catch on the Labrador and Grand Banks. At least twenty countries were overfishing. In 1975, Canada responded to one of the worst offenders by closing her ports to the Soviet fleet. Canada became even more protective after that, declaring a two-hundred-mile limit in an attempt to insure "control" over what fish were left in this corner of the Atlantic. This move, which angered much of the international fishing community, helped Nova Scotian fishing companies to survive, but it may have proven to be merely a postponement.

Nonetheless, Canadian catches were up for five years after that and government began to speak of something called a Groundfish Management Plan. But if the fish were somewhat protected, the biologists, oceanographers and even the companies involved in fishing were not. In 1978 the federal fisheries lab in Halifax was closed. In 1981 and into 1982, there was a financial crisis in the industry because of high interest rates, huge inventories and a lack of interest on the part of buyers. Ironically, the market was glutted with fish and it was wrecking the business. In response, the feds poured fifteen million bucks into "inventory relief" for the companies.

The Scale of Social Disruption

So, while businessmen were still trying to figure out how to "manage" the resource, government was slashing the Department of Fisheries and Oceans on into 1985 and 1986—at the very time that more research should have gone into insuring a stable future for fish in the sea, not in the can or freezer.

Then something weird happened in 1987: a very good year. The Atlantic Provinces Economic Council called it the "best year ever for the Atlantic fishery [with] landed value of $791 million." But those few scientists left working for DFO saw forces other than economic ones at work on the fish population. They saw populations of haddock and cod going down not up and allowable catch limits were tightened. This led to the closing of fish plants in Newfoundland and Nova Scotia; foreign fishing companies with plants ashore here pulled out.

In May of 1990, the Atlantic Fisheries Adjustment Program was announced and APEC would cry out that "the scale of social disruption caused by proposals to rationalise the sector is unprecedented." People would lose their jobs, companies—big and small—would go belly up and fishermen would cease to fish. Coastal towns would die and an entire way of life was close to disintegration. And all the while, the once-bountiful cod was headed toward extinction.

That same APEC report argued that fishing was the single most important industry in our region, with more than 100,000 people directly employed in harvesting and processing, and many towns entirely dependent on the resource. That was then.

As the federal government screwed the lid down tightly on the fishing business, it created other massive spin-off losses in shipbuilding and repair, manufacturing, transportation and the like. All this came on the heels of the unprecedented short fishing boom that resulted from initiation of the two-hundred-mile limit. In a short time, more fishing licences had been issued, more families had become dependent on fishing income and more people had become dependent on the Unemployment Insurance factor, allowing them to go on "pogie" for the time they could not fish. Young people quit school and fished because it all looked so attractive. Then the bottom dropped out and these under-educated young men and women became part of the fallout from a very short golden age of fishing.

Inshore/Offshore

The whole fishing industry is a pretty complex entity rarely understood by anyone who is not directly involved in it. The so-called "fishery" employs everyone from corporate managers to trawler captains to the lone inshore fishermen with one boat and on to the coastal dweller who harvests Irish moss. Fishermen has also given way to simply *fishers*, to include the many women who work in the industry.

While larger ships have traditionally left port in Nova Scotia to harvest from the Grand Banks (once the richest fishing ground in the world, now an undersea desert), men and women with smaller vessels fish in the Gulf of St. Lawrence's Northumberland Strait, the Bay of Fundy and the Scotian Shelf which stretches from Yarmouth to Cape Breton.

The harvest is divided into groundfish, pelagic and estuarials, shellfish and seaweed. Groundfish refers to fish that feed on the ocean floor such as cod, turbot, haddock, halibut, hake, plaice and sole. Pelagic and estuarials are the surface-schooling variety—herring, mackerel, hark, smelts, tuna and salmon. Atlantic shellfish include lobsters, crabs, clams, mussels and shrimp, among others. Seaweed is also considered a fisheries resource. Dulse and Irish moss are primarily the only two varieties harvested here.

Important distinctions have been made between the inshore and offshore. Inshore fishermen have smaller boats and use traps, weirs, gill nets, long-lines, seines or trawls. This area of the industry employs the highest numbers, while offshore fishermen work from ships over thirty metres long and travel further out to sea to fish. The line between the two industries begins to blur as inshore fishermen, out of necessity, buy advanced technical gear and go further out to catch fish. It seems that everything about the industry is at the whim of a whirlwind of economic, governmental and biological factors.

Economic cycles prompt a boom-and-bust scenario; environmental factors may be doing the same. Government friendliness to the industry appears idiosyncratic, and to top it off consumer interest in fish seems to ebb and flow like the tides and not always in sync with any of the above. Nothing is new about this haywire condition, but it makes life quite difficult for a fisher or an employee in a small-town fish plant who needs a dependable wage to feed a family.

If You Can't Fight 'em, Join 'em

Meanwhile, back to the sorry saga of how the fishing business went bust. The federal government came to the aid of the big fish companies, such as Nova Scotia's National Sea Products. Now companies like NSP would operate with a quota system which should have allowed them to avoid the glut/shortage syndrome. They'd fish to maximize profits by catching only what the market demanded. This was a good trick, if it all worked according to plan. They had bigger, "better" ships—draggers that cost over a million bucks each and needed heavy financing. A new ship with all the latest gear was designed to pull in two hundred tons a year and that should have taken the guessing entirely out of fishing.

Inshore fishermen, on the other hand, would argue that they were being squeezed out by the giants. It was harder to compete with a big company's prices and their control of the market. The inshore fishermen had a few good years, as well, and in order to keep up with the big guys, invested in new boats, taking on significant debts with the hopes it would all pay off sooner or later.

By 1990, it was clear that all the good intentions for a modernized industry had run afoul. The fish were disappearing, thanks to all this efficiency. Consumers weren't all that hungry for fish and there were too many fishermen fishing too few fish. The government intervened again by cutting fish quotas. Processing companies closed down and the buzz word in government circles was "rationalization."

The years 1976 through 1990 saw an array of massive government reports, policy statements, task forces, reviews and adjustment packages. Common themes included controlling domestic and foreign fishing (well, overfishing, really), conserving and rebuilding the fish populations, community survival and new options. The Harris Report of 1990 spoke of extending the two-hundred-mile zone. The author of the report suggested that "serious thought be given to the possibility of participating in the rape of the 'Nose' and 'Tail' of the Bank...since European Community countries already take every fish they can possibly catch." If you can't fight 'em, join 'em, the rationale seems to have been.

But Leslie Harris, author of this report, was just being facetious. In an interview with Silver Donald Cameron, he was willing to come clean and tell it like it really was, stating flatly, "Our technology has outstripped our science. We have underestimated our own capacity to find, pursue and to kill.... The state of our ignorance is appalling. We know almost nothing of value with respect to the behaviour of fish. We don't even know if there's one northern cod stock or many, or how they might be distinguished. We don't know anything about migration patterns or their causes, or feeding habits, or relationships in the food chain. I could go on listing what we don't know."

The problem the scientists faced seems like a simple one. Nobody knew exactly how to come up with an accurate fish count. Counting the catch didn't necessarily tell you how many fish were in (or left in) the sea. I'm not exactly putting the blame for the death of the fishery on the poor researchers who couldn't figure how to count fish. It was a pretty daunting task and becoming more difficult as funds dried up. One method was known as "catch-per-unit-of-effort," but as the technology kept changing, it grew ever more difficult to find the right measuring stick.

The word "management" was often tossed around at DFO, but the net effect was that there was little control when it was most needed. Unhappily, everyone saw the "biomass" shrinking and began to tighten the total allowable catch. But it was all too little and too late. Just when we needed those dedicated but somewhat befuddled DFO researchers the most, Ottawa had slashed funding, closing that Halifax fisheries lab in 1978 and the Marine Ecology Lab in 1986, and cutbacks went on and on toward the end of the century. It's a classic case of the eighties and nineties slash-and-burn scenario, whereby diminished funding in the name of shrivelling the deficit would wreak economic ruin far into the future. Bad political moves dictated by the corporate agenda continue to come back to haunt not only the corporations themselves but the people of Atlantic Canada as their livelihood from fishing disappears.

Death by Dragger

This all leads us back to the big question: exactly who or what killed off all the fish? The federal government thought they were "managing" the underwater stock as if it was a rambling herd of cattle. But it was not. Whether it was foreigners or our own fleet, much of the blame can be placed on the draggers. Technology ruled the sea and if it was bigger, it was considered better—more efficient. Around the world, draggers have devastated the ocean floor and they continue today, hauling in everything they can scrape up, tossing back the unwanted species and only keeping the desirable catch. The so-called by-catch is dumped back into the sea, dead. Some of it includes the big numbers of the desirable species like cod that are considered too small. Those adolescent cod, however, are never going to have a chance to grow up. It didn't take a DFO Ph.D. to figure out that this style of fishing was very bad news. Since the 1960s or earlier, inshore fishermen on the wharves of Causeway Road in Seaforth or out on Big Tancook Island could tell you that the big fleet of draggers was killing the sea.

Aside from killing millions of unwanted fish, the other problem with the draggers is that they rake across the bottom of the sea floor. Afterwards, there's nothing left in many cases for fish to eat. The feeding grounds *and* breeding grounds have been decimated as if by some all-out military assault. All this could be avoided if fish were simply caught with baited hooks "the old fashioned way." Even a massive array of long-liner hooks and lines wouldn't inflict the kind of damage the draggers have on the Atlantic waters. Only bigger fish would take the larger hooks and there would be relatively little by-catch.

As you might guess, Canadians were not alone out there on the Grand Banks with their draggers. They were kept company on the Nose and Tail and elsewhere by the Spanish, Portuguese, Mexicans, Soviets, South Koreans, Panamanians and Americans. NAFO was supposed to have some control but everybody blatantly ignored the rules, including member nations. In 1986, the quota for all of Europe was set at about 23,000 tons, but the entire European Community hauled in more than 172,000 tons, with Spain and Portugal taking the lion's share. In 1988 when NAFO tight-ened the symbolic belt, the EC still took more than 66,000 tons, possibly because the fish population was already in a crash dive.

Was Canada as bad as the rest? Well, draggers were still chewing up the floor and dumping the by-catch, all perfectly good fish, just not what was needed for the market and possibly not what was in their licence to catch. The system was turning out to be both illogical and punitive to the fisher-men and to the fish. In an all-out war (and what else could this eradication of a species be called?) the generals might call it collateral damage. There were too many draggers and, in southwest Nova Scotia in particular, too much illegal fishing of all sorts. The Halifax *Chronicle-Herald* reported, in fact, that it was likely that fifty per cent more fish were taken by inshore fishermen than were actually reported. It was estimated that the illegal fish-ing business was netting a solid $100 million or more.

As the fish began to die off, fishermen had to sail further out on the Scotian Shelf. They needed bigger boats as they headed way out toward Sable Island or George's Bank. To buy the big boats, they had taken out loans and had to pay back the banks. They *had* to come up with a big catch if they wanted to stay solvent. So they fished further out and they took more fish—illegally if necessary. Some were actually getting quite rich in the short run, but, like the big draggers and the foreign fleets, they were devastating their future.

Seals for Scapegoats

When the cod started to disappear, some Nova Scotian fishermen and spokesmen for the big corporations decided to look for a scapegoat. Instead of blaming government or themselves, they blamed it on the seals. Seals ate too much cod and they carried cod worms and disease. Grey seals, in partic-ular, were seen as competitors. Some fishermen from Cape Breton to the South Shore took the matter into their own hands and carried rifles to shoot seals on sight. Television footage showed frustrated and brazen fishermen recklessly massacring seals at sea or near shore in front of the camera, and calling for another all-out war, this time directed against these benign crea-tures who had fed and lived in the North Atlantic long before man had arrived on the scene.

The debates raged as to whether seals were responsible for the loss of cod. The number crunchers who had been so inept in tallying the fish stocks came to the fore, arguing that the grey seal population in the Northwest Atlantic was 200,000 and growing. Supposedly they were munching up 40,000 tons of cod a year. Nova Scotians, still mostly embarrassed and enraged by the bloody sight of fishermen butchering seals for worldwide TV, were slightly relieved when Dalhousie University researchers in 1994 came up with a birth-control vaccine for seals that could be fired into a seal with an air rifle. The best place to find the female seals was on Sable Island and that's where Dr. Robert Brown and his sixteen-member team injected the first two hundred seals. The program is in its infancy, and while it sounds better than blasting seals into extinction, one might worry over the ethics of it all. Is it right to sterilise one species to suit the needs of another? Brown suggests that if each seal eats a ton of fish a year, that much can be saved for our consumption with each baby seal that is prevented from coming into the world. This might well be a moot point if the cod never make a comeback anyway.

Dr. David Lavigne, a zoologist at the University of Guelph, however, opposes the birth-control campaign, arguing that as fish stocks fall, so too will the population of seals. This sounds like death by starvation to me and I'm not sure that's more humane than a birth-control bullet in the butt of a mamma seal.

Still other researchers who monitor the sea suggest that the death of all those once-plentiful fish might simply be chalked up to "change of habitat." The water temperature has dropped slightly, reducing reproduction. Perhaps global warming has led to an increased melt in the polar ice, ironically producing colder water and colder water makes it less likely for fish to breed. Another argument put forward is that tiny but persistent quantities of oil, heavy metals or other chemicals are doing the damage.

Ray Rogers, an environmentalist who spent twelve years as a fisherman in southwest Nova Scotia, has an altogether different theory. He believes that the problem may relate to the size of cod "schools." Codfish move en masse with the smaller fry following the bigger ones who have adapted and know the ropes of sea survival. Rogers surmises that it's possible that all the larger cod have been caught, leaving the immature fish to guide the rest. If the "teenage" cod don't know what they need to know for survival, then the whole school is in real trouble. They don't know where and when to migrate, so the patterns for natural survival are altered toward an inevitable kind of mass suicide.

There is no precise, clear and certain answer to the question of who destroyed the cod, but it is obvious that humans were part of the equation. And the problem is not a simple one. The cod may be gone and they may be gone for good, fished until they were no more.

Imagining the Alternatives

In Atlantic Canada, as the sorry truth of the fish business settles in, governments are spending nearly two billion dollars over a five-year period to help workers forsake the fishing industry forever and learn to do something else. This means, in many cases, leaving the fishing communities.

In the 1990s, money continued to drain out of the government agencies responsible for research and for protecting the fish. Powerful *laissez-faire* advocates in the industry now say that government should get out of the mess altogether and let the experts—fish corporations—manage what's left of the ocean's resources. Forget the little guys; they're not as efficient as the larger operations, the argument goes. Big business favours the ITQ option. That's an individual transferable quota whereby a company could harvest *or sell* its right to a certain fixed quota of fish, whichever is most profitable.

Most independent fishermen don't like this idea, fearing that they and the smaller companies would soon be swallowed up into one mega-company that controls everything. This concept is modelled on a frightening Reaganistic policy of deregulation, leading to *private* ownership of natural resources. It's partly based on the false assumption that the new owners of the depleted ocean stock would look after their fish in their own best interest. If private enterprise has done little to protect the fish in the past, one might wonder, why would this change in the future? In Iceland, the introduction of ITQs was met with widespread strikes and in Norway, protests made the government back away from the same plan.

Nova Scotia has been far too slow to invest in a big way in the most obvious of alternatives: aquaculture. Salmon is the biggest crop, worth about $48 million in Atlantic Canada in 1988. Norway, far ahead of Canada in salmon aquaculture, apparently made good use of research done in the 1960s at Bedford Institute of Oceanography in Nova Scotia to speed ahead its own industry.

In this province, many traditional fishermen have fought aquaculture, fearing it would infringe on territorial rights or otherwise interfere with what is left of the natural fish stock. The government has been slack in getting the engine of aquaculture really going. We have fallen behind neighbouring New Brunswick and have a long way to go to catch up. The potential is good but possibilities remain relatively unexplored for the farming of salmon, cod, halibut and all manner of shellfish.

"The Dog That Walked..."

In 1991 John Crosbie of Newfoundland, former fisheries minister, had this to say about federal attempts at managing fish in Atlantic Canada: "Like the dog that walked on its hind legs, it is remarkable not because it walks poorly but that it walked at all." Such was Crosbie's way of summarizing the situation. It would be another Newfoundlander and federal fisheries minister, Brian Tobin, who, to follow Crosbie's simile, would have to shoot the walking dog, shutting down the cod and flatfish industry in the Atlantic in 1994, putting 35,000 workers out of jobs.

NAFO had hired a group of scientists in 1991 to look into the decline in the fishery and the report that emerged recommended a moratorium on cod and reduction in redfish quota. NAFO member countries voted to ignore the report and keep on fishing. A well-intentioned but gutless (or gutted) organization, NAFO had little leverage in making the facts work toward solving or reducing the problem.

In 1994, the federal government tossed some more money at the human victims in this story. The TAGS program (The Atlantic Groundfish Strategy) put nearly two billion dollars into an assistance package for fishers and plant workers. It was a kind of unemployment program that would also include money for skills training, counselling and generally getting people out of the fishing economy. Few glowing stories of overnight financial recovery and new, permanent jobs have come out of the program, and as the money runs out, fishing families long to return to the relatively good days of the past when a fishing man or woman could be self-employed and relatively independent. Not only have the fish disappeared, but a way of self-sufficient living, cherished by shore-dwelling Nova Scotians, is gone forever.

Chapter Forty-five

Fish Sheds and Federal Politics

Abandoned lobster traps and fish shacks at East Chezzetcook waiting to be claimed by the advancing seas.

The Politics of Place

In January of 1996, the Halifax *Mail-Star* reported that Nova Scotia premier John Savage was interested in opening up a dialogue with the other regional premiers concerning a new form of Maritime Union—consolidating New Brunswick, PEI and Nova Scotia into one province. Nobody, however, is jumping up and down in wild enthusiasm for this idea.

Consolidating and downsizing government, it seems, has become a sort of infectious disease. In 1995, Halifax, Dartmouth, Bedford and all of Halifax County were rolled into a new "supercity." Now, everybody along this shore from Hubbards to Ecum Secum, officially at least, has become a citizen of the new, modified if not improved, Halifax. There was, of course, no referendum. If there had been, the vast majority would have been opposed to the move, one deemed as being good for us, leading to leaner government, supposedly lowered debt and all of the et ceteras. So, one night I went to sleep in my own bedroom at Lawrencetown, the next morning I woke up and I was in Halifax. Like magic. It's a little bit too reminiscent of the way Nova Scotia was dragged against its will into Confederation by Charles Tupper, a wise man, a visionary of sorts, but certainly not a politician who saw his mandate to uphold the will of the populace. Far from it.

In 1995 Quebec came perilously close to separating from Canada. Invariably, the news commentators, when they spoke of Atlantic Canada, talked of how we'd be "cut adrift." Here was a fright even more chilling than being folded into a supercity or blended into a single, bland Maritime province. Would we slip backwards into the past as the rest of the world raced on without us into the future? Would we truly feel cut off from the rest of Canada, our voices drowned out in the new political battle lines drawn up by the reformers? Or would we, like Jonah, be swallowed up by a whale as we drifted away from the centre of a Canada that could not hold fast to us. The whale, in this scenario, of course would be the United States. And then, once digested by the beast, would we become some kind of Third World appendage, a cheap labour pool for wealthier American industrialists to draw on? Blessedly, none of these questions would have to be answered for now. Who knows? Perhaps it was the pity bestowed upon us by that minute percentage of Quebeckers that saved us from drifting out of Canada in the wake of separation.

The Inspirational Province

Oddly enough, I'm not as troubled by all of the political uncertainties as I could be. For me, personally, the politics of Nova Scotia has always performed on a small stage compared to the more grandiose venues of culture and environment. My vision of this province as it exists today is of an intoxicating mix of people and places, stories and storms.

At a book-launch party in West Chezzetcook for a local history book, a seventy-six-year-old Acadian man pulls me aside and tells me about the good old days when thousands of metal containers of booze were smuggled up and down the inlet on barges lightly covered over with a layer of stone and sand as if it's just an everyday shipment of gravel going down the shore. Another local Acadian, an artist from Grand Desert named Joe Purcell, tells me nearly true and fabulous tales about growing up around here in the 1960s among some of the craziest, friendliest people on the face of the earth.

When I turn on the radio, I hear that Nova Scotian Celtic music has found its way into the mainstream. The Rankin Family, the Barra MacNeils and Ashley MacIsaac, to name a few, have found the right studio mix to blend traditional heart-piercing sounds and songs with contemporary stylings. A morning drive to Cape Breton or even Antigonish County, and I'd have no trouble tracking down a fiddle-player or a bagpiper who would be more than happy to give me a rendition of something even closer to the roots—maybe a tear-magnet of a tune, like the air titled "Neil Gow's Lament for the Death of His Second Wife."

I open a book and read the poetry of Black writers like Maxine Tynes, George Elliott Clarke or David Woods and realize that these are voices speaking truths of Nova Scotia that are revelations to us all. Eskasoni poet Rita Joe writes with eloquent sadness,

> I am the Indian,
> And the burden
> Lies yet with me.

and I am haunted by the evocation. In another poem she sums up with a gentle irony the centuries of despair brought on her Mi'kmaq people by the invasion of Europeans:

> Seeing
> What wrongs have been wrought,
> Native ways seem not so wild.

For me, the words of these writers transcend the myopic wisdom of government departments and news commentators.

In looking for an image for a book cover, I go to Halifax to the office of Visual Arts Nova Scotia where I search through a collection of photographs and images of paintings, sculpture, weaving and other crafts. I am stunned by the sheer volume of beauty created by artists living and working in this province and walk back out onto the grey Halifax street with explosions of colour swimming in my head, having viewed en masse the work of such artists as Al Chaddock, Charlotte Wilson Hammond, Carol Kennedy, A.J. Gray, Geoff Butler, Margo Metcalf, Jeff Amos and dozens more.

Not a stone's throw from my house, a sculptor named Luigi Costanzo creates exotic, erotic shapes from chunks of marble the size of old Volkswagen Beetles. Down on the South Shore of the province, a retired street musician named Darren Arsenault finds beach rocks, and takes them back to his workshop in the town of Rosebud and crafts them into zen-like pieces of art. But when asked what he does for a living, he smiles and says that he "just drills holes in rocks."

The phone rings as I walk in from a cold, clear snowy day and a Vietnamese refugee living in Halifax asks if I would be willing to look at her autobiography—her story of escape from war-torn Vietnam, her struggle to stay alive in a Thai refugee camp, her exodus to Canada. I say yes. I know that her story is as much a part of this province as that of the Loyalists who came here in the nineteenth century. Not long after that I receive another call, from a Bosnian man, another immigrant who moved here in retreat from war, searching for sanity and peace. He has written poetry about his experience and wonders if I would take a look at it.

I moved here myself in 1979, as a sort of refugee from a life and a lifestyle that simply felt alien to me. I had scouted the planet for that "sane and safe and beautiful place to live," and nowhere felt like here. If reincarnation is a reality, it wouldn't take a psychic to convince me that I lived here in another life but, alas, I have no concrete memory of any of it. I just know that when I'm walking the shoreline, studying the waves, feeling the sand and stones beneath my shoes, the sky still blue and generous, at those moments, I am at peace with both myself and with history.

Writing this book has not always been pleasant. History is an unhappy business. Before I began my wrestling match with Nova Scotian history, I was primarily familiar with the here and now—the sane and beautiful place that is *still* out there every morning when I look out my bedroom window across the wide Lawrencetown Marsh. But now I know more about what went *wrong* here than I know about what went right. History, as far as I can tell, is mostly the legacy of mistakes. Mistakes and failures, perhaps, are what make history interesting. Survival, too, is part of that legacy. Survival in the face of disasters is sometimes a matter of stamina, persistence, sheer willpower or, quite often, pure luck. The Halifax Explosion was an accident of profound magnitude. But if we had had nuclear weapons in 1917, the Halifax Explosion might have destroyed most of the province, not just a chunk of North End Halifax.

Beyond the greed and the exploitation, Nova Scotia's history is also a story of recovery, self-reliance and searching for something better. Nova Scotia was a disappointment at first to many of the Loyalist refugees like

Jacob Bailey who found the appearance of the coast inhospitable and the citizens on the Halifax wharves uncivilized. To modern immigrants like myself, however, the landscape is rugged but inviting, the society relatively kind, gentle and civilized compared to the rest of North America. Economically we are poorer than many, but in terms of quality of life, I am certain we are much richer than most.

Ice Islands in the Sea

An important part of the story of contemporary Nova Scotia takes us back to where we began. This is ultimately a province shaped by the sea. Here is a chunk of land, nearly an island, that is surrounded by water and influenced by the great elemental forces of the North Atlantic.

In April of 1987, after a very cold winter, the pack ice moved out of the Gulf of St. Lawrence, pushed out past Cape Breton and drifted down along the Nova Scotian shore as far as Halifax Harbour. Only once before in the previous forty years had ice closed down the harbour, halting ferry services and the movement of huge container ships. At Lawrencetown Beach, the amazing blue-white islands of ice, in an infinite assortment of fantastic shapes, stretched out to sea as far as the eye could behold. I walked with my young daughter along the shoreline, dazzled by the ice islands beaching themselves like crystalline whales upon the shores here. Later, alone, I foolishly danced myself from one ice island to another far out to sea where I had never before stood on anything solid. When the wind shifted so that it was now blowing off the land, I had to make a hasty retreat as the pans began to shift and buckle and to drift away from the coast. My heart was pounding by the time I took my final step ashore onto solid land and lay down on the sand to watch an immense armada of white boats of ice set sail for southern waters and dissolution.

The Flood Tides of Christmas

Just three days before Christmas of 1995, I watched as storm surge waves slammed up and over the natural beach barrier of stones at Lawrencetown, flooding my neighbours who live in houses built in low-lying grasslands near the sea. There is no question that the sea is attempting to reclaim big portions of coastal Nova Scotia. Records show that storms and excessive high tides along the Atlantic coast have accounted for flooding up to six metres above the usual high tide markers at regular intervals. There are certain pieces of real estate around here that the sea would like to consume.

The tropics may come ashore here as well every few years with a blast of warm tropical wind strong enough to knock down power lines or reduce a barn to a pile of kindling but it is only a rowdy tourist with a temporary visa.

For this sea, this Atlantic beyond our shores, is a northerly thing. We live in a cold place, shaped by the whims of the *North* Atlantic. Unaware visitors from America or Ontario are still paralysed by the cold as they jump into those clear, enticing blue waters of Martinique Beach on a warm summer day. Even in summer the ocean water stings, electrifies, even burns, because it is so cold. The arctic ice remains there to the north, forever venting its cold. The cold water slowly drifts south on the Atlantic side of Nova Scotia and saves us from ever having to worry about air-conditioning in the summer.

The Grey Rocks of Fishermen's Beach

"Farewell to Nova Scotia, your seabound coast, may your mountains dark and dreary be." So goes the vintage song that Helen Creighton saved for us as she travelled the province to collect traditional music of these shores. "Dark and dreary" are not usually two words found in any tourist brochure, but along with the appreciation of stunning clear days and bright sunshine, I've cultivated a love for the infinite shades of grey that haunt the sea and the sky of this coast.

It was on such a grey day in November that I was hiking a remote headland—or what was left of a headland—at the mouth of Chezzetcook Inlet, with a photographer friend, Len Clifford. We drove the twisting, turning road of the east side past Deep Cove, Gaetz Island, Roasts Hay Island, Red Island and across the bridge of Little River. I parked the car at the end of the road and we had about one and a half kilometres or so to walk out along a long, grim, stony spit known as Misener's Island (although it wasn't really an island, not yet, anyway). We had a northeast wind howling at our backs as we stayed on the landward side of Story Head, headed toward a place labelled on the topographic map as "Fishermen's Beach." The grey rocks bloomed with orange lichen, choppy waves rattled the stones of the shoreline and the inlet of Chezzetcook looked dark (yes, even dreary), deep and ominous.

We hiked out to the remains of what had once been a thriving fishing village thirty years ago. In three short decades so much had changed. The fish had diminished, the fishermen and -women had retreated inland to tether their lives more securely to mainland life. But something else was gone as well. The land. There wasn't much left here but sea, stone and stubbles of drifted wood.

Once there had been a road out here. Once there had been solid soil, grass, dunes and stunted spruce trees, but the sea was moving landward, drowning the coast, shipping the soil away, leaving only this. If the tide was higher, we'd have to take a boat to get here. As it was, we could stay almost dry on our hike here to the haunting but beautiful remains of the fishing village where old houses, boat sheds and wharves still remained.

The sea continues to carve away at Nova Scotia. In the most basic way, we remain shaped by the sea. The sculpting is not at some beginning or anywhere near some end point. But we are in the midst of it. It was going on long before we arrived and will continue on long after we are gone. We are still just barely beginning to learn how to live with it, to use this momentum, to understand that the immense power of tide and wave and storm and erosion is *both* a curse and a blessing.

With a photographer's eye, Len pointed out a great piece of sea-ravaged wood sculpted into something that looked like caribou antlers. Other driftwood, the remains of the roots of a tree, looked like bizarre alien creatures, yet others presented themselves like carved figurines. When we arrived at the fish shacks, our ears stinging with the cold, we noticed that several of the buildings were jammed into each other at odd angles. Higher tides had floated them off foundations and bumped them together as if they were cars with clumsy drivers. As the tide withdrew, they remained parked like this. Property lines once recorded in legal documents in Halifax would have little meaning now that the sea had called the mortgage on the soil.

Inside a boat shed, wavy lines of salt along the rough plank walls marked the intrusive tides of spring and fall. All the furniture inside one small saltbox house had been moved into the cramped quarters of the upstairs as if to imply that as the sea took over the real estate, all you had to do was move one flight up. Other buildings had given up all hope already and collapsed into the rubble of rock. One remaining house, with curled asphalt shingles of bright blue crowded over with brilliant yellow orange lichen, look oddly out of place, like some gaudy oriental pagoda.

Broken lobster traps littered the community of ghosts. Shards of yellow rope were everywhere. No other human soul walked the stones here, but the inlet was alive with the cacophony of Canada geese and the sea oats were hung with small grey and brown migrating birds. Len spotted one lone weasel who followed us from pillar to post as we surveyed this amazing ghost town. He watched our every move from beneath a dozen fish sheds, always wary but intensely curious. Did he remember raucous, happy summer parties here where bottles of beer were emptied and the air was alive with human noise, a time when scraps of food and living mice were once plentiful? Or was he just a tourist like us, passing through?

As the wind increased from the north and began to blow an impertinent snow in our eyes, we retraced our steps back to shore as the tide began to spank against the higher stones. And I kept asking myself why this place, today so stark, so sea-weary and so "dark and dreary," was also so amazingly beautiful? But it was, without a doubt, beautiful.

The Spiritual Link to the Sea

We cannot hold back the sea on this drowned coast, although we've tried. We've experimented with tapping the energies of tidal forces and wind power, but not since the days of sailing ships have we been truly comfortable with harmonizing our needs with what the sea could provide. The sea has at once diminished our land and enhanced it in a multitude of ways. It has given life and taken life. It will take little notice of the politics of Quebec or a Maritime Union or who has won the latest provincial or federal elections.

The wood of the shacks of the East Chezzetcook village will eventually rot or float away. What's left of that bit of land will be a rocky shoal, a good shallow place for undersea plant life and, if we're lucky, fish. Lawrencetown Lake, where I first learned to sail my little Laser, will have successfully been reunited with its parent, the sea. The waves will have swept away the living-room furniture of my neighbours who built their homes in the lowlands, entrusted to the care of the barrier rocks above the beach that try their best, but fail, to hold back the sea.

If the current trends of rising sea levels from global warming continue to enhance the natural advance of the ocean, all of the above may happen much sooner than expected. We aren't talking about a thousand years here, not necessarily even centuries. A generation, perhaps, and the sea will lap at the foot of my driveway.

Water Street in Halifax at that time will be exactly that. The sea will prove to be the most successful privateer ever to make port at that historic city.

I'm hoping that we learn well the lessons of the past. We cannot undo the mistakes we've made but we may yet learn to avoid repeating them. The sea, even as it has intruded into our lives, may be gracious enough to bring back the fish, the forest may be benevolent enough, given time, to undo the pillage of clear-cutting. May we gently tap the tides and the winds and leave the coal in the ground to compress further into diamonds and spare the lives of miners.

Here at the tail-end of the twentieth century, Nova Scotia remains a unique and singular place. As the sea has shaped the land and its history, so too has it shaped a spirit that is intrinsic to our individuality and our culture. This spirit, so obvious in our literature, our art, our music and the tales that are told in the kitchens and backyards around the province, is our greatest strength and certainly worth preserving. Let the wharves wash off to sea. We can always build new ones. But we cannot afford to let drift the spiritual link to the sea that sustains who we are.

Select Bibliography

Africville Genealogical Society. *The Spirit of Africville*. Halifax: Formac, 1992.

Armour, Charles. *Sailing Ships of the Maritimes*. Toronto: McGraw-Hill Ryerson, 1975.

Barkhouse, Murray. *Famous Nova Scotians*. Hantsport, NS: Lancelot, 1994.

Bell, John, ed. *Halifax: A Literary Portrait*. Porters Lake, NS: Pottersfield, 1990.

Bell, W. P. *Foreign Protestants and the Settlement of Nova Scotia*. Toronto: University of Toronto Press, 1961.

Bird, Will R. *Atlantic Anthology*. Toronto: McClelland and Stewart,1959.

— *This Is Nova Scotia*. Toronto: Ryerson, 1972.

Blakeley, Phyllis. *Nova Scotia: A Brief History*. Toronto: Dent and Sons, 1955.

Brown, Craig. *The Illustrated History of Canada*. Toronto: Lester and Orpen Dennys, 1987.

Clarke, G.E. *Fire on the Water*. Volumes 1 and 2. Porters Lake, NS: Pottersfield Press, 1991.

Degen,Terry. *The History of Lawrencetown*. Lawrencetown, NS: Lawrencetown Historical Society, 1979.

De Volpi, Charles. *Nova Scotia: A Pictorial Record*. Toronto: Longman, 1974.

Doane, Benjamin. *Following the Sea*. Halifax: Nimbus, 1987.

Elliott, Shirley B. *The Nova Scotia Book of Days*. Halifax: Province of Nova Scotia, 1979.

Fingard, Judith. *Dark Side of Life in Victorian Halifax*. Porters Lake, NS: Pottersfield, 1989.

Forbes, E.R., and D. A. Muise. The *Atlantic Provinces in Confederation*. Toronto: University of Toronto Press, 1993.

Grant, Ruth Fulton. *The Canadian Atlantic Fishery*. Toronto: Ryerson, 1934.

Halpenny, Francess. *Dictionary of Canadian Biography*. Toronto: University of Toronto Press, 1974.

Howell, Colin, and Richard Twomey. *Jack Tar in History: Essays in the History of Maritime Life and Labour*. Fredericton: Acadiensis, 1991.

Jobb, Dean. *Bluenose Justice*. Porters Lake, NS: Pottersfield Press, 1989.

— *Crime Wave*. Porters Lake, NS: Pottersfield, 1991.

Laurier, La Pierre. *Canada, My Canada: What Happened?* Toronto: McClelland and Stewart, 1992.

MacMechan, Archibald. *At the Harbour Mouth*. Porters Lake, NS: Pottersfield, 1988.

McCreath, Peter, and John Leefe. *A History of Early Nova Scotia*. Tantallon, NS: Four East, 1982.

McKay, Ian. *The Quest of the Folk*. Montreal: McGill-Queens University Press, 1994.

Morrison, James, and James Moreira. *Tempered By Rum: Rum in the History of the Maritime Provinces*. Porters Lake, NS: Pottersfield, 1988.

Nova Scotia: *Gazeteer of Canada*. Ottawa: Canadian Board of Geographical Names, 1961.

Pacey, Elizabeth. *Historic Halifax*. Toronto: Hounslow Press, 1988.

Paul, Daniel. *We Were Not the Savages*. Halifax: Nimbus, 1993.

Payzant, Joan, and Lewis. *Like a Weaver's Shuttle*. Halifax, Nimbus, 1979.

Peabody, George, et al. *The Maritimes: Tradition, Challenge and Change*. Halifax: Maritext, 1987.

Raddall, Thomas. *Footsteps on Old Floors*. Porters Lake, NS: Pottersfield, 1988.

— *Halifax: Warden of the North*. Toronto: McClelland and Stewart, 1971.

Reid, John. *Six Crucial Decades*. Halifax: Nimbus, 1987.

Roland, Albert E. *Geological Background and Physiography of Nova Scotia*. Halifax: Nova Scotia Institute of Science, 1982.

Roland, A.E., and E.C. Smith. *The Flora of Nova Scotia*. Halifax: The Nova Scotia Museum, 1969.

Ryan, Judith Hoag. *Coal in Our Blood*. Halifax: Formac, 1992.

Spicer, Stanley T. *Masters of Sail*. Halifax: Petheric, 1968.

Thurston, Harry. *Atlantic Outposts*. Porters Lake, NS: Pottersfield, 1990.

Whitehead, Ruth Holmes. *Stories from the Six Worlds*. Halifax: Nimbus, 1988.

— *The Old Man Told Us: Excerpts from Micmac History 1500-1950*. Halifax: Nimbus, 1991.

Index

Illustration Credits

Illustrations from the following are used with permission:

Public Archives of Nova Scotia: pages 8 (Norwood Collection), 12 (Norwood Collection), 163, 169 (both), 175, 188, 195 (Boutilier Collection), 210 (Halifax Relief Commission), 219 (Halifax Relief Commission), 244 (Norwood Collection), 254 (Norwood Collection), 260 (Bob Brooks Collection), 266 (Norwood Collection), and 278 (Norwood Collection).

Special Collection, Killam Library, Dalhousie University: pages 17, 22, 29, 35, 37, 42, 53, 65, 72, 78, 88, 92, 100, 106, 112, 119, 126, 142 (J.J. Stewart Collection), 150, 155, 181, 202, 224, and 272.

The Archives, Dalhousie University: pages 231, 237, and 249.

New Brunswick Museum: pages 46 (Webster Canadian Collection), 59 (Webster Canadian Collection), and 135 (Webster Canadian Collection).

Len Clifford Photographer: pages 1 and 289.